Literary Simulation and the Digital Humanities

Literary Simulation and the Digital Humanities

Reading, Editing, Writing

Manuel Portela

BLOOMSBURY ACADEMIC
NEW YORK · LONDON · OXFORD · NEW DELHI · SYDNEY

BLOOMSBURY ACADEMIC
Bloomsbury Publishing Inc
1385 Broadway, New York, NY 10018, USA
50 Bedford Square, London, WC1B 3DP, UK
29 Earlsfort Terrace, Dublin 2, Ireland

BLOOMSBURY, BLOOMSBURY ACADEMIC and the Diana logo are trademarks of
Bloomsbury Publishing Plc

First published in the United States of America 2022

Copyright © Manuel Portela, 2022

For legal purposes the Acknowledgments on pp. 207–9 constitute an extension of this copyright page.

Cover design by Daniel Benneworth-Gray

All rights reserved. No part of this publication may be reproduced or transmitted in any form or by any means, electronic or mechanical, including photocopying, recording, or any information storage or retrieval system, without prior permission in writing from the publishers.

Bloomsbury Publishing Inc does not have any control over, or responsibility for, any third-party websites referred to or in this book. All internet addresses given in this book were correct at the time of going to press. The author and publisher regret any inconvenience caused if addresses have changed or sites have ceased to exist, but can accept no responsibility for any such changes.

A catalog record for this book is available from the Library of Congress.

ISBN:	HB:	978-1-5013-8538-4
	PB:	978-1-5013-8539-1
	ePDF:	978-1-5013-8541-4
	eBook:	978-1-5013-8540-7

Typeset by Integra Software Services Pvt. Ltd.

To find out more about our authors and books visit www.bloomsbury.com and sign up for our newsletters.

Dedicated to António Rito Silva

Contents

Incipit: Evolutionary Textual Environment — 1
    A Digital Humanities Experiment — 1
    From the *Book* to the *Archive* — 5
    Modeling Literary Performativity — 11
    Cross-over View — 16

1 From Archive to Simulator — 19
    Metamedia and Simulation — 19
    The Persistence of the Codex — 24
    Digital Scholarly Editing — 26
    From Textual Marks to Textual Fields — 30
    Modeling a Virtual *Book of Disquiet* — 36
    Beyond the Bibliographic Horizon — 42
    Reader-function — 48
    Editor-function — 49
    Author-function — 50
    Book-function — 51
    Simulation Layers — 52

2 Reading as Simulation — 57
    Modeling the Life of Reading — 57
    Marginalists and Extractors: Traces and Trails — 62
    Intertext as Hypertext: A Network of Quotations — 66
    Critical Reception as Reading Practice — 73
    Reading Protocols — 79
    Social Media Reception as Reading Practice — 88
    Visualizing the Spacetime of Reading — 94

3 Editing as Simulation — 101
    From Edition to Meta-Edition — 101
    Document, Text, Book, Work — 107

	Exploding the Book: Editing as Process	115
	Encoding and Visualizing Variation	117
	From Meta-Edition to Virtual Edition	121
4	**Writing as Simulation**	**131**
	Writing Acts in the *Book of Disquiet*	131
	The Kinetics of Writing	143
	Fragment, Book, Self	153
	From Handwriting to Language Processing	159
	Disquiet Variations	163
	Machines of Disquiet	169
5	**Living on in the Web**	**179**
	Digital Libraries and Networked Books	179
	Textual Instability and Modular Variability	188
	The Dynamic Digital Archive and the Library	191
	The Monograph, the Work, and the Archive	194

Explicit: No Problem Has a Solution	**199**
Foresight	199
Hindsight	204

Acknowledgments	207
References	210
Index	227

Incipit: Evolutionary Textual Environment

Actors are always already on the stage, within the terms of the performance.
Judith Butler (1988: 526)

A Digital Humanities Experiment

How can we use digital media to understand reading, editing, and writing as literary processes? How can we design the digital medium in a way that goes beyond the printed codex? This book is an attempt to answer those fundamental questions by bringing together a performative theory of literary action and a highly dynamic computational environment. The modernist masterpiece *Book of Disquiet*, by the Portuguese writer Fernando Pessoa (1888–1935), is the work selected for this simulation of the social multidimensionality of textual experience. Algorithmic procedures have been imaginatively used to show how the literary is brought into being through a network of open-ended interventions according to a role-playing rationale.

Starting from the premise that literary experience is sustained through the actions of reading, editing, and writing, subjects are invited to explore multiple reading paths, create virtual editions, and write their own variations on texts from the *Book of Disquiet*. The literary simulation consists of abstracting the actions of reading, editing, and writing as roles that subjects can perform within this textual environment. Their actions become part of the textual field and the entire system evolves as users experiment with those literary processes. Pessoa's work-in-progress thus becomes a model of how a book assumes an emergent textual form resulting from the collaborative interventions of readers, editors, and writers. This playful engagement enables users to shift perspectives and change roles, consciously experiencing the processes through which the literary is dynamically constituted during the improvisational interactions between different agents.

The experiment described in this book is also an attempt to answer the challenges posed by textual modeling and interface design according to humanistic principles. The work known as *Book of Disquiet* has been the point of departure for engaging with contemporary literary theory through computational media. As a digital humanities experiment, the *LdoD Archive: Collaborative Digital Archive of the Book of Disquiet* is informed by the complexities of poststructuralist critical theories, performative theories of culture, systems theory, software studies, and materialities of literature, among others. Rather than merely a functional digital artifact or an operational digital platform—produced according to representational models of textuality and engineering principles of transparent human-computer interaction—it is a conceptual and technical experiment whose result can be described as an evolutionary textual environment.

The notion of evolutionary textual environment refers to its evolving structure and functionalities as researchers continue to experiment with what is possible in this medium, on one hand, and to the changes in its content and uses as interactors perform their scripted and unscripted role-playing actions, on the other. The dynamic and socialized functions of the *LdoD Archive* offer an interpretative interface through which subjects are asked to see how their actions are constitutive of the textual environment itself and how they are constrained by the conventions that are available for playing, including those that they bring to the game. In this reading-editing-writing space, the conditions of production and reception of the web have been integrated into the ecology of its literary and computational form. The *LdoD Archive* changes its content and the relations among its elements as interventions by this community of users modify the configuration of its textual and computational space over time.

Not only are interactors invited to see the processuality of reading, editing, and writing as it is being presented from multiple perspectives through the *LdoD Archive*'s contents and functions, but they can also experiment with their own acts of reading, editing, and writing by inscribing them into the system. The system evolves as those inscriptions and the analyses of the interactions are iteratively used for changing and adapting its own affordances and constraints. Our modeling of literary performativity operates according to a double logic, both as representation and simulation, and generates a textual environment whose content and structure evolve to register the interventions of its interactors and foster their creativity. This open textual system is the unanticipated result of the attempt to offer a theoretical and computational answer to the question "what is the *Book of Disquiet?*"

The project was triggered by the initial desire to model the relation between two answers to that question: first, the *Book of Disquiet* is an unfinished work, composed of a semi-determined set of modular texts in various stages of composition; secondly, it is also a set of specific editions that have used diverse criteria for transcription, selection, and organization of their texts. Once we began to model the relation between those two perspectives, our focus shifted from representing the actuality of those relations as documented in the work's authorial and editorial archive to simulating the processes through which a work becomes a work. These processes were referred to, in the redesigned model, as literary performativity, by which I mean the set of material and social processes that sustain the production and reproduction of literary meanings, forms, and experiences. These time-based processes have been abstracted as reader-function, editor-function, author-function, and book-function.

The *LdoD Archive* thus gradually morphed into a complex software architecture, based on a data model and a series of functionalities that are meant to express the relation between a representation layer and a simulation layer. The evolving dynamics between those layers addresses an additional set of fundamental questions: how can we represent and simulate the processuality of the book under construction (as material production and conceptual operator)? How can we represent and simulate the processuality of the acts involved in its construction, such as reading, editing, and writing? How can we open them up to further acts of reading, editing, and writing through which our own interpretative interactions become recursively inscribed in its bibliographic and imaginary space? How do we use the knowledge generated by the experiment to change the conditions at the level of code and interface?

Each of those dimensions of performativity is modeled as a representation: writing acts by encoding the *Book of Disquiet* as a set of autograph materials; editing acts by encoding the *Book of Disquiet* as a set of expert editions of autograph materials; reading acts by showing the *Book of Disquiet* as a set of actual reading paths. At the same time, the simulation of those actions as a range of possibilities requires them to be experienced through interventions on the textual materials that feed back onto the representational layer. Modeled through this simulation layer, the *Book of Disquiet* within the *LdoD Archive* is transformed into an open set of role-playing interactions—that is, an open set of readings, editions, and writings constellated by the gravitational force of an imagined book—and, ultimately, an evolutionary textual environment (including its own source code).

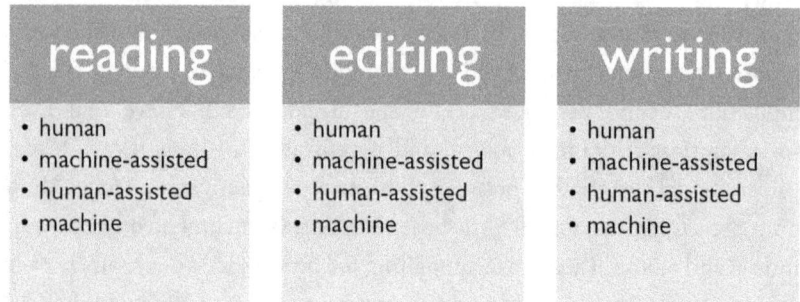

Figure 0.1 From manual-only to fully algorithmic: experimenting with the medium.

Insofar as the contents and structure of the system respond to the ongoing actions of its subjects, the processuality and performativity of those literary actions are experienced as constitutive of the system. Taking into account that reading, editing, and writing have been conceived to explore a wide range of human-only, machine-assisted, human-assisted, and machine-only actions, the model can also be understood as an experimental digital environment in which a large suite of digital tools and applications can be adapted, used, and transformed. Our modeling of this dynamic textual environment thus becomes a combinatorial experiment with the performativity of the code through an ensemble of techniques, algorithms, and methods (Figure 0.1).

Interactors experience their actions not only as a series of textual possibilities that emerge from a range of predefined values and parameters, but also as an open exploration of literary performativity itself. What is a reading act? What is an editorial act? What is a writing act? According to its simulation rationale, each output is the result of a collaborative action in which the algorithmic production of the system is modified by intentions and procedures of the interactor. Outputs—whether taking the form of reading trails, edited sequences, classification taxonomies, macro-visualizations, or new texts—are not entirely determined by the system's internal logic since they will capture the human processing of its programmed processing. The constrained improvisations fostered by the *LdoD Archive*'s rationale contribute to the emergent nature of readings, editings, and writings as possible actualizations of the experience of the work.

This openness of the *LdoD Archive* to the interpretative action of its subjects takes place at two entangled levels of performativity. On one level, interpretative action happens according to flexible and shifting perspectives on its textual representations. On another level, interpretative action works according to game-like practices in role-playing simulations. As users inscribe their reading, editing, and writing acts, the *LdoD Archive* documents the results of those interactions and offers them for further reading, editing, and writing acts, and further analysis. Both user-created content and reflexive analyses are part of the open textual system. The evolutionary textual environment itself could be redescribed as an evolving socialized literary practice in networked programmable media. Its fusion of technical and conceptual model, on one hand, with actual acts of reading, editing, and writing, on the other, bring into being the unbounded and iterative nature of the textual condition.

If we think of it in ethical terms, we could say that the *LdoD Archive* is not a system for automating literary production, reception, or analysis. In this respect, it sets itself apart from dominant engineering approaches to computational creativity in artificial intelligence systems and from dominant digital humanities approaches to textual processing and analysis. On the contrary, its ecology of machine-assisted human action and human-assisted machine action turns algorithmic processes into literary procedures for opening up textual spaces to critical and creative explorations. The result is an environment fed by the unpredictability and creativity of human interactors in a live, time-distributed, and collaborative social process. One in which the rules and roles of literary play can be deprogrammed and reimagined.

Its purpose is to instantiate the conditions that allow the reiteration of the relation between potentiality and actuality for each individual role-playing action. Given that this complex computational environment originated in an attempt to model the processuality of bringing a book into existence (in this particular case the *Book of Disquiet* by Fernando Pessoa), we can say that the bibliographical imagination itself is reconfigured as a linguistic and physical force in the dynamics that produces the literary as material poetics and social semiotic practice. It becomes a living model of the improvisational and emergent identity of the literary work of art as a cultural construct.

From the *Book* to the *Archive*

And I offer you this book because I know it is beautiful and useless. It teaches nothing, inspires no faith, and stirs no feeling. A mere stream that flows towards an abyss of ashes scattered by the wind, neither helping nor harming the soil …

I put my whole soul into making it, but without thinking about it as I made it, for I thought only of me, who am sad, and of you, who aren't anyone.

And because this book is absurd, I love it; because it is useless, I want to give it away; and because it serves no purpose to want to give it to you, I give it to you …

Fernando Pessoa, *Book of Disquiet*[1]

Among several unfinished book projects by Fernando Pessoa, there was a prose work begun in 1913 titled *Livro do Desassossego* (*Book of Disquiet*). This work has been translated into many European languages during the past forty years and is now generally regarded as one of Pessoa's masterpieces and a major modernist work. What many foreign language readers of the *Book of Disquiet* do not know is that the first Portuguese edition only appeared in 1982, forty-seven years after the author's death. It was only one of many posthumous works that editors have excavated (during the past eighty-seven years) from the *c.* 28,000 autograph papers left by Pessoa and which have been in the possession of the National Library of Portugal since the late 1970s. Pessoa's works continue to be re-edited and studied by a new generation of scholars, at the same time that their popularity grows outside the Portuguese-speaking world.

The composition of most texts for the *Book of Disquiet* has been dated from two distinct periods: 1913–20 and 1929–34. Texts explicitly assigned by Pessoa to *Livro do Desassossego* contain the annotation "L. do D." (hence the name we adopted for our digital experiment: "LdoD Archive"[2]). However, there are more than two hundred texts without the "L. do D." annotation that also belong (or have been ascribed by editors as belonging) to the *Livro*. Editions vary both in relation to the set of texts and also, in some cases, in relation to the internal structure and specific readings of selected texts. Thus, we can offer two distinct answers to the question "What is the *Book of Disquiet*?" The *Book of Disquiet* is an authorial project. The *Book of Disquiet* is an editorial construct based on the authorial project.

As an authorial project, it may be described as an unfinished and unorganized work written between 1913 and 1934, whose set of witnesses contains typescripts,

---

[1] "Perystile," *c.* 1913, in Fernando Pessoa, *The Book of Disquiet*, edited and translated by Richard Zenith (Penguin Books, 2002). Texts are referenced by their title or by their number in Richard Zenith's edition. All translations, unless noted otherwise, are also by Richard Zenith. Full text available at https://ldod.uc.pt/fragments/fragment/Fr449/inter/Fr449_WIT_ED_CRIT_Z (BNP/ E3, 9-39-41r-31; Coelho 246, 247, 250; Sobral Cunha 5, 6; Zenith 507; Pizarro 17).
[2] *LdoD* is pronounced ɛl–du–de. Its English translation would read BofD for *Book of Disquiet*.

manuscripts, and printed texts. As an editorial construct, it is the set of printed editions based on that authorial project. Editions vary in the interpretation of Pessoa's intentions as inferred from textual witnesses. They vary in terms of selection, transcription, as well as division and organization of textual units. Editions may vary also in heteronym attribution—Pessoa assigned many of his works to fictional authors, each of which had a particular style, psychology, and biography. He used the word "heteronym" to describe such authorial personae. The first heteronym for the *Livro* (1913–20) was Vicente Guedes, but the work was later (1929–34) reassigned to Bernardo Soares, a persona described by Pessoa as a "semi-heteronym."

Our initial intention was to create a computational artifact that would allow us to examine the *Book of Disquiet* as both an authorial project and an editorial construct. Those two dimensions would be fully integrated through a radial representation that would take any fragment (understood as the minimum textual unit of composition of the *Book*) as the unit of organization of the *Archive*. While the authorial facet would be represented by digital facsimiles and new transcriptions of the autographs, the editorial forms of the work would be represented by the four major editions published between 1982 and 2012. Each version of each text would be marked up at an extremely granular level so that all types of variation would become comparable across the textual corpus of each interpretation of the witnesses, but also within the structure of each edition.

In this way there would be no single dominant hierarchical structure in the *Archive*, but only a series of dynamic perspectives offered by various possible structures that would allow users to move from authorial view to editorial view or from one editorial view to another editorial view. Users could thus see how the edited and published book (as a conceptual and material entity that instantiates a given idea of the work) had emerged from the archive in various shapes, according to specific editorial models of what the *Book of Disquiet* was or should be. Each edited book could be seen in the context of the authorial archive and in the context of other possible edited forms of itself. This multifaceted scholarly approach to editing according to the hypertext rationale would eventually give way to a series of more fundamental research questions about the performative dimension of textual forms and practices.

The modularity of the *Book of Disquiet* as a series of discrete texts, which could be assembled and ordered according to multiple criteria, was ideally suited for experimenting with the modularity of digital objects as programmable entities.

Thus the dynamic features of the *LdoD Archive* expanded beyond the initial concept of comparing multiple versions of the *Book* in order to turn the archive into a participatory and socialized space for reading, editing, and writing. This was the moment when the technical and conceptual development of the archive morphed into an experimental textual environment. From the original intentions of using Pessoa's work as a research probe into the modernist imagination of the book we came to this innovative notion of the *Book of Disquiet* as a hypertextual place for literary simulation.

Since reading the *Book of Disquiet* could be experienced not only as predefined sequence, but as an exploration of alternative paths, we multiplied the reading traversals. Because the editorial process of constructing the *Book of Disquiet* by its editors (which we had represented through its four major editions) could continue in the virtual space of the archive itself, we added a virtual editing functionality. Because the writing process of the *Book of Disquiet* could be not only observed in the autograph documents at a very granular scale but also expanded as a new writing process, we added a virtual writing functionality. The actual multiplication of reading, editing, and writing acts emerged as model of literary performance in which interactions could take the form of role-playing.

So the self-description that users of the *LdoD Archive* now find in the website sums up the history of the project briefly outlined in the previous paragraphs:

> The *LdoD Archive* is a collaborative digital archive of the *Book of Disquiet* by Fernando Pessoa. It contains images of the autograph documents, new transcriptions of those documents and also transcriptions of four editions of the work. In addition to reading and comparing transcriptions, the *LdoD Archive* enables users to collaborate in creating virtual editions of the *Book of Disquiet*. It also includes a writing module which will allow users to write variations based on fragments of the *Book*. Thus the *LdoD Archive* combines a representational principle with a simulation principle: the first is expressed through the representation of the history and processes of writing, reading, and editing the *Book*; the second is embodied in the fact that users are given the possibility of playing various roles in the literary process (reading, editing, writing), using the flexibility of the digital medium for experimenting with the *Book of Disquiet* as a literary machine.
>
> (https://ldod.uc.pt/about/archive)

As you can see, the simulation function has been explicitly articulated as one of the guiding principles of the archive. The inadequacy of the "Archive" designation was already clear in presentations and articles about the project written in 2013.

I now believe that a more appropriate designation would be *LdoD Simulator*, since we have gone beyond the remediation rationale that has governed digital archival projects developed during the last twenty years.

In its current textual, socialized, and dynamic instantiation, the *LdoD Archive* would be more accurately described as a public textual collaborative environment, where reading, editing, and writing are theoretically and functionally integrated. I have decided to retain the name *LdoD Archive* because of the familiarity of the concept "archive" in digital scholarly editing, but I am aware that the categorization implied by the established form of the concept is partially inadequate for the ensemble of functionalities that we have already implemented or are currently under development. So one of the major difficulties of this decade-long experiment in Digital Humanities is a communication problem: how can we convey a new concept and new technical construct using familiar concepts and tools, but without submitting them to earlier frames of perception and use?

This question takes us to what is perhaps the most challenging aspect of any project that attains this level of complexity: how can we make it understandable and usable by different kinds of users—from the general reader who encounters the *Book of Disquiet* for the first time, to students of Pessoa's work at various stages of their experiencing the work, and to scholarly experts in the *Book of Disquiet*? These are questions that have to be answered by any digital scholarly editing project as part of their public engagement and outreach objectives, but which are often impossible to address in an entirely satisfactory way—either because the complexity of the digital textual apparatus is impenetrable for expert users and beginners alike, or because editors have not designed multiple interfaces and aids that avoid making the initial approach a daunting task.

We have tried to address this problem by structuring the archive into six different interfaces, each of which encapsulates only one dimension of the *LdoD Archive*, allowing access to functionalities related to that particular dimension:

1. Reading: reading the work according to different sequences.
2. Documents: listing of all fragments and information about sources.
3. Editions: visualizing autographs and comparing transcriptions.
4. Search: selecting fragments according to multiple criteria.
5. Virtual: creating virtual editions and their taxonomies.
6. Writing: writing variations based on the fragments.

We have also carried out several usability tests for each set of functionalities using mixed groups that included both users with no knowledge of the *Book of Disquiet* and users with various levels of knowledge and expertise. These tests have provided invaluable insight about strategies for designing the interactions with the textual database, but also about the need for various levels of granularity in the meta-information provided about each menu and each set of tools (from short mouse-over prompts to detailed explanations of the editorial principles by means of FAQs). A step-by-step guide (with a series of video tutorials) was made for each interface, with a particular focus on the virtual editing function, which was the most difficult concept for beta-users to grasp. The virtual writing functions are currently under computational development. Of course, even these strategies are no guarantee that the *LdoD Archive* will become the multipurpose collaborative textual environment that we want it to be: available for leisure reading, for teaching and learning, for creative writing experiments, and also for advanced research, including future critical editions of the work.

We continue to work closely with selected reading-editing-writing communities to learn more about the actual uses of the textual environment and about how we can improve its design and make the concept of digital literary simulator intelligible for everyone. We also want to expand the archive into a multilingual textual space, but this will take a few more years of development and, given copyright restrictions, it will depend on the collaboration of many translators and publishers. The first release of the *LdoD Archive* contains Pessoa's text only in Portuguese, although the interfaces for the various sections of the archive as well as all meta-information are already presented in three languages: Portuguese, English, and Spanish. In future releases we intend to include a multi-language version of the *Book of Disquiet* itself in which a selection of texts will be translated into as many languages as possible.

The *LdoD Archive* facilitates the creation of multiple reading paths that explore the modularity of the *Book of Disquiet*; it enables the construction of narratives about the composition of the *Book of Disquiet*, based on the observation of images and transcriptions of the autograph documents; and it helps the production of narratives about the editions of the *Book of Disquiet*, based on the comparative analysis of four critical editions as possible versions for this work. More importantly, it sustains a collaborative textual environment that models processuality through the simulation of the acts of reading, editing, and writing as dynamic constituents of the literary experience of text and language. Now that this digital experiment has gone live, only time will tell if it will catch the imagination of readers and scholars of the *Book of Disquiet*, or if it will become one more future evidence of a failed solution to an imaginary problem.

Modeling Literary Performativity

The *Book of Disquiet* contains several references to reading, writing, editing, and books, including self-references to the acts of reading, writing, and organizing "this book." Images of reading and images of writing are used to characterize the writing self as the empty being of fictional imagination: "As my feet wander I inwardly skim, without reading, a book of text interspersed with swift images, from which I leisurely form an idea that's never completed" (Text 181).[3] Describing the self as "a book of text interspersed with swift images," this passage links reading-writing and self-creation with the imagination of the book. The swiftly skimmed book becomes an image for the inscrutability of the self, but also for the shifting projective nature of the book as a moving desire for form. The "idea that's never completed" suggests the incompleteness of self-production through reading-writing feedbacks, but also the ongoing process of creating and perceiving form in literary acts.

In the *LdoD Archive*, processuality has been modeled through the notion of literary performativity. Our aim is to engage the constructedness of literary experience as a shared social practice dependent upon acts of reading, writing, and editing. In this performative space, programmed affordances and constraints enable subjects to move across different positions in its field of literary action: from reading to editing, from reading to writing, from editing to reading, from editing to writing, from writing to reading, and from writing to editing. Interactors are asked not only to observe and iterate a parametrized set of reading, editing, and writing forms and relations modeled on Pessoa's textual corpus, but also to reiterate and transform those forms and relations by engaging them according to variable positions in the field (Figure 0.2). The "idea that's never completed" can be extended as a metaphor for the *LdoD Archive*'s attempt to represent and simulate processuality as an open-ended unfinished (and unfinishable) machine.

---

[3] Full text available at https://ldod.uc.pt/fragments/fragment/Fr112/inter/Fr112_WIT_ED_CRIT_Z (BNP/E3, 2-37r; Coelho 183; Sobral Cunha 585; Zenith 181; Pizarro 320).

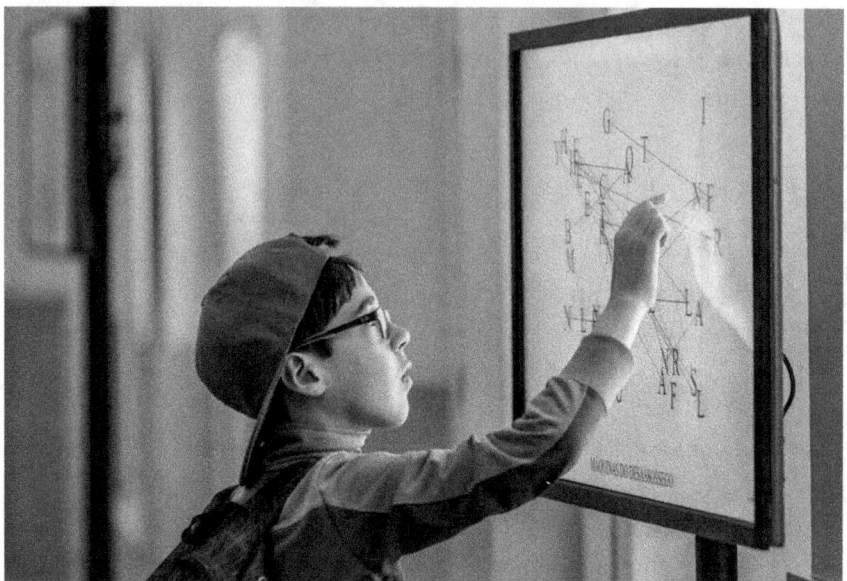

Figure 0.2 Modeling performativity: process as representation and simulation. *Machines of Disquiet*, May 2018, Criatek, Aveiro. © Filipe Cunha. Reproduced with permission.

The *Book of Disquiet* offers several examples of position shifts which can be equated with the role-playing setting of the *LdoD Archive*. For example, the shift from reading to writing instantiates the relation of reader-function to author-function:

> I know no pleasure like that of books, and I read very little. Books are introductions to dreams, and no introductions are necessary for one who freely and naturally enters into conversation with them. I've never been able to lose myself in a book; as I'm reading, the commentary of my intellect or imagination has always hindered the narrative flow. After a few minutes it's I who am writing, and what I write is nowhere to be found.
>
> (Text 417)[4]

Similarly, the change from reading to editing expresses the relation of reader-function to editor-function:

> In one of those spells of sleepless somnolence when we intelligently amuse ourselves without the intelligence, I reread some of the pages that together will form my book of random impressions. And they give off, like a familiar smell,

---

[4] Full text available at https://ldod.uc.pt/fragments/fragment/Fr040/inter/Fr040_WIT_ED_CRIT_Z (BNP/E3, 1-46r; Coelho 18; Sobral Cunha 694; Zenith 417; Pizarro 273).

an arid impression of monotony. Even while saying that I'm always different, I feel that I've always said the same thing; that I resemble myself more than I'd like to admit; that, when the books are balanced, I've had neither the joy of winning nor the emotion of losing. I'm the absence of a balance of myself, the lack of a natural equilibrium, and this weakens and distresses me.

(Text 442)[5]

The shift from writing to reading, in turn, can be equated with the movement from author-function to reader-function:

> In the faint shadows cast by the last light before evening gives way to night, I like to roam unthinkingly through what the city is changing into, and I walk as if nothing had a cure. I carry with me a vague sadness that's pleasant to my imagination, less so to my senses. As my feet wander I inwardly skim, without reading, a book of text interspersed with swift images, from which I leisurely form an idea that's never completed.

(Text 181)[6]

The split between embodied self as phenomenological entity and fictional self as an imaginary character constituted by written language is at the heart of Pessoa's account of literary depersonalization. In "The Art of Effective Dreaming for Metaphysical Minds," depersonalization is divided into three stages, of which the last one leads to the performative ability to be several selves at the same time: "The highest stage of dreaming is when, having created a picture with various figures whose lives we live all at the same time, we are jointly and interactively all of those souls" (Text 495).[7] This multiplication of being is manifest in the proliferation of heteronyms or writing selves:

> We are mere ashes endowed with a soul but no form—not even that of water, which adopts the shape of the vessel that holds it. With this □ thoroughly established, complete and autonomous plays can unfold in us line by line. We may no longer have the energy to write them, but that won't be necessary. We'll be able to create secondhand; we can imagine one poet writing in us in one way, while another poet will write in a different way. I, having refined this skill to a considerable degree, can write in countlessly different ways, all of them original.

(Text 495)

---

[5] Full text available at https://ldod.uc.pt/fragments/fragment/Fr142/inter/Fr142_WIT_ED_CRIT_Z (BNP/E3, 2-71r; Coelho 294; Sobral Cunha 473; Zenith 442; Pizarro 303).
[6] Full text available at https://ldod.uc.pt/fragments/fragment/Fr112/inter/Fr112_WIT_ED_CRIT_Z (BNP/E3, 2-37r; Coelho 183; Sobral Cunha 585; Zenith 181; Pizarro 320).
[7] Full text available at https://ldod.uc.pt/fragments/fragment/Fr549/inter/Fr549_WIT_ED_CRIT_Z (BNP/E3, 144D(2)-46r-47-48-49; Sobral Cunha 113; Zenith 495; Pizarro 54).

Writing selves appear as fictional authors and become independent of Pessoa's self by virtue of their way of writing. Ways of writing are precursors of ways of being, that is, entangled forms of perception and action that relate the self to its environment and to itself. The inner autonomy of those unfolding "autonomous plays" in effective dreamers also suggests that selves are emergent forms taking their shape from specific discourses and roles—formless souls retroactively produced by their linguistic performance. Pessoa's fictionalization of heteronymic writing as the multiplication of selves may also be equated with the author-function. The act of writing "in a different way" constitutes the heteronymic author as an emergent function of a specific writing practice (including each heteronym's projected books). In turn, Pessoa's role, in this meta-literary system, is to perform as the author-producing author, i.e., as a second-degree manifestation of the author-function, a sort of writing program.

The production of the book in the *Book of Disquiet* contains textual and material evidence of the performativity of literary action that we have tried to model in the *LdoD Archive*. Additionally, there are more than a dozen external references to the *Book of Disquiet* in letters to friends, notes, title lists, and plans for publication. Imagining this particular book through self-description is only one instance of the continuing imagination of books as expression of his various heteronyms, on the one hand, and as expression of Pessoa's meta-authorial condition on the other. Their existence as fictional authors, as well as his existence as author of authors, depend upon the complex workings of the book-function as a constitutive element of literary performativity. At once assemblage of written discourse in search of conceptual and material unity, on one hand, and imaginary horizon for each new act of writing, on the other, the book-function is both a physical and metaphysical operator.

The incompleteness of the *Book of Disquiet* as a book in progress reincarnates in the processuality of reading, editing, and writing as acts of inscription of consciousness in the duration of time. Appropriating the time-based nature of digital media, the *LdoD Archive* places representation in a dynamic and complex relation with simulation, showing them as expressions of the fundamental performativity of meaning production and perception. In effect, representation could be described as a reified instantiation of textual processuality, a particular set of textual forms that must be reperformed again and again.

Beyond the archival representation of the unique and historical occurrence of a set of texts in several stages of completion, the *LdoD Archive* attempts to model and experiment with the flows of reading, editing, and writing that constitute and maintain a literary field through the living imagination of the book. The flexibility of digital inscription and reinscription is used in the *LdoD Archive* to explore the potentiality of those actions as an iterative ongoing process, and the material and conceptual operator we designate as *book*, which has become one of the main producers of the literary as a set of practices of evocation and intensification of the human experience of the world.

As we will see, the performativity of reading is expressed as (1) multicursal visualization of reading paths, (2) analysis of specific reading practices (such as the history of the *Book of Disquiet*'s expert critical reception or its current social media reception), and (3) reading of one's own reading trails, resorting to human-assisted and computer-assisted processes. The performativity of editing enables interactors to (1) compare authorial witnesses against their various transcriptions, (2) compare expert editions against each other, and (3) produce their own editions and selections (including annotations and taxonomies) using both manual and automated processes. Finally, the performativity of writing takes the form of (1) exploration of autographic writing processes, (2) new writing acts anchored on specific passages, (3) new writing acts based on machine-assisted procedures and constraints. Each process (reading the book, editing the book, and writing the book) can be experienced in relation to other representations or simulations of itself, and also in relation to all other processes.

The *LdoD Archive* may, ultimately, be described as a conceptual, material, and technical experiment that attempts to simulate literary functions as a dynamic field of discursive interactions for imagining our being in the world through fictional written language. Electronic remediation of Pessoa's text has been reimagined as a meta-reading, meta-editing, and meta-writing exercise that allows interactors to play with and investigate the social dynamics of textual production. They are invited to engage reading, editing, and writing as performative actions that constitute and sustain a literary field. The problem of writing, editing, and reading a book about the inner existence of a written self becomes a material experiment with the potentiality of the literary imagination that takes advantage of the procedural and collaborative affordances of the medium.

Virtualizing the *Book of Disquiet* in a dynamic archive-simulator is our way of modeling literary performance for the current environment of networked reading, editing, and writing spaces. This implies reimagining the dynamics between editing and the codex, and between reading and writing in ways that fully engage the possibilities and constraints of the digital medium, including its diverse layers of encoding, programmability, visualization, transaction, and interaction. The *Book of Disquiet* is the ideal work for an attempt at reimagining the textual condition in ways that fully explore the computer as an expressive medium and the web as new kind of textual ecology. To engage reading, editing, and writing—inside and outside bibliographic structures—through simulations in a time-based medium is a material exploration of the medium's processing and participatory affordances for literary potentiality.

Cross-over View

The first chapter explains the concept of literary simulation according to a double rationale: first, by looking at the metamedia features of the digital medium and showing how they provide a second-order representation of the bibliographic structures of codex-oriented processes of reading, editing, and writing; secondly, by describing this critical level of representation as a conceptual and material space for simulative experiments that engage actual acts of production—that is, acts for producing reading, editing, and writing. Because these three acts are fundamental acts for the production of literary communication, the possibility of enacting those specific interactions within this textual environment is theorized as a simulation model of literary performativity. The digital archive thus becomes a literary simulator: through a series of programmed functionalities, the metamedia representation of the situational nature of the codex as a dynamic literary object is able to open up a generative space for experimentation with textuality. The book itself—as conceptual structure in search of an ergonomic, cognitive, and enactive material embodiment—is seen as a fourth dynamic operator whose gravitational force constellates readers, editors, and writers in multiple configurations.

The second chapter explains the reading functionalities of the *LdoD Archive* as a reading space where user-readers can explore multiple reading paths while registering their own interactions within this reading space. Readers can move across the various reading sequences (editions) offered by its reading space: expert sequences, user-generated sequences, and algorithmic-based sequences. Those reader-based movements and reading sequences will be available for visualization and analysis, according to various strategies. Readers are thus able to explore their own reading maps along with machine-assisted sequences as second-order representations of traversals of the reading space. Reading is experienced as a recursive back-and-forth focus between close attention to individual signifiers and large-scale abstraction of earlier engagements. The simulation of reading thus consists of enabling a certain number of reading operations to become registered in the textual field as a new semiotic field open to further explorations.

The third chapter describes the editing functionalities of the *LdoD Archive* as the comparative visualization of various editions and the dynamic addition of user-generated virtual editions based on the selection and annotation of textual fragments from four expert editions. These expert editions can be compared and analyzed at different levels of granularity: from the micro-variations of punctuation, orthography, and word variants to the macro-variations of internal textual structure of each fragment and global structure of the edition. The historical canonical editions produced between 1982 and 2012 are presented as a set of distinctly realized editions, to which the virtual editing level adds an open set of other possible editions. Understood as an open process of textual selection and organization, this editing functionality, in the context of the *LdoD Archive*, refers to any act of selection and organization of the text, whether aiming at producing an entire edition of the work or just a brief selection of texts. Virtual editions can also be produced according to computer-assisted methods, for instance, on the basis of frequency of citations from particular fragments in a given social media network. Once published, virtual editions themselves can be appropriated for the production of further virtual editions in an endless cycle.

The fourth chapter explains the writing functionalities of the *LdoD Archive* under the notion of simulation at three related levels: as a site for observation of various types of material inscription that document authorial script acts; as a site for exploring narrative, cognitive, and affective thematizations of self-conscious acts of writing (a significant topic in the *Book of Disquiet* itself); and as a site for engaging in new writing acts that expand and re-signify the fragments through compositional variations. Through acts of observation, exploration, and engagement, the *LdoD Archive* enables reader-writers to experience both the external and internal experience of writing, i.e., writing as inscribed form and writing as the invention of textual form through the extended cognition provided by recursive acts of writing and rewriting. The addition of writing variations to the *LdoD Archive* also follows a double principle: human writing using text-processing tools and computer-assisted writing (including multimodal forms of writing) using programmed compositional processes.

The fifth and last chapter examines the relation between the book, the digital archive, and the library in the transliterary environment of the World Wide Web. The *LdoD Archive* is considered in terms of the phantasmal presence of earlier paper-based inscriptions of the autographs and of their radical transformation through the affordances of machine-readable text, programmable temporal media, and social collaboration. Thanks to their modularity and metamedia features, computational media subsume and emulate other media, partially dissolving the material and formal boundaries that constituted earlier forms and genres, including their classificatory systems. A second-order manipulation of the first-order acts of reading, editing, and writing brings together simulation principles and socialized processes in the *LdoD Archive*. Redescribed within the ecology of the web and in relation to concept of digital library, the form and idea of the book emerges as an imaginary function in the field of practice that produces the literary as material poetics and social semiotic practice. In the final section, the transmedia condition involving this monograph, the *Book of Disquiet* and the *LdoD Archive* is analyzed.

The book closes with a retrospective look at its own historicity. The research project that led up to this point is briefly recapitulated in a coda, in which the collaborative environment of the *LdoD Archive* is described as a new kind of literary experiment: an evolutionary textual environment based on a model of literary performativity. Exploring the inseparability of textuality and materiality, *Literary Simulation and the Digital Humanities* demonstrates how computability can fully engage with the complexities of contemporary literary theory. Its unique combination of theoretical speculation, literary analysis, and artifactual construction represents a significant critical intervention and a key advance in the invention of the digital medium as a humanistic interface for modeling processes of textual production and interpretation. The foregrounding of the foundational practices of reading, editing, and writing will be relevant for several fields, including literary studies, scholarly editing, software studies, and digital humanities.

1

From Archive to Simulator

Metamedia and Simulation

The concept of simulation as scientific modeling of a natural or social process or system is used in many fields of research, from meteorology to political science. It is also widely used in the field of learning to refer to individual training practices in performing operations that, in an environment of controlled variables, emulate the actual conditions of a particular procedure—in an operating theater, in a theater of military operations, in an emergency situation, in a space station. The concept is further used to refer to technology testing in order to optimize its design and performance.

A search using the word *simulation* in databases of scientific articles shows how the concept has become the object of a complex theorization, particularly in the fields of social studies and cognitive sciences, in which simulation tends to be seen as a practice for modeling knowledge about the social world and about individuals. One example would be the notion that different forms of fiction could be analyzed, from a cognitive point of view, as simulating practices that provide individuals with models of social relations and the minds of others (Reisenzein 2009; Lavocat 2014; Wright-Maley 2015; Oatley 2016; Tamir et al. 2016). The application of quantitative computational methods for modeling and simulating creative processes is another use of the concept in the field of the arts and humanities. The very notion of simulation as an epistemological concept has become the subject of historical and critical analysis (Grüne-Yanoff et al. 2011; Wise 2017). Another semantic network comes from social theories that define simulation as a false representation of social relations, associating it with both the mass media of the earlier electronic age and the current info-sphere of cybercapitalism and global surveillance (Wilson 2012; Opitz 2017).

Given its procedural nature, the digital computer has often been described as a simulation machine, that is, a medium whose programming is oriented to the modeling of objects and processes. Insofar as its materiality can be described as a cascade of abstractions, which transform machine-code into media objects perceptible by the human senses, its functioning is based on simulation principles. The perceptual representations that result from the execution of code generate effects of continuity sustained by the algorithmic processing of discrete data structures. Modeling and simulation are thus defining operations of digital materiality. They derive from the allographic ontology of the computer's mode of inscription, that is, from the fact that the execution of instructions that determines its operation is based on recursive computational processes of reading and writing that represent other processes (Kirschenbaum 2008; 2016).

From the point of view of the history of modes of representation in art and science, the pre-modern logic of mimetic representation, which seeks to produce a surrogate for the object, has given way to a modern conceptual logic, which develops models of objects—assessing the adequacy of models through conditions of theoretical possibility of these models. With the adoption of computer science in the second half of the twentieth century, modern conceptual systems are further transformed by a postmodern logic of simulation and gaming (Frischer 2011), which creates a parametric space of interaction that generates dynamic, procedural, and responsive representations, endowing them with temporal and transformational complexity, features that are inherent to the very phenomenological processuality of the modeled events.[1]

This awareness of the simulative nature of computer-based representation appears in early texts by visionary engineers, such as Alan Kay or Theodor Nelson. Referring to Dynabook, the first prototype of the graphical user interface that recreates programmed interactions in an intuitive learning space, Alan Kay writes:

> What kind of a thinker would you become if you grew up with an active simulator connected, not just to one point of view, but to all the points of view of the ages represented so they could be dynamically tried out and compared? I named the notebook-sized computer idea the Dynabook to capture McLuhan's metaphor in the silicon to come.
>
> (Kay 2002: 125)

---

[1] Development of computational parametrized approaches exploring the generative productivity of factorial permutations became a research tool in both the sciences and the arts. See, for example, Liao and Li 2020 (materials science), Brown and Mueller 2019 (architecture), and Tatar and Pasquier 2019 (music).

The "silicon to come," referred to by Alan Kay, is the ubiquitous metamedia of technical mediation, capable of simulatorily absorbing previous media. Lev Manovich emphasizes precisely this universal simulative function of software in his detailed analyses of how historical techniques for producing images and moving images have been algorithmically encoded (Manovich 2013). For Manovich, media become software through this second-order mediation of a medium. It should be noted that the simulatory nature of the graphical user interface is not only a result of the dynamism conferred by its digital operationality and by its algorithmic modeling of analog techniques and materials, but it also lies in the graphical user interface itself as a simulation of the functioning of cognitive processes, in particular of the relation between figuration and iconic manipulation, on the one hand, and abstract symbolization, on the other. Kay actively seeks to transform the computer into a medium whose processes are cognitively internalizable to the point of transforming the scale of thought and human interactions. The graphic user interface thus brings together a model of specific real-world proprioceptive enactive perceptions and a cognitive model of learning which links visualization, manipulation, and abstraction in recursive trial and error user actions.

The extraordinary effectiveness of the graphical user interface comes from its adaptation to the ergonomics of manipulation, perception, and symbolization insofar as it contains a theory of learning and cognition in the way it encodes the digital medium as an exploratory interactive space. The enactive, iconic, and symbolic stages of child development are integrated with each other in the graphical user interface. It was this deep understanding of the nature of human cognition that allowed Alan Kay to design the graphical user interface as a kinesthetic environment in which learning occurs through recursive processes of manipulation-visualization-abstraction, which he synthesized in the formula "Doing with images makes symbols" (Kay 2002: 128).

A similar understanding of the networks of hypertext and hypermedia led Ted Nelson to envision the hypermedial writing of the future as "transclusive all-media interactive literature," that is, as a field of reconfigurable links that offers multiple perspectives on itself:

> It would be hyperarchical, permitting the same material to be organized into simultaneous alternative structures—hierarchies, sequences, hyperplexes. It could permit no embedded codes, would make all changes by optional additions and structural overlay. As a deep revision server and project tracker for writers, scholars and programmers, it would manage reuse and instance comparison

in all projects and publications. Users trying many possible organizational strategies could maintain all of them to express the unified fullness of their exact ideas. And this single user console would scale up directly to groupware and a mighty on-line publishing server for tomorrow's transclusive all-media interactive literature.

(Nelson 1995: 32–3)

This scalability—presciently imagined by Nelson—from individual console to collaborative online writing, is already explicit in the notion of "open hypertext network" (Nelson 1987: 0/12), formulated in *Literary Machines*, but present since his seminal article of 1965 (Nelson 1965), and it can be related to current forms of collaborative writing and editing in cloud computing practices. Moreover, in considering that this open hypertextual network was a simulation of the associative structures of thought—"an interwoven system of ideas (what I call a structangle)" (Nelson 1987: 1/14)—an idea he adopted from Vannevar Bush's memex (1945), Nelson regarded hypertext, first and foremost, as a cognitive device:

> It is my belief that this new ability to represent ideas in the fullness of their interconnections will lead to easier and better writing, easier and better learning, and a far greater ability to share and communicate the interconnections among tomorrow's ideas and problems.
>
> (Nelson 1987: 1/19)

The possibility of dynamically reconfiguring interconnections among digital numerical representations, by means of graphical user interfaces and hypertextual structures, has given digital materiality an intrinsically simulatory capability, since the elements and relations among the elements in a representation become susceptible to a multitude of variations. This possibility of internal reconfiguration of the relations among the elements that constitute a form creates representations that have the parameterizable provisionality of a set of values. For a given set of algorithmic conditions, a given form. This definition of a range of values allows digital objects to acquire their simulating virtuality as a probabilistically distribution across an actualizable space.

Inspired by Jerome McGann's ideas about the relationship between bibliographic structures and hypertextual structures, and by Johanna Drucker's notions of speculative computing, the project of creating a dynamic digital archive dedicated to Fernando Pessoa's *Book of Disquiet* developed from the notions of radiant textuality (McGann 2001a) and performative materiality

(Drucker 2009, 2013a). The idea of a de-hierarchized archive—in which any text could be connected to any other and become the center of a reconfigurable constellation of associations—was combined with the idea of a textual space where user interventions could be inscribed, exploring the potentiality of the acts of writing, reading, and editing in the re-materialization of the *Book of Disquiet*. My initial idea of constructing a meta-critical textual space evolved into the conceptualization of new kind of artifact: a literary simulator, in which the distributed principles of digital ontology would be experimentally used for engaging with the production of the literary as an intersubjective, collaborative, game-like, and open process (Portela and Rito Silva 2015b).

The following sections trace the conceptual and technical trajectory of the *LdoD Archive*, from a dynamic scholarly editing environment to a fully-fledged theory of literary action. The critical exploration of the simulation capabilities of the computer opened up a cognitive landscape with transformative consequences for our imagination of the literary.[2] This book is my attempt to explain how this artifact embodies several new ideas subsumed under the notion of literary simulation. Since its programming and interfaces have been designed as both models of literary processes and as literary tools, the whole environment may be described as large-scale literary experiment whose aim is to understand the performativity of literary action. Computational creativity and simulation are not to be understood as referring to the development of an autonomous system for modeling reading, editing, and writing, but rather to the creation of a parametrized space for literary action that impacts on our textual practices and textual theories, and on the development of humanistic interfaces.

The plasticity of the *LdoD Archive* reflects its data model, its textual encoding, and the programming of a set of functionalities that allow users (a) to construct various perspectives on its textual corpus; (b) to manipulate its literary materials at different scales of intervention; (c) to register their own actions of reading, editing, and writing within this interpretative and semiotic space, whose content and structure evolves over time. By taking on the role of readers, for example, they can explore the alternative paths offered by various editions as possible versions of the *Book of Disquiet*. By acting as editors, they can construct virtual editions of the *Book of Disquiet* through the exploration of the modularity of the fragments in order to instantiate new aggregations of the texts of this work.

---

[2] For a brief history of computers and interfaces as augmentation systems and cognitive tools, see Douglas Engelbart (1962), Alan Kay and Adelle Goldberg (1977), Bret Victor (2013), and Michael Nielsen (2016a, 2016b).

When they move to the role of authors, they can relate to the text of the *Book of Disquiet* through the act of writing—expanding and transforming the text itself.

The Persistence of the Codex

Digital remediation of bibliographic forms of the past has been focused on representing the appearance of the codex and mimicking its visual structure. Our current ability to construct large databases containing thousands of digital facsimiles is reflected in the growth of documentary editing across humanities disciplines (literature, history, philosophy, etc.). Thus the primary mode for the scholarly engagement with books in the digital environment has been representational, i.e, as a textual, visual, and metatextual presentation that refers back to an original manuscript or print source. Similarly, the design of digital books has been focused on emulating the familiar structures of organization and navigation of the printed codex.

Studies of the editorial process of hybrid publication (understood as multiplatform publication, i.e., the simultaneous publication in both print and digital format) suggest that changes in the design of books brought about by digital technologies have not yet translated into a standard set of production and organizational practices that incorporate the hybridism of the current situation into their processes. Even if we consider that, since the 1990s, most printed books are merely the output of digital processes, the fact remains that the process of designing and printing books through digital media continues to be attached to the symbolic and financial value of the printed book as a marketable commodity and to the function of the codex as communication artifact. This strong media legacy is also a material and formal attachment to the graphical layout and bibliographical structures of the printed codex. The current situation seems to embody a media paradox: while books are digitally designed to circulate in print form, the flexibility of the digital medium for generating multiple formats for electronic circulation and reproduction is rarely explored in ways that go beyond the facsimile and the emulation of the printed page.

Thus books are designed with digital tools with a print output in mind, and both the production workflow and the actual graphical design of the layout follow the division of work of print publishing and the formatting conventions of print book layout. This means that e-books are conceived of as a digital output of a print output, which was itself the output of a series of digital processes (from word processing and editing to designing and printing). The digital format often appears as an afterthought of the print format, and the affordances of the digital medium for modularized structuring of information, responsive design, and multiple interfaces are rarely explored, despite the fact that most information has been processed as computer code for most of the production chain. The result of this process is the erasure of a set of processing possibilities that would enable the simultaneous conception of the dual form of the book (printed and digital) to be produced as output from a single digital workflow.

The printed codex is such a powerful cognitive and rhetorical structure that we seem unable to think about the digital book other than as a mirror remediation of the print form. Even when we design scholarly archives we remain attached to our source documentary inscriptions, using many resources for replicating their formal appearance as a way of authenticating our digital re-encodings and transmediations (Deegan and Sutherland, 2009a, 2009b; Mandell 2015). The printed codex is the dominant model in our imagination of the scholarly edition: we create digital editions as remediations of printed books; and then we reprint books based on digital editions that were already remediations of printed books. In other words, the printed form of the book constantly replicates itself in electronic space, so that many electronic books are not yet digital books in a full sense. And why should this be?

In my view this question has to be addressed from two perspectives: from a book design perspective, and from a marketplace perspective. From a book design perspective, a strong connection persists between the design program of a print book as a model of information flows within a publishing organization (such as a university press or a trade publisher) and its design program as a model of formal templates (in terms of both graphic layout and digital standards for encoding and publication). This means that the division of work between graphic designers, on the one hand, and web designers and software developers, on the other, does not encourage a design approach that conceives of the print and digital publication as an integrated process in the production and communication workflow.

On the other hand, since the economic rationale of the publishing industry depends on the market for publications, the decision to publish in both media is necessarily determined by the demand for each genre and type of book, and for the effects that each media format has on the market for the other. The set of processes according to which decisions are made about which print works are also produced and distributed in digital format, and vice versa, is fundamentally dependent on these market dynamics. In addition, more than just determining whether to publish in both print and digital format, the market dynamics seem to determine the multimedia design program for a publication in the sense that it determines the amount of time and resources that publishers are willing to commit to digital affordances in the digital versions of books. Although here we are specifically concerned with the case of scholarly editions, this way of framing the problem can be applied to other types of books, including technical books, textbooks, and children's books, for example.

To the extent that the commercial dynamics (and its feedback with the technological apparatus) influences the degree of hybridity in multiplatform publication, one of the theoretical problems in shaping the organizational flowchart of a hybrid design program for the book is precisely the need to understand the implications of these commercial dynamics in the programmatic hybridization of the book, according to specific types, genres, markets, and platforms (online platforms, tablets, e-book readers, smartphones). This is a reflection that applies more clearly to certain types of publication—such as academic journals, scientific research monographs, or didactic works—but which is nevertheless relevant for the critical editions of literary works, which also participate in this hybrid editorial context.

Digital Scholarly Editing

Over the past thirty years, the evolution of technologies and technical standards has significantly modified digital critical editing models. During the 1990s, the CD-ROM (and later the DVD) were the preferred media for these editions, usually developed as commercial projects, resulting from collaboration between academic publishers and philologists. The possibility of aggregating numerous texts and documentary images, representing them through hyperlinks and expanding the possibilities for automatic search of the text and its metadata were the three most important functionalities explored in this initial process of migration of the critical edition into the digital medium.

The first major modification in the paradigm of printed critical edition is precisely the possibility of relating the documentary facsimile edition (with a full representation of the material witnesses of the texts) with a critical and genetic edition, reconfiguring the critical apparatus and redesigning the layout according to the specific flexibility of the digital medium, for example through parallel synchronization, in separate windows, of the image of the text and its transcription, or presentation of the image, transcription, and translation, as can be seen in the early editions on CD-ROM of texts from the classical, medieval, and Renaissance periods. The edition on CD-ROM also implied the insertion of the digital critical edition in the modes of production and distribution of the book sector and the possibility of proprietary control over the textual contents and the software applications developed for each edition.

Starting in the mid-1990s, critical digital editions are gradually transferred to the web, often taking the form of databases and archives. Proprietary models based on the massive digitization of thousands of texts were followed by research projects focused on the development of new methods for editing and publishing our literary heritage. These digital archives are usually born within the context of a funded research project and are developed within an academic ecosystem whose partners may include the information services of the institutions and a group of experts in the specific textual corpus. Given the cultural value and canonical nature of many of the corpora selected for electronic editing, these multipartner projects usually involve university libraries, often in collaboration with national libraries, which add as a new aim of their mission to develop forms of digital access to their literary and bibliographic heritage.

This change entails three significant transformations in the ecology of digital critical editing: the need for a technical adaptation to web standards, namely compatibility with browser markup languages (SGML, first, and XML, later), adoption of international standards to ensure interoperability—such as the Text Encoding Initiative—and a predominantly open-access publishing practice, often developed in a context of peer review and validation that is independent from the context of the book industry. Some of the major North American digital archives, funded by the National Endowment for the Humanities and various foundations and developed in centers for technology in the humanities, contributed to the affirmation of this open-access model during the second half of the 1990s.

At the same time, some of the leading academic editors were developing ambitious digital publishing platforms on the web, seeking not only to commercially exploit the possibilities of distributing new editions but also to take advantage of their valuable bibliographical catalog—for example, in relation to works of reference and dictionaries, but also to critical editions—as was the case of Cambridge University Press and Oxford University Press. The commercial dynamics of creating a new market for the online digital edition of works in the public domain can be seen in ProQuest's Literature Online project, originally launched in 1996, and continues to the present in many large databases and datamining services.

As anticipated in the early 1990s, modular genres—dictionaries and encyclopedias, technical manuals and textbooks, newspapers, magazines, and scientific journals—were the forms that most quickly transitioned to hybrid production or to digital-only formats (Nunberg 1996). In the case of the genres of continuous reading, it was necessary to wait for the development of reading devices such as the Kindle or the iPad for the distribution and sale of digital versions of certain categories of books, such as fictional narrative genres, to surpass their printed versions, as happened in the English-language market after 2010. In any case, many of these publications adopt EPUB, MOBI, and PDF as standard or choose formats dependent on specific software-hardware assemblages, and very few companies produce cross-platform versions compatible with various devices and operating systems. Issues of compatibility and rapid obsolescence of devices and systems are determined both by the pace of technological innovation and by the consumerist logic of market competition.

At present, the process of coexistence between print and digital formats covers a spectrum that ranges from simple remediation to full digital transcoding of the print. The relation between print and digital editions could be conceptually summarized through three modalities, with variable degrees of intersection among them:

> 1. Migration of works from the (handwritten and printed) bibliographic heritage to the electronic medium: all digital facsimile representations of manuscript or printed books, for example, but also those text editions that mimic the printed page. Most digitization projects of national libraries were developed according to this model. The Google Books project can also be described in terms of this rationale, with the added functionality of making the entire multilanguage and multiwriting corpus of their texts searchable. After an initial stage of development working with library collections around the world, the project was extended to include many publishers and current publications.[3]

---

[3] For a brief history of library digitization, see (Darnton 2009, 2015), (Purcell 2016), and (Hoffman 2019). For the early history of Google Books, see https://www.google.com/googlebooks/about/history.html.

2. Production of digital editions that respect the modularities of printed forms and genres, but which reorganize them according to the structures and features of screen display: most examples of the current market would fit here, as is the case of simultaneous publication of printed and electronic versions of books. Generally, this hybrid publication does not imply a restructuring of the information structures of the codex or other printed formats such as the newspaper and the magazine. In these cases, we can speak of the cognitive preponderance of print and the transfer of bibliographic forms and genres to the digital medium, in which electronic hypertext is used as a remediation of bibliographical structures: indexes and notes function as internal links; references, citations, and bibliography as external links. As the hybrid edition has become more frequent, particularly with regard to large commercial and academic publishers, a flexible design approach has also become more frequent in the design of the edition, which conceptually integrates the printed and digital outputs. This is reflected, for example, in a page layout responsiveness that becomes adaptable to different screen resolutions and sizes, and in general in a more careful marking up of the metadata and XML file structure.

3. Invention of specifically digital forms: all examples that completely assimilate the features of digital textuality, such as procedurality, networkability, multimediality, and participation, would fit in this group. In this case, the multiple reinscription as property of the electronic page and the digital book as processable binary code are fully assimilated as informational structures, generating forms and genres that are not replicable on paper. This recoding of bibliographical structures gives rise to new interfaces and new possibilities for manipulation, as well as to the expansion of the intermediality and of programmable components, both in textual content and textual structures, as well as navigation and search capabilities.

For the most part, critical digital editions carry out processes of remediation of the literary archive that correspond to the first two modes of migration, that is, to a media logic of transfer centered on a mimetic relation with the original documents, including the digital reconstitution of their handwritten, typographic, or printed modularities. Interaction design is almost exclusively focused on enhancing the user's relation with the accuracy of the representation within predefined conventions. Interfaces are rarely transformative in changing the modes of perceiving the materials or providing awareness of user-presence in the interface.

From Textual Marks to Textual Fields

Reconstitution of the autograph archive and its editions in digital critical editions follows a representational principle, whose aim is to authenticate its own authority as both facsimile image and textual transcription of the document, supplemented by a comprehensive critical apparatus that explains autographic inscriptions and their editorial transformations. The interpretative nature of the editorial act is minimized due to the transparency effect obtained by the facsimile presence of the object, through exhaustive description in metadata and notes, and also through textual encoding for automatic processing. This principle of exhaustive representation for digital processing manifests itself in the content and structure of the different modules of the Text Encoding Initiative, whose hierarchical tagging system contains extremely granular descriptors of very large sets and subsets of textual forms and events (The TEI Consortium 2021).

Although deeply aware of the remediating specificity of digital media, research carried out in the field of digital critical editing has focused almost exclusively on the transfer and expansion of the critical edition model in the new environment (Bryant 2002; Shillingsburg 2006, 2009, and 2017; Sahle 2016). The emphasis is placed on exhaustiveness, inclusivity, and scale, and the electronic edition remains attached to a document-centric approach (Roland 2011; Apollon et al. 2014; Van Hulle and Nixon 2011–21). This scholarly editing model has been extended to the universe of born-digital texts, adapting document editing approaches to electronic inscriptions (Kirschenbaum 2008, 2013). Digital scholarly editing has been less concerned with the reconceptualization of the relationship between document and transcription, or between text and critical apparatus, or between reader and text (Robinson 2013, 2016a, 2016b; Pierazzo 2015; Driscoll and Pierazzo 2016).

Computational affordances have been understood as tools for doing more extensive annotation and description of holograph documents in ways that reinforce the social division of literary work established by print media. Despite the theoretical and technical sophistication of discussions of digital representations of literary texts, including the problem of modeling (Ciula et al. 2018; Flanders and Jannidis 2019), their focus is rarely placed on the ways in which digital scholarly editing and archiving are framing literary objects and prescribing interactions. Theoretical explorations of the ontology of digital objects for interpretative action is still relatively rare (Zundert and Andrews 2017; Drucker 2020).

The strong mimetic power of digital visual representation has limited experimentation with other possibilities for modeling textual objects. Intentionalist editing, social editing, and genetic editing models remain dominated by a representational descriptive logic and a comprehensive emulation of the document. The possibility of facsimile representation of the original in high resolution and the consequent mapping of textual marks by means of topographical transcriptions—made according to a grid system of spatial coordinates—testifies to this fetishism and monumentalization of the material object. The principle of exhaustiveness in description contains an ingrained desire for transparency and coincidence between transcription and inscription, as if transcription or facsimile representation could finally evade the process of abstraction and modeling of its textual object.

Digital editions in which the mimetic logic in the representation of marks is expressed through an extensive spatial mapping of writing marks according to a topographic coordinate system can help us understand how the logic of transparency has dominated our imagination. Three significant examples are the *Samuel Beckett Digital Manuscript Project* (2011–), the prototype for Marcel Proust's *Cahier 46* (2012), and *Woolf Online* (2013).[4] Their marking up of the topography of the source documents can be related to the extension of the TEI tagset for genetic editions. Although *Woolf Online* does not follow TEI semantics and syntax, the encoding of spatial coordinates follows similar principles. In 2011, an encoding model for genetic editions was integrated into the TEI guidelines, introducing new sets of tags for topographic encoding of documents (e.g., <surface> and <zone>) which encouraged editors to intensify this emulation component in their transcriptions.[5]

---

[4] Van Hulle and Nixon 2011–21 (https://www.beckettarchive.org/), Pierazzo et al. 2012 (http://peterstokes.org/elena/proust_prototype/), and Caughie et al. 2013 (http://www.woolfonline.com). Samuel Beckett's digital manuscript project is perhaps the most ambitious and complex genetic editing project currently in progress. Besides the extensive marking up of Beckett's autographs, it also includes the Beckett Digital Library, a digitized reconstruction of Beckett's personal library with the aim marking up Beckett's reading traces and linking them to the autograph manuscripts, typescripts, and proofs. Since the first release of the SBDMP in 2011, the autographs for the following works have between critically edited: *Stirrings Still / Soubresauts* (1988); *Comment dire / What is the Word* (1989); *L'Innommable / The Unnamable* (1953); *Krapp's Last Tape / La Dernière Bande* (1958); *Molloy* (1951); *Malone meurt / Malone Dies* (1951); *En attendant Godot / Waiting for Godot* (1952), and *Fin de partie / Endgame* (1957). Besides the genetic electronic edition, the composition of each work is thoroughly analyzed in a series of dedicated volumes (*The Making of Samuel Beckett's …*) published by Bloomsbury.

[5] The proposal was made in 2010: "An Encoding Model for Genetic Editions" (https://tei-c.org/Vault/TC/tcw19.html). See also the latest version of the *Guidelines* (The TEI Consortium 2021), particularly chapters 11 ("Representation of Primary Sources") and 12 ("Critical Apparatus"), for the current list of tag sets.

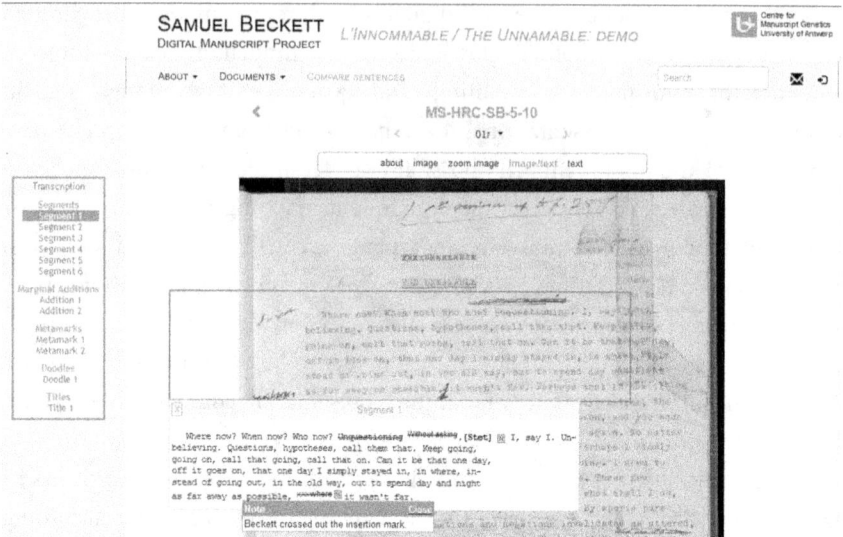

Figure 1.1 *Samuel Beckett Digital Manuscript Project*: digital facsimile and linear transcription as approximation to the original. First page of typed manuscript of *The Unnamable*, completed June 1958 (MS-HRC-SB-5-10), as presented in the image/text interface.

The *Samuel Beckett Digital Manuscript Project* represents the compositional complexity of multiple successive drafts in Beckett's writing through a combination of topographic and linear transcription, thus attempting to bring together the granular and chaotic layering and branching of script acts with a genetic interpretation that reconstitutes the sequentiality of writing and revisions (Figure 1.1).[6] According to its "Editorial Principles and Practice":

> The BDMP works with a text-oriented approach, but not without taking "toposensitive" (Ferrer 1998: 262) data into account. The "record" ("Befund") is represented by means of digital facsimiles, while the transcriptions are regarded as forms of "interpretation" ("Deutung") of the manuscripts because they are never fully free of interpretation. ... Yet, these two diverging viewpoints are not irreconcilable. On the one hand, a topographic transcription is not always that "simple"; on the other hand, a linear transcription does not necessarily imply a "reduction." They are both transformations, and the combination of a topographic with a linear transcription proves to be an adequate way to perfect

---

[6] https://www.beckettarchive.org/writingsequenceofinnommable.jsp

the approximation of the original, according to the principle formulated by Almuth Grésillon: "L'objectif de la transcription n'est pas la perfection, mais la perfectibilité" (Grésillon 1994: 129).

(Van Hulle and Nixon, SBDMP, 2011)

Perfecting "the approximation of the original" becomes the general principle behind the reification of the inscriptions as the site for insight. In the case of genetic editing, this approximation may be used for analyzing and visualizing the inscription and reinscription protocols through which a given text comes into being. The granular reconstruction of script acts samples the analog traces of writing on the sheet of paper according to the discretizing principles of digital representation: numbering sentences, making them traceable within the coordinates of a grid applied to the manuscript draft, mapping them onto the published sentence sequence, and then temporizing the hypothetical writing sequence through animation. The *Samuel Beckett Digital Manuscript Project* offers five visualizations of this process in relation to *L'Innommable* which show how the logic of digital tracing enabled by current technologies has been obsessively applied in digitizing Beckett's writing process. Digital tracing and visualization reinforce each other in the positivist reification of the mark. The emulation of the visible thus becomes the major critical method for transcoding texts into digital code.

The justification for the TEI encoding prototype of Proust's *Cahier 46*, which uses the new spatial tags to rehearse a timelime of composition, also underlines the gain in representing the process of writing as a gain of mimetic fidelity (Figure 1.2):[7]

> Ultra-diplomatic online editions are generally presented facing the facsimile of the manuscript, but this representation is not satisfactory, and this for several reasons: first, imitation is never perfect; then, it is up to the user/reader to relate the transcription to the document; finally, because of the spatial constraints of the screen, we must be content to present one page at a time, and not, for example, a double page spread—which, in the case of Proust's notebooks, betrays the reality of the manuscript, since the double page is, in Proust, the space of writing.
>
> (André and Pierazzo 2013: 155; *my translation*)

Although aware of the necessary distortions of digital remediation—such as treating the single page as the unit of transcription instead of the double

---

[7] http://peterstokes.org/elena/proust_prototype/

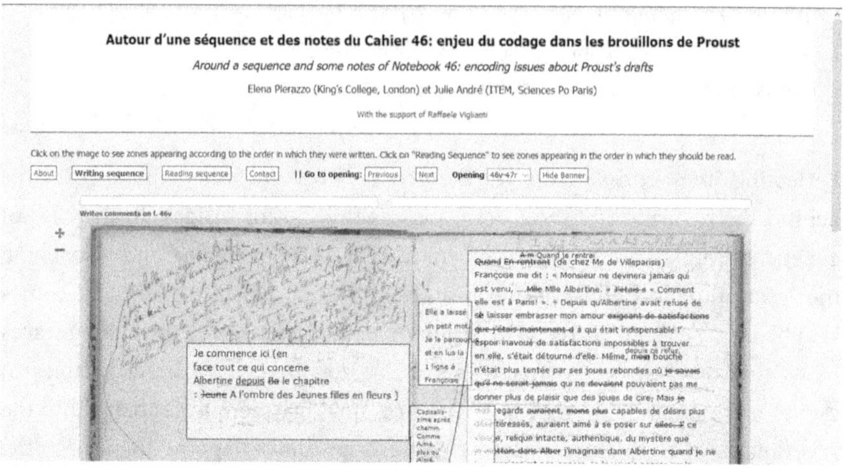

Figure 1.2 Proust's *Cahier 46* prototype: a temporized representation of spatial marks for folios 46v and 47r (Pierazzo et al. 2012).

spread or leaving the mapping between transcript and image in the hands of readers—the rationale for a topographic transcription is presented in terms of the imperfection of the imitation. The mediating function of the data model for processing remains subordinated to the enactment of the visual fidelity of digital representation to a specific material instantiation of the source document.

If, in the cases of Beckett and Proust, topographic encoding of textual marks serves a principle of genetic analysis of the sequence of inscriptional acts, translating spatiality into temporality, in the case of the Virginia Woolf's *To the Lighthouse*, the topographic transcription of the typescript results in a strange combination of redundancy and transparency, suggesting the coincidence between inscription and transcription, while exhibiting, at the same time, the ontological un-coincidence between object and model of the object (Figure 1.3).[8] Although enriched with the possibility of separating or overlapping the display of layers of visualization and transcription inherent to the photo-electronic materiality of the screen, those three digital critical-genetic editions can be described as remediations of the ultra-diplomatic edition that expand its mimetic principles by overlaying text and image. This means that the

---

[8] http://www.woolfonline.com/?node=content/text/transcriptions&project=1&parent=2&taxa=17&content=5584&pos=1.

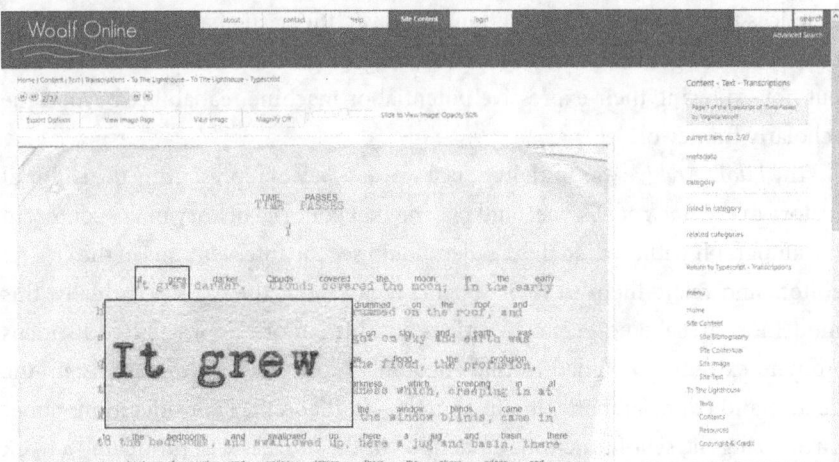

Figure 1.3 *Woolf Online:* mapping encoded transcription onto a digital image facsimile of Virginia Woolf's typescript *To the Lighthouse* (50 percent opacity and magnifier). Page 1 of the typescript of "Time Passes" by Virginia Woolf.

bitmapping of the latter and the character codes of the former are subordinated to a representational positivistic logic of literal correspondence between machine-readable representation and physical object.

Providing a combination of documentary editing with critical edition, integrating image and text in the same environment, often with the added value of aggregating many primary and secondary resources for the study of the remediated texts, books, or artworks, digital archives developed between the 1990s and 2010s redefined scholarly editing and art history in digital media as a complex hypermedia network. We took as our initial models those first- and second-generation archives, informed by both genetic criticism and social editing theories, such as the *Rossetti Archive*, *The William Blake Archive*, *Dickinson Electronic Archives*, *The Walt Whitman Archive*, *Radical Scatters*, *Samuel Beckett Digital Manuscript Project*, or the *Shelley-Godwin Archive*.[9] Providing access to digital representations of source documents, creating complex networks of documents, and structuring navigation and search functions became the standard goals of digital archives. Web 2.0 functionalities were gradually added to the intermedia integration of artistic and literary facsimiles, opening up textual

---

[9] Cf. http://www.rossettiarchive.org/, http://www.blakearchive.org/, https://www.emilydickinson.org/, https://whitmanarchive.org/, http://radicalscatters.unl.edu/, https://www.beckettarchive.org/, http://shelleygodwinarchive.org/.

practices to new types of interaction. However, the participatory affordances in these projects generally involve transcribing or glossing the primary sources, but not exploring their expressive potential or machine readability beyond the scholarly framework.

The *LdoD Archive* was initially conceived as a way of representing the editorial history of the *Book of Disquiet*, and placing that editorial history in the context of the autograph witnesses so that readers could see the interventions of the critical editors and relate them to their specific ideas about the work. Gradually, this model for virtualizing Pessoa's writings and his editors' books shifted its focus from an extremely detailed textual encoding—concerned with marking up the genetic and editorial marks in our sources—to theoretical considerations about virtualizing the set of functions embedded in the processes of producing a work as work. Thus our data model of the *LdoD Archive*, which had established the textual fragment as the basic unit for processing and presentation, expanded to include Web 2.0 interactions that would enable users to change the content of the archive and perform actions on the text according to specific roles. The TEI modeling of the documents as a hierarchical processable representation of textual marks was critically transformed by a theoretical and processing model whose aim was to simulate the dynamics of the textual field itself.

Modeling a Virtual *Book of Disquiet*

Fernando Pessoa is a major Portuguese modernist writer. His work, most of which was only published posthumously, continues to fascinate and intrigue new generations of readers, editors, and writers.[10] Readers are attracted to the multiplicity of voices and perspectives that can be found in his writings. Editors persist in their renewed attempts at making sense of his paper archive and giving form to his many unfinished publication projects. Writers look at the invention of multiple fictional authors as experiments in subjectivity that show the discursive nature of being as a linguistic function. His range of modes, genres, and forms further testifies to Pessoa's attempt at appropriating and transforming a large body of literary sources. In effect, Pessoa's self-description as "not only

---

[10] The publication of a new thoroughly researched biography in August 2021 testifies to the growing worldwide interest on Fernando Pessoa: Richard Zenith, *Pessoa: A Biography*, New York: W.W. Norton & Co.

a writer, but a whole literature,"¹¹ and whose immediate reference is the alterity of heteronyms as stylistic and fictional practices of multiplied authorship, also expresses this omnivorous assimilation of diverse writing practices.

Among his many works in progress, the *Book of Disquiet* stands out as a long-term unfinished book project. Pessoa wrote more than five hundred pieces of text meant for this work between 1913 and 1934. Some of these pieces are several pages long, but most fragments are brief texts consisting of a few paragraphs. Pieces meant for *Livro do Desassossego* are generally typed or handwritten on loose sheets, with only a few written in notebooks. Pessoa drafted a preface for the book and left several fragmentary and incomplete plans for organizing the work, but there is no final authorial revision, selection, or ordering of the pieces. Pedro Sepúlveda has identified several lists of publishing projects by Pessoa in which the *Book of Disquiet* appears, and also a few structuring plans for this particular work. Pessoa's repeated plannings show the persistence of the idea of the book in the ways he conceived of the works assigned to his different heteronyms, but they also document his changing ideas and the postponement of any final closure. In the case of the *Book of Disquiet*, the very partial and shifting lists of texts to be included confirm that his concept evolved over time, leaving this project open and incomplete (Sepúlveda 2013, 2014).¹²

Texts for the *Book of Disquiet* were first assigned by Pessoa to heteronym Vicente Guedes, but the work was later reassigned to Bernardo Soares, a persona described by Pessoa as a "semi-heteronym." The concept of "heteronym" was developed by Pessoa: heteronyms are fictional authors who have a specific writing style and a unique biography and psychology. Many of Pessoa's works have been written by heteronyms, the most well known of which are the poets Alberto Caeiro, Álvaro de Campos, and Ricardo Reis. The editors Jacinto do Prado Coelho and Richard Zenith have assigned the *Book of Disquiet* to Bernardo Soares; Teresa Sobral Cunha has assigned the first part to Guedes and the second to Soares; Jerónimo Pizarro assigns the *Book* to Pessoa himself.

Our model of the electronic reading, editing, and writing space for the *Book of Disquiet* attempts to constellate in radial form all existing textual

---

¹¹ "Aspectos," c. 1918. Full text available at https://ldod.uc.pt/fragments/fragment/Fr585/inter/Fr585_WIT_MS_Fr585a (BNP/E3, 20-70r-71r-72r; Coelho—prefatory material; Sobral Cunha 325; Pizarro 456).

¹² For further information, see the ongoing digital edition of the autograph documents related to Fernando Pessoa's publishing projects and content lists for planned works: Sepúlveda and Henny-Krahmer 2017, http://www.pessoadigital.pt. See also my review of this electronic edition (Portela 2018).

witnesses: digital facsimiles (autograph materials) and editions 1 to 5 (JPC, TSC, RZ, JP, and LdoD), or those that will exist in the future as a result of user-created editions (edition n) (Figure 1.4). The procedural, participatory, spatial, and encyclopedic affordances of the digital medium (Murray 2012) are fully engaged in order to create a complex network of documentary relationships and a set of functions of dynamic interaction within this open documentary network. Our programmatic virtualization of the *Book of Disquiet* is a performative intervention in the work's archive that takes place also at the level of reading, editing, and writing. Besides the genetic dimension (composition of *LdoD* by the author) and the social dimension (construction of *LdoD* by its editors), the *LdoD Archive* provides a virtual dimension (reconstruction of *LdoD* by its readers), with a set of interactive and open-ended features explicitly programmed in the model.

As shown in Figure 1.4, the structure of the database and the textual encoding of its array of texts establish a network of relations between each and every one

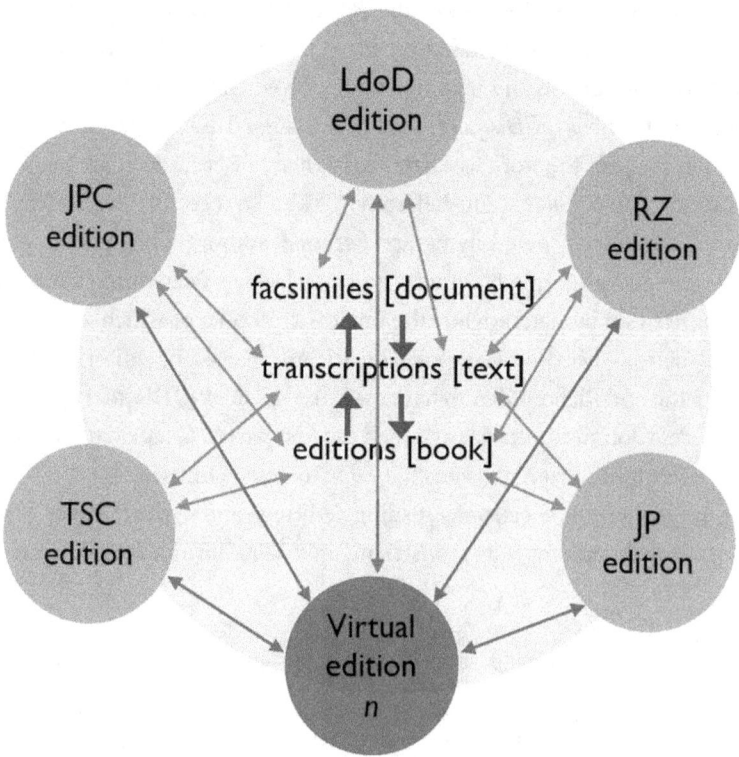

Figure 1.4 Radial structure of the *LdoD Archive*. © Manuel Portela, 2012.

of the manuscript and typescript fragments so that from each one of them we can automatically reach any other as its variant. Moreover, any fragment from any of the seven possible scholarly transcriptions—LdoD edition [autograph version 1, autograph version 2, autograph version 3], edition 1 [JPC], edition 2 [TSC], edition 3 [RZ], edition 4 [JP]—can become the center of the constellation. This flexibility extends to all virtual editions (edition n), whose texts are based on the scholarly transcriptions. This virtual dimension is an extension of the social dimension in the collaborative environment of the web.

The archive's datamodel and the electronic encoding of textual fragments support radial configurations that respond to multiple interactions in each of those three dimensions: genetic, social, and/or virtual. As seen in Figure 1.5, the genetic dimension (A) supports narratives of composition; the social dimension (B) supports narratives of editing; the virtual dimension enables users to explore permutations of A and B in constructing new editorial versions, and also the processes and mechanisms of reading and writing. The virtual dimension opens up the textual field to general processes of literary performance and semiosis.

Our conceptual and technical integration of these three dimensions constitutes an experiment in interaction design for literary archives with the aim

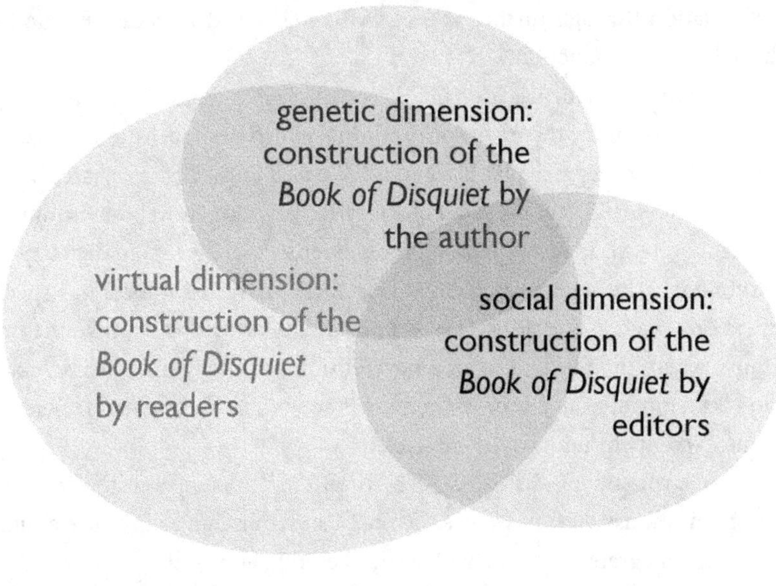

genetic dimension: construction of the *Book of Disquiet* by the author

virtual dimension: construction of the *Book of Disquiet* by readers

social dimension: construction of the *Book of Disquiet* by editors

Figure 1.5 Three dimensions of the *LdoD Archive*. © Manuel Portela, 2012.

of extending current textual theories and practices. Besides the usual search, retrieval, and display interactions, the dynamic functions enable readers of the *LdoD Archive* to perform textual interventions that change the content of the virtual dimension of the archive. These interventions can be performed according to the literary roles of reading, editing, and writing, thus becoming part of the archive's simulation of the general dynamics of the literary field through its engagement with Web 2.0 tools. This model of the reconfigurative iterability of the genetic and editorial archive of the work enables users to virtualize Pessoa's book project according to four functions: reader-function, editor-function, author-function, and book-function (Figure 1.6). Through interaction between textual representation and transformation, the *LdoD Archive* has become a computational engine and a textual field for the experimental simulation of literary processes (Portela and Rito Silva 2015b and 2016a).

"Author-function" in this context contains an allusion to authorship as a discursive function (as described in Michel Foucault's 1969 essay [Foucault 1997]), but it also expresses our approach to an understanding of textual form through the actual experience of writing. Instead of reifying the text as a material object that we (as readers and/or editors) can only perform through representation and interpretation, the *LdoD Archive* also approaches the work through a playful engagement with the writing process itself. Authorship is socialized and distributed as the textual field becomes open to expansion and transformation through further acts of writing. The text remains open to new authorial acts of production.

"Social editing," in turn, is used in this book in two different but related senses: one is derived from the theory of social editing, which describes the socialization of texts embodied in particular bibliographic codes in the historical archive; the other refers to social editing as a collaborative practice in web environments. This second sense is to be understood as an extension of the first in digital media environments. The socialization of editing through Web 2.0 tools has specific implications, such as the possibility of continuous re-editing—unlike the print medium, where the production of a new edition only happens when an earlier edition is no longer available or when there is enough market demand for several editions to compete amongst themselves.

The construction of the *LdoD Archive* attempts to answer the following research questions: (1) Can we use a Web 2.0 environment to produce a digital archive that integrates a genetic with a social editing approach?; (2) Is it possible to structure and encode genetic and editorial witnesses for dynamic interactions that feed back into the contents and structure of the archive itself?; (3) As we remediate and simulate reading, editing, writing, and bibliographic processes in the construction of the *Book of Disquiet*, can we rethink the relations between acts of reading, editing, and writing and forms of the book as they are imagined and performed in our literary practices?; (4) By virtualizing reading, editing, and writing processes, can we remodel the archive as a space for autopoiesis and allopoiesis, i.e., as an exploratory space for multiple remakings rather than a fixed, immutable, and authorized repository?

The participatory affordance of the digital medium has two major facets: the definition of a semiotic environment for collaboration and social interaction, on the one hand, and the possibility of marking material changes at the level of code, on the other. These features of networked computational media can be used to redesign the digital archive as a living environment for different kinds of practice, not limited to research and teaching. A scholarly remediation of the *Book of Disquiet* according to tested principles of electronic philology and genetic criticism becomes part of a larger interactive environment where reading, editing, and writing practices around the *Book of Disquiet* are to be socialized, visualized, and analyzed within the digital medium itself. Aggregation of authorial and editorial witnesses according to criteria defined by readers occur within a virtual space that allows users to visualize their own reading trajectories, assemble and annotate selections of texts, or write variations based on the fragments. Thus knowledge of textual form and textual transmission is complemented by poetic experiments with reading, editing, and writing processes and with bibliographic structures.

According to this theoretical framework for virtualizing the *Book of Disquiet*, the archive becomes a space for visualizing and analyzing particular historical configurations of Pessoa's book project in actual authorial and editorial versions, but also a space for experimenting with reading, editing, and writing. The problem of creating a space for interaction and dynamic addition to archive material has been formalized in a number of cases (Bénel and Lejeune 2009; Fraistat and Jones 2009; Siemens et al. 2010, 2012; Muñoz et al. 2013). However, there is no satisfactory model or solution for the integration of the genetic, social, and virtual functionalities as defined here. This conceptualization of the virtual dimension of the *LdoD Archive* implies finding a satisfactory technical solution at the level of encoding and programming operations. Pessoa's writing process (including his invention of writing selves) and his many plans for organizing his works (including his projects for the *Book of Disquiet*) are in themselves significant for an understanding of the dynamics between writing and book forms, and for a general investigation into the nature and functions of literary discourse and practice. The rationale for virtualizing the *Book of Disquiet* in this way stems from our understanding of digital materiality as a medium that is capable of simulating both the actuality of extant witnesses and recorded events, on the one hand, and the potentiality of its processes and structures, on the other.[13]

Beyond the Bibliographic Horizon

Although the *LdoD Archive* contains a representational logic similar to those that define the technical standards and theoretical principles in the field of digital scholarly editing, I would argue that it embodies a radically different model of remediation, i.e., a model that uses the processability of the digital medium for reconfiguring modes of textual presentation, as well as modes of interaction with these textual reconfigurations. It is this redesign of text and reader's interaction with text—or "intra-action" (Barad 2003) if we look at it from the point of view of the performative entanglements constitutive of the various elements in the system—that lets us add a simulatory function to the representational function. The goal of the simulation is to create an evolving machine that enacts the relations and transactions between the archival, the readerly, the editorial, and the authorial dimensions of literary practice. The *LdoD Archive* is not there to be perceived as a predefined bibliographic structure, but rather as an experiment in enacting the performative conditions for literary action.

---

[13] The code for the *LdoD Archive* is available at https://github.com/socialsoftware/edition. It may be shared according to a FreeBSD license. António Rito Silva designed the software architecture and a significant part of the code for the platform. New features integrated into *LdoD Archive* since its publication in December 2017 include the following applications: "LdoD Classification Game" (2018, https://ldod.uc.pt/classificationGames); "Citations on Twitter" (2018, https://ldod.uc.pt/citations); "LdoD—Virtual Edition: Citations on Twitter" (2018, https://ldod.uc.pt/edition/acronym/LdoD-Twitter); and "LdoD Visual" (2019, https://ldod.uc.pt/ldod-visual). In the list of cited works, readers will find the bibliographic entries and links for accessing all the components of the source code. Can this model be applied to other corpora? Although conceived for this particular work, its general principles can be tested on other literary corpora, particularly for those works that pose similar editorial problems. Projects for modularizing the various components of the *LdoD Archive* in order to make them reusable have been developed by the project team (Cruz 2018; Gonçalves 2019). If we think of the *LdoD Archive* as a prototype for the redesign of our literary practices and concepts for computational environments, then it could have a much wider impact, particularly in challenging the normative divide between scholarly and creative practices.

Textual variability is not only presented as a record of variations that are historically attested in the work's reading, editing, and writing processes. It is also experimentally produced as a consequence of the virtualization of the *Book of Disquiet* at the levels of reading, editing, and writing. Through the development of an infrastructure and a set of programming principles that allow users to modify both the text and the organization of the text, the *LdoD Archive* opens up a set of possibilities for intervention and manipulation that exceeds a merely representational logic, thus virtualizing the book as a potentiality. The processuality of the book as conceptual and material horizon of writing, editing, and reading can be experienced as a remediation of the past archive and can be actively explored as the future production of the archive (Portela and Rito Silva 2015a).

The *LdoD Archive* thus proposes a simulatory modeling of the procedural nature of textuality, similar to what has been imagined by Jerome McGann:

> But suppose, in our real-life engagements with those physical objects, we experience them as social objects, as functions of measurements that their users and makers have chosen for certain particular purposes. In such a case you will not want to build a model of one made thing, you will try to design a system that can simulate all the realized and realizable documentary possibilities—the possibilities that are known and recorded as well as those that have yet to be (re)constructed.
>
> (McGann 2006: 60)

Instead of reifying the objective nature of the material instantiation of one particular text (its textual marks), the technical and conceptual model of the *LdoD Archive* is focused on the processuality through which the text is produced as "literary" (its textual field). Literary practices can be modeled on the actions that produce a text as a literary object and as a literary event, that is, as an object and event that meets a given set of rules of production and perception. Produced as a literary object, it is also perceived as a literary object, and it is through this double production that its literary condition emerges.

Its literary condition is intentionally produced by an act of writing and is retroactively produced by the inscription of a reading act in the field of intentions and meanings of this writing act. Among the actions that mark an object or an event as literary, we can highlight the actions of writing, editing, and reading. Literary performativity consists of performing the set of roles associated with those actions. The separation and division of roles—which originates in the functional differences between writing, editing, and reading—resulted in the historical development of specific figures and institutions: the institution of the author as the original creator; the editor as an expert in the form and transmission of the text; and the reader as an interpreter and commentator open to the ambiguity of signs.

Furthermore, the material and conceptual instantiation of the work in the form of a book is the space where those actions converge. The book can also be postulated as another powerful actant since it constitutes itself as a conceptual, material, and discursive space through which the particular network of actions and roles are constellated and mutually determining. It is at once a body in motion and a gravitational force binding the system together. We can thus postulate a *book-function* as another structuring aspect of literary performativity. Writers write with a certain idea of the book as the horizon of their creative process, assuming the *author-function* within the discursive fields of language and culture; editors, in turn, are involved in the bibliographic materialization of the text, that is, in giving it a textual and material form capable of reproduction and circulation, that is, they assume the *editor-function*; finally, readers act on the textual field by performing a set of manipulative and interpretative operations that the body of signs of the book-text and the discursive fields of language and culture provide them, exerting the *reader-function* (Figure 1.6).

In book-based literature, the production of the literary involves a social and cognitive dynamics sustained by those actions. Those four actions can be conceived as discursive functions or roles whose performance brings the literary field into being. Instead of essentializing the conditions of production through the institutional and technical modes that define the roles that I can play, what is proposed in *LdoD Archive* is to use the technical flexibility of the digital medium to break the rigidity of the print medium performance. Thus, the *Book of Disquiet* can be reimagined as a literary space for playing with the nature and conditions of literary performance. By co-producing different positions in this variable space, and experimenting with features that allow them to read, edit, write, and analyze, interactors can observe literary performativity itself as a set of actions that generate a given work and its conditions of existence and interpretability for a given subject. Subjects are reflexively engaged in performing a range of possible roles.

What is literary performativity and what is its relation to other theories of performativity, such as those put forward by phenomenology, speech act theory, deconstruction, poststructuralism, actor-network theory, feminist and queer theory, or posthumanism? The notion of literary performativity is an

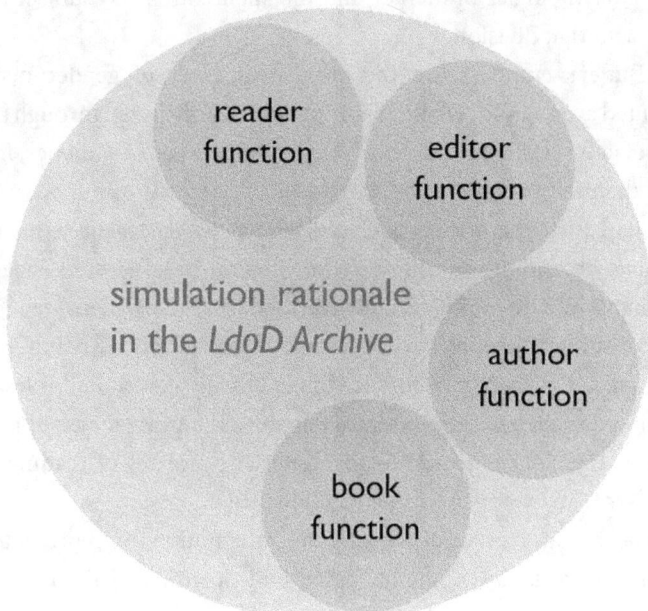

Figure 1.6 Four conceptual and technical features in the simulation rationale of the *LdoD Archive*: reader-function, editor-function, author-function, and book-function. Users interact with the archive according to several roles. The dynamic aspects of the software are used to show the performativity of those literary functions. © Manuel Portela, 2013.

attempt to describe the production of the experiential category of the literary in terms of the social semiotics of reading, editing, and writing as collaborative processes. The literary is a field of action and interpretation dependent upon the continuing performance of those specific roles. These roles, in turn, are cultural and material devices that situate individuals in particular networks of symbolic action.

Although I refer to role-playing as a way of abstracting the actions through which specific configurations of the literary (as form, practice, and experience) are produced, I am not implying that roles are predetermined or preconstituted. They are moving historical formations that interpellate individuals according to particular conventions for regulating literary action, but they are also produced anew by the ways in which subjects perform and materialize their actions of reading, writing, and editing. The literary identity of subjects as readers, writers, and editors are contingent on their performative acts, diffracting the division of labor of the technologies of literacy and the apparently fixed subject positions associated with that division.

Judith Butler's emphasis on the performativeness of gender displaces a preconstituted agency and redefines it as "an identity instituted through a stylized repetition of acts" (1988: 519) in which the "mundane social audience, including the actors themselves come to believe and to perform in the mode of belief" (520). Similarly, the literary is conceived here as an emergent set of relations based on acts of reading, editing, and writing that become fluid engagements with ongoing symbolic production. Readers, editors, and writers are temporary identities constituted through particular modes of enacting and being enacted by written language. Their reperformance of historically constituted roles sustains the field in which their action becomes possible. The discreteness of their roles is defined by their participation in the material processes of reading-editing-writing rather than by any preconstituted identity.

One aspect that is crucial for the reconfiguration of representation as performance—that is, as a practice-based and open-ended engagement with processes—is that the *LdoD Archive* attempts to model the relations between analog and digital technologies beyond the notion of remediation as the transfer of medium-specific features from one medium to another. Its purpose is not to make legacy features (those that derive from earlier media) and new features recognizable as such in terms of an old medium/new medium dialectics. Emphasis on medium-specific features tends to reinforce their separation and thus the perception of material form as direct reflection of the technical medium, as if the properties of the medium were not also retroactively produced by their historicity, that is, particular uses and conventions. Instead, the digital modeling of print materials has been used for opening up their material and discursive form to further acts of transformation, while the digital modeling of digital materials engages with the shifting boundaries of human and non-human acts of production at all levels of the system.

Its posthumanistic logic is an operational manifestation of its simulation rationale according to diffractive principles. I am adopting Karen Barad's notion of diffraction as a critique of representationalism (2003, 2007). Her theory of agencial realism extends quantum entanglement to an onto-epistemological framework that aims to understand "naturalcultural practices, including different kinds of knowledge making practices" (2007: 90). The *LdoD Archive* can be described as a material-discursive experiment in which the ontology of textual production and the epistemology of textual knowledge are brought together. Its diffractive methodology is sustained by a performative engagement with the phenomena of literary textuality. The becoming text of text, and the emergence of textual subjects and textual objects through intra-actions are critically programmed into the conditions of the experiment.[14] They are meant to provide intra-actors with awareness of the patterns of interference and entanglement created by their actions, including those involving "non-conscious cognizers" in N. Katherine Hayles's terminology (2017).

The crucial aspect is that the *LdoD Archive* is not primarily a space for representing and archiving textual objects, but rather an ongoing experiment about the modeling of performative materiality. This concept, developed by Johanna Drucker (2013a), serves both as a critique of literal definitions of materiality and a program for designing digital interfaces that are capable of modeling the performative dimension of interpretation:

> In a model of materiality as fundamentally performative, we can show how forensic, evidentiary materiality and formal organization serve as a provocation for the creation of a reading as a constitutive interpretative act. The specific structures and forms, substrates and organizational features, are *probability conditions* for production of an interpretation.
>
> (Drucker 2013a: §17)

The conceptual model of performativity that we offer as description and explanation of the simulation rationale of the *LdoD Archive* can be further related to the actor-network metaphor. The set of four functions explained below, for instance, could be redescribed as a set of actants whose action constitutes a specific network-tracing of meanings, practices, and objects. The codependence of actants and network in the system's software architecture, including both human and non-human actions (such as algorithmic readings, editings, and writings), attempts to capture their fundamental embeddedness. Modeling literary action as an evolving process in a digital environment highlights the performative generativity of the multiple agencies involved. The literary is provoked into existence through their relationality: "No net exists independently of the very act of tracing it, and no tracing is done by an actor exterior to the net.

---

[14] For a summary of her critique of representationalism, see Barad 2007 (particularly the table on pp. 89–90). In Barad's methodology, the concept of "intra-action" refers to the internal differentiation that constitutes the relationality of elements: "It is through specific agential intra-actions that the boundaries and properties of the 'components' of phenomena become determinate and that particular embodied concepts become meaningful" (Barad 2003: 815).

A network is not a thing, but the recorded movement of a thing" (Latour 1996: 378). The *LdoD Archive* is an attempt to model this "recorded movement of a thing" as an evolving performance rather than a bibliographic structure.

Reader-function

> I don't dare reread. I can't reread. What good would it do me to reread?
> (*Book of Disquiet*, Text 63[15])

The main goal of the reader-function is to support a contextualized reading of fragments from the *Book of Disquiet*. Contextualized reading means the ability of visualizing fragment variations according to several authorial and editorial witnesses. Thus, variations fall into two groups: authorial revisions, which originate in authorial manuscripts, typescripts, and texts printed during the author's lifetime; and editorial variations, those that result from the interpretation of a posthumous editor. Variations in authorial witnesses can occur within a single documentary source or across different sources. Variations within a single source include autograph changes made in manuscript, typescript, or print text. Variations across two or more authorial witnesses describe differences between the different sources of the same fragment. Editorial variations may be the result of conjectural readings—such as interpretations of illegible words—the choice of a particular authorial variant—and of editorial revisions, such as corrections of the original text (either by standardization of spelling and punctuation, or by error correction) or internal reorganization of paragraphs. Editorial variations also occur at higher levels of granularity, including aspects such as heteronym attribution, fragment selection, and fragment order.

Reading is also represented within the *LdoD Archive* through reception documents, including both the critical reception by experts and the current online reception in social media by general readers. Additionally, reading paths of users within the archive can be captured and analyzed by the system. Visualization of interpretative protocols map quotations of the work made in critical reception documents and in the online reception to their source texts in the *Book of Disquiet*. Features associated with the reader-function enable the simultaneous visualization of facsimiles and their textual transcriptions, as well

---

[15] Full text available at https://ldod.uc.pt/fragments/fragment/Fr205/inter/Fr205_WIT_ED_CRIT_Z (BNP/E3, 3-54r-55r; Coelho 427; Sobral Cunha 501; Zenith 63; Pizarro 239).

as a comparative reading sequence interface. Textual transcription also provides a certain degree of topographical representation. Additionally, when viewing a fragment, it is possible to access its critical texts and view their semantic tags. These critical texts and semantic tags may be associated with the fragment as a whole or a part of it. In sum, there is a retroactive process involving representation and simulation at several levels: reading the work according to predefined editorial sequences; reading the work according to computer-assisted sequences; reading the work according to macro-visualizations of reader-generated criteria; reading through the lens of critical readings or online quotations of the work; and reading one's own process of reading the work. Reading is experienced as a dynamic process of shaping the text through our traversals, quotations, and interpretations.

Editor-function

> This book, furthermore, could form part of a definitive collection of dregs, the published depository of the unpublishable—allowed to survive as a sad example.
> (*Book of Disquiet*, Note concerning the actual editions[16])

The main purpose of the editor-function is to support interpretations of the *Book of Disquiet* as a book project, that is, as an attempt to assemble and organize a series of texts. Support to this editorial assemblage must be achieved through the manipulation of metatextual information on the fragments and on the *Book of Disquiet* as a whole. Besides displaying variability in aggregation and sequencing, the archive also integrates annotations and semantic tags necessary to classify the genetic and expert editorial versions of the *Book of Disquiet*. Such meta-information makes it possible not only to represent and compare actual existing versions of the book, but also to generate further editorial versions. Editorial projectuality is recreated at three levels: as an unfinished authorial project; as a series of published critical editions based on the authorial project; and as an open set of virtual editions based on the first two levels. Editorial functionality thus consists of opening up the projectual organization of the book both to its historical instantiations and to its hypothetical ongoing constructions.

---

[16] Full text available at https://ldod.uc.pt/fragments/fragment/Fr580/inter/Fr580_WIT_ED_CRIT_Z (BNP/E3, 9-12r; Coelho 7; Sobral Cunha 748; Zenith 538; Pizarro 458).

The virtualization of the editorial function takes place through a series of collaborative affordances for finding, selecting, and ordering texts, including the ability to annotate them by means of comments and tags. Comments and tags may be associated to entire texts from the *Book of Disquiet*, or to specific passages within those texts. Each set of tags associated to a virtual edition of the *Book of Disquiet* constitutes the taxonomy of that particular virtual edition. Tags thus provide an additional meta-information layer through which the interpretative rationale for arranging the texts can be explicitly declared. Editions can be structured on the basis of a sequence defined by their virtual editors or on the basis their taxonomy. The editorial function is expressed through both layers of the archive: at the representational level, it offers a meta-editorial view of the editorial function as performed by the expert editors; at the simulation level, it gives the interactors the ability to try out multiple selections, arrangements, and annotations of the texts, based on a range of computer-assisted interventions.

Author-function

> Writing is like the drug I abhor and keep taking, the addiction I despise and depend on.
>
> (Text 152[17])

The author-function is also expressed through both layers. Insofar as Pessoa's autograph materials are photographed and genetically transcribed, interactors are able to look at temporal and compositional manifestations of authorial script acts. The author-function becomes observable through the very marks of writing that constitute the traces of a writing self. On the other hand, the author-function can be programmed in the virtual model as a writing affordance to be performed by another writing self. The authorial evidence of a writing self—inferred from the handwritten and typewritten autograph inscriptions on paper—is abstracted as a literary role to be performed by a new writing self. By taking the written marks as their point of the departure, new acts of writing experiment with word and language-processing tools. At once corpus of language and texture of discourses, the *Book of Disquiet* opens itself to writing further selves. This opening up of language through further acts of writing expresses the simulatory

---

[17] Full text available at https://ldod.uc.pt/fragments/fragment/Fr009/inter/Fr009_WIT_ED_CRIT_Z (BNP/E3, 1-14; Coelho 190; Sobral Cunha 711; Zenith 152; Pizarro 269).

dimension of the author-function. Expanding the dynamic component of the model, the author-function socializes the act of the writing in a way that parallels the socialization of reading and editing.

The main objective of the author-function is the extension of the *Book of Disquiet* with new texts based on original fragments from the work. Thus, a reader of the *LdoD Archive* is able to write a new text derived from fragments of *Book of Disquiet*, becoming an author in the context of a virtual writing edition. Central to the author-function is the functionality that provides capabilities of extension, which range from the ability of modifying sentences and using sequences of words from the *Book of Disquiet* to automatic permutations and generation of sentences. To be considered an extension, references must be maintained to the sentences and sequences of words of the original fragment. The extension of fragments must be done in the context of a virtual writing edition, in which Pessoa's textual witnesses are socialized at the level of writing processes by the users of the archive. After the extension, the extended fragment becomes part of a virtual writing edition and it will eventually become part of other virtual editions through the functionalities provided by the editor- and book-functions.

Book-function

> I ask what remains of me why I bothered with these useless pages, dedicated to rubbish and dispersion, lost even before existing among Destiny's ripped up papers.
>
> (Text 442[18])

Unlike the other functions (reader, editor, and author)—which describe literary performativity as constituted by sets of distinct actions—book-function is meant to refer to the *changing relation between textual production and the imagination*. It is an attempt to capture the speculative dance between the book as a process of invention and the book as a process of production. Reading, editing, and writing take part in these conceptual and material processes because their modes of action depend on the operation of the book-function in the imagination of the subject. In effect, the act of calling a book "book," as in *Book of Disquiet*, could

---

[18] Full text available at https://ldod.uc.pt/fragments/fragment/Fr142/inter/Fr142_WIT_ED_CRIT_Z (BNP/E3, 2-71r; Coelho 294; Sobral Cunha 473; Zenith 442; Pizarro 303).

be analyzed as an explicit invocation of this literary function. The material unity of discourse and book form as signifiers of the literary suggests the centrality of this function in organizing the imagination and the actions of readers, editors, and authors. The *LdoD Archive* uses the dynamic and metamedia features of the digital medium to show the book-function as a force field of actions, relations, and possibilities.

The main purpose of the book-function is the continuing (re)construction of the *Book of Disquiet* based on predefined information, including information that is algorithmically generated through various analyses. This predefined information originates in the static representational layer, such as the table of contents or taxonomy of an expert critical edition. It also derives from the dynamic simulation layer, including, for example, the structure of virtual editions, networks of reading trails, or new writing sequences. In the context of this function it is possible to generate one "instance" of the book based on textual and metatextual information in the archive. This feature makes it possible to navigate among fragments according to multiple criteria. From the point of view of the functional implementation, its main feature is search, which is associated with navigation, which in fact may be defined as a contextually defined search. A search results in a set of fragments that meet the search criteria and offer entry points for fragments of the *Book of Disquiet*, using the navigation features. Because this type of search serves as an entry point for fragments from the *Book of Disquiet*, it can be said that it is a generation of an "instance" of the *Book of Disquiet*. The mutability of the network of connections and textual associations in the *LdoD Archive* is an attempt to model the book-function as an open feedback between imagining and producing a book.

Simulation Layers

Through an infrastructure and a set of programming principles that enable the rereading, re-editing, and rewriting of Pessoa's text, the *LdoD Archive* offers a set of possibilities for manipulation and intervention that go beyond a representational logic, virtualizing the acts of reading, editing, and writing as living potentialities. Given its material and conceptual nature, the *Book of Disquiet* appears as the ideal object for an experiment like this. Existing as a modular set of several hundred texts, but also as a set of fragments in varying degrees of completion, the *LdoD Archive* makes it possible to observe their emergent nature. Its writing, editing, and reading history as a book under construction provides us with the opportunity of focusing our attention on the processuality of the actions that constitute its discursive field.

Through its thematizing of self-awareness and its use of writing to intensify the processes of conscious perception and sensation, showing them as writing in process—from the fragmentary and preliminary annotation to the clean typewritten final draft—the *Book of Disquiet* allows us to think about acts of writing as performative acts, that is, as acts that do what they write and thus show writing as an illocutionary action (Portela 2016a and 2017). In addition, by constituting itself as an unfinished and fragmentary work, whose text has to be repeatedly edited and organized, the *Book of Disquiet* shows us the editorial process as another element in the construction of the book. Editing can be heuristically primed as another kind of performative literary action. Finally, and because the relation between writing and editing must be mediated by reading, the specifics of reading in action can be added to the simulation model. Those three actions have been modeled not only as representations of acts of reading, editing, and writing but as functions that interactors perform in an iterative simulatory process.

Working with the horizon of the book as an imaginary operator for ordering the awareness of existence and the proliferation of thought-in-writing, the *Book of Disquiet* makes it possible to apprehend and model a fourth material and conceptual actant in the production of the literary: the book as dynamic function, the energy vortex for the actions of writing, editing, and reading. Finally, by offering itself as an object for multiple readings, that is, as a machine for generating interpretations that become registered through new inscriptions, the *Book of Disquiet* bears witness to the codependence between writing and reading, and shows us the retroactive production of meaning through acts of reading. The open iterability of the chain of written signs is foregrounded in an ongoing reading-writing cycle.

The *LdoD Archive* moves away from intentionalist editorial principles, replacing them with socialized principles. However, its goal is not only to create a meta-editorial perspective that allows us to observe specific editorial interventions on the documentary *corpus*. It is also to extend that meta-editorial function to a level of virtualization in a way that makes it possible to realize new hypotheses of editorial organization, opening it up to a play of possible futures. Its goal is also to show the multiplicity of reading paths and mark our own reading traversals in its textual space. It is further to think about the potentiality of textual construction not only at the level of editing but also at level of writing. The authority of the text as an exclusively hermeneutic object, that is, an object designed for acts of interpretation and reinterpretation that take place outside its closed field of signs, gives rise to acts of rewriting that inscribe themselves, verbally and cognitively, in the discourse of the work.

Instead of unconsciously adopting the meta-discursive protocols of reading as an institutionally regulated practice of interpretation, the *LdoD Archive* sets itself up as a new kind of literary environment. Its goal has been fully extended to a simulation level, which uses textual encoding and programming to increase textual flexibility, i.e., its projectuality—the fact that it is a work in progress that remains in progress. The ideas of book-concept and book-object can be disconnected from a principle of mimesis and emulation, and can be explored through the differential system established by means of the human and computational processability of text at level of writing, editing, and reading. The heuristic of digital procedurality in the *LdoD Archive* is to express deep principles about literary procedurality through the features and functionalities of its multiple interfaces.

The reader-, editor-, author-, and book-functions have been virtualized in this digital reimagining of the *Book of Disquiet*, making it possible to experiment with the production of the literary as a result of a dynamic field of relations whose material and discursive form can be apprehended through role-playing. Reading that reads itself, editing that edits itself, writing that writes itself, a book that becomes a book—four processes whose reflexive processuality the *LdoD Archive* attempts to model. The performative awareness of linguistic self-production inherent in a writing process, which is the basis of heteronomy theory in the writings of Pessoa, is extended to the potentiality of self-production that originates in the actions that produce the literary as an experience. *Subject-reader*, *subject-editor*, *subject-author*, and *subject-book* would be the four heteronyms of this experience.

In the *LdoD Archive*, the *Book of Disquiet* was transformed into a machine-readable text whose machine readability constitutes itself as a device for generating multiple literary speech acts, that is, acts that allow us to experience the dynamics that sustains a literary field. To this extent, the *LdoD Archive* is a machine—an assemblage of heuristic interfaces—that offers us the possibility of discovering processes of reading, editing, and writing whose conceptual and material horizon is the production of the discursive occurrence we refer to as the *Book of Disquiet*, i.e., the instantiation of the readerly, editorial, and authorial projectuality in the book-as-work.

The encoding and programming of the *LdoD Archive* integrates a genetic and critical representation of autograph features that show the cumulative process of authorial writing and revision recorded in the witnesses. It further shows the passage from this archive of documents into a set of four editions, which have selected and organized, internally and externally, the text of each single witness. All of these materials are embedded in a series of reading, editing, and writing interfaces that offer functionalities for exploring the processes through which a textual field comes into being. The closed set of autograph materials and editions of those autograph materials define a representation layer. The open set of role-playing interactions and reading, editing, and writing productions resulting from those interactions constitute the simulation layer (Figure 1.7).

Figure 1.7 shows the functional distinction between representation layer and simulation layer. The first refers to the documentary materials of the archive (autographs and expert editions) and to a set of functionalities for searching, retrieving, comparing, and visualizing those materials. The second refers to the *LdoD Archive*'s dynamic and creative space, and to the set of functionalities for interventions on those materials (selecting, ordering, annotating, glossing, mapping, writing, etc.). All interventions (*reading, editing, writing*) have been designed as an ecology of human and machine tools, which range from human-assisted computational action to computational-assisted human action. Automated processes are part of the heuristics of discovery and creativity,

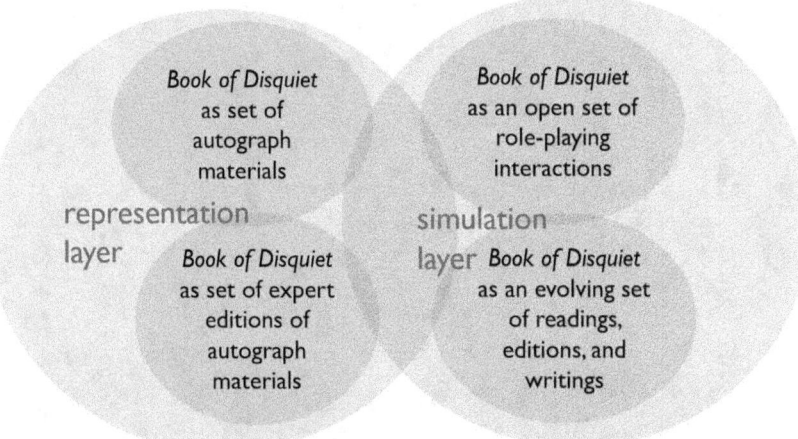

Figure 1.7 The representation and simulation layers in the *LdoD Archive*.

and they have been conceived for extending the range of human practice and human thought.

To the strictly editorial and meta-editorial component, the *LdoD Archive* adds a set of functionalities of simulation of literary performativity, that is, the field of relations between the acts of writing, reading, and editing with the possibility of visualizing reading protocols, of creating virtual editions, and of writing variations on the texts. Through the functionalities for visualizing readings and witnesses, comparing transcriptions and editions, creating virtual editions, and rewriting and recombining texts, the representation layer is subsumed into the simulation layer. By making the *Book of Disquiet* a readable, editable, writable, and computationally manipulable object, at multiple scales and from different perspectives, the *LdoD Archive* makes it possible to experiment with literary speech acts. Its result is a new way of thinking about the interaction between the situated and emerging dimensions of literary performance which has the potential to extend our cognition and transform our practices.

2

Reading as Simulation

This chapter examines the reading facets of the *LdoD Archive*. First, it highlights how the variability of reading sequence as an inherent feature of the *Book of Disquiet* has been modeled in the interface. Secondly, it discusses the multiple traces and trails of reading, and also how the *Book of Disquiet* itself contains marks for scripting the reading motions of its writer. Thirdly, the productivity of reading is analyzed through the protocols of different communities, including expert critical readers in scholarly journals and common readers in social media platforms. The concepts of hypertext and intertext as models of textual connectability are discussed. Finally, the movements from macro-visualizations of textual structure and textual properties to actual strings of characters are analyzed in terms of immersive and emersive reading practices.

Modeling the Life of Reading

How can we model the process of reading a particular work so that it contributes to the retroaction between the representational layer and the simulation layer in the *LdoD Archive* as described in the previous chapter? Which instances of actual reading marks of the *Book of Disquiet* should we document and encode? How can the platform foster and register multiple reading practices within its own literary environment (Figure 2.1)? How should we integrate those tracings of reading, i.e., the traces that we can collect and analyze from external sources (both historical and contemporary) and the traces that we can collect from the archive itself as a constrained experiment in the performance of reading? What about those dimensions of the reading passion that, as Leah Price mentions, leave no trace?

> The most impassioned reading destroys its own traces. The greater a reader's engagement with the text, the less likely he or she is to pause long enough to

leave a record: if an uncut page signals withdrawal, a blank margin just as often betrays an absorption too rapt for note taking. Can a book mark us if we mark it?

(Price 2004: 312–13)

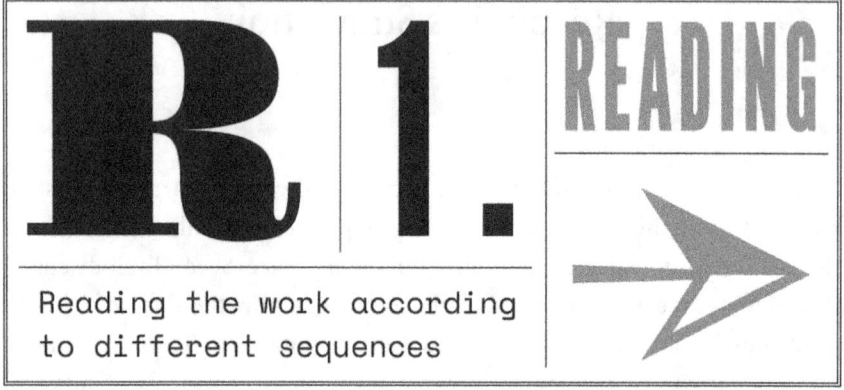

Figure 2.1 Graphic representation of the reading interface. This interface has been designed to take readers directly to a plain reading version of the text without any additional layers of meta-information.

Historical and sociological approaches to reading tend to focus on economic evidence about the availability of specific texts in order to determine their circulation among various social groups during particular periods. Additional evidence about the social impact of reading and about actual reading practices is often collected from occasional references in letters, diaries, and notebooks, or based on marginal annotations written by readers on their own or on borrowed copies (Price 2004, 2019; Colclough 2007; UK RED 2011). Current networked systems for electronic books have made it possible to gather more specific and structured information about reading behaviors, including reading time, highlighted passages, or marginal comments, all of which can be shared within a given reading community. The traversal of a textual field and the engagement of readers with that textual field can become scripted in the textual field itself (or in paratextual spaces linked to the text—such as fan sites and other discussion forums), and these collective assemblages of inscriptions can be analyzed for evidence of reading practices and interpretative protocols.

One of the features of the *Book of Disquiet* that is most relevant for digital representation derives from the fact that it has no established reading sequence. Each edition of the work has to determine not only the word-by-word transcription of the individual texts and the slightly variable set of texts to be assigned to the *Book*, but also their sequential arrangement, as we have seen. Because of this fact, we can argue that the interpretative dimension of editing is enhanced: editors are asked not only to turn the marks in the autograph documents into readable text (deciphering difficult passages, deciding on variants, sequencing textual blocks, etc.), but they are asked to perform a major intervention at the macro-compositional level by determining reading sequence according to specific criteria such as thematic clustering, stylistic affinity, documentary similarity, chronology of composition, heteronym attribution, or any combination of these. They have to engage in the conjectural construction of a reading sequence of their own.

The *LdoD Archive* interface has been designed to enhance the productive nature of the act of reading. Readers have to decide how they are going to read the text, since there are always many possibilities. Reading is not only the first interface that interactors are encouraged to explore, but when they enter the *Archive* they are already in the middle of reading. Every time the browser is refreshed a short passage (usually only one sentence) from a text in a specific edition is presented (Figure 2.2). When they click on it they go directly to the reading interface: they encounter that particular text within the reading sequence of its edition, and they are also made aware of its relative position in other editions (Figure 2.3).

The reading sequences presented through this interface include the four critical editions and, additionally, an automated sequence that is being generated

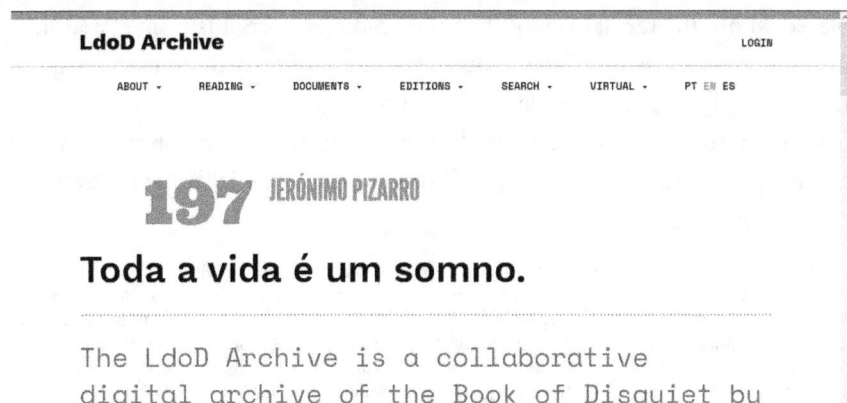

Figure 2.2 Starting off *in medias res:* in the *LdoD Archive*'s homepage, the random generation of a quote from a particular edition takes users directly to that text in the reading interface. Reading always starts in the middle.

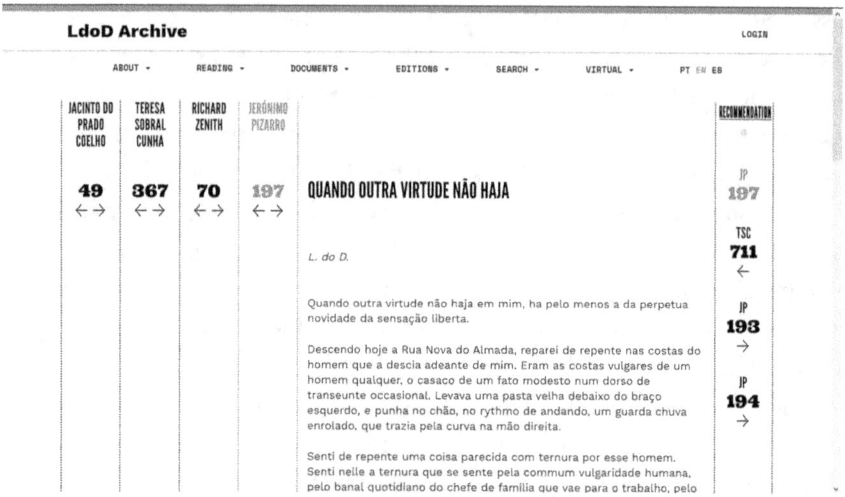

Figure 2.3 *LdoD Archive*'s reading interface showing the text containing the quoted sentence or phrase, and also its relative position in the four critical editions (left-hand columns) and in automated recommendation sequence (right-hand column).

on the fly. This recommended reading sequence suggests the most similar fragment to the one currently being read (excluding those that have already been read). Similarity between the edition fragment and the recommendation fragment is calculated according to a combination of four criteria (adjustable by users): heteronym, date, text, and taxonomy. This way readers are always already placed within the textual labyrinth. Their reading traversal is primed and they get an immediate sense of the multicursal nature of textual sequence, making the archive's hypertext rationale the default reading mode of the system. Readers have to create their own reading trails by choosing among a number of possible reading paths.[1] The singularity of each reader's traversal highlights the eventive nature of reading.

---

[1] This was one of the features that was clearly understood by the first critical review of the *LdoD Archive*: "Any description of the navigation experience of *LdoD*—or at least one that intends to be coherent with the way the project conceives itself—inevitably pays heed to two features made prominent in the website: mutability and immersion. By the former we refer to the site's ongoing recreation of a sense of uniqueness and infinitude, that is, of the impression that no two navigation experiences will ever be the same. This is evident right from the start: the homepage (composed of a brief description of the project followed by links to the site's five main sections: 'Reading,' 'Documents,' 'Editions,' 'Search,' and 'Virtual') is introduced by a random quote, from the *Book of Disquiet*, that changes every time the site is refreshed or re-entered. This rotating quote not only makes room for literary interpretation, as a common epigraph would, but also is accompanied by a link to the entire fragment where it is originally found. This means that the first and most visible link users encounter is one which immediately takes them to the gist of the site: any random fragment that inevitably blurs the notion of a starting point. Thus, by entering the site, users are only one click away from finding themselves amongst the labyrinthine abundance of the *Book of Disquiet*" (Barbosa and Pittella 2017: 726).

The way readers are constituted by the interface—i.e., their position within the textual environment and the perspective on their own traversal and exploration of the materials—suggests the cognitive and enactive role of reading actions in giving structure to the textual field. One of the consequences of making hypertext (rather than a hierarchical table of contents) the default reading mode is the emphasis on the labyrinth as a figure for the motions of reading, which are based on recursion, divergence, and convergence. Once the associative and the hierarchical structures are flexibly combined in multiple ways by reader-generated structures and trails, the reading experience becomes labyrinthine, open-ended, and exploratory. At this level, the editorial problem of producing a bibliographic structure for the *Book of Disquiet* is experienced as a physical and cognitive engagement with the materiality of reading processes.

The movement from one quoted sentence in the initial screen to the entire source text, and to a graphic representation of the relative position of this text within five reading sequences (four of which are the major editorial versions of the *Book*, while the fifth is an algorithmic sequence that is being generated in response to the text currently being read), highlights the variability of reading sequences as an intrinsic feature of one's experience of the work. It further suggests processes of contextualization and decontextualization through which textual strings produce meaning within specific discursive fields. The single quote, which takes readers into the middle of the text and into the middle of the *Book*, also functions as an epigraph, that is, as a strong reading trace through which a reader's appropriation of the text takes place. This multicursal model for *Book of Disquiet* within the *LdoD Archive* establishes a link between representing the work according to a particular reading form, on the one hand, and simulating the acts through which the work assumes a given reading form, on the other.

The *LdoD Archive* attempts to represent the social life of reading the *Book of Disquiet* by looking at diverse reading traces and reading practices of several groups of readers, including the author as reader. Resources include a sample of significant historical readings, as expressed in critical essays; current online readings, as collected through extracted quotes shared on social media; the *Book of Disquiet* itself as an assemblage of reading traces by Fernando Pessoa, many of which are trackable to his personal library; and also the reading acts that take place within the *LdoD Archive* itself, as captured through the analytical and visualization tools of the system. As shown in the following sections, reading is simulated in three ways: as a map of trails and traces; as a mosaic of quotations; and as a process of textual immersion and emersion.

Marginalists and Extractors: Traces and Trails

Reading can be represented through its reading marks, such as marginal annotations and citations. When describing the types of reading traces left by writers, Daniel Ferrer distinguishes between "marginalists"—those who inscribe their reading marks in the textual surface—and "extractors"—those who prefer to write notes in a separate notebook (2001: 18). As reader, Fernando Pessoa combined those two types of reading annotations: there are many underlined passages and marginal comments in the books of his private library, but also passages from his readings transcribed onto his notebooks or paraphrased and transformed in his works.[2] The marking up of the reading traces of Fernando Pessoa within the *LdoD Archive* is one specific component of the representation of reading. Traces related to philosophical topics and literary ideas for the *Book of Disquiet* are being marked up for visualization and analysis.[3] This will be relevant also for mapping the relations between writing and reading acts in Fernando Pessoa's creative process.

One frequent example of how reading traces itself in the textual field is offered by underlined passages. An underlined passage is a sign of the heightened attention that comes from rereading, indicating that it resonated strongly with the reader, and it is often a marker for future reference and appropriation, as we can see in the following example. Fernando Pessoa's private library contains two works with texts by William Blake: an edition of the letters, which includes a biography of Blake written by Frederick Tatham (*The Letters of William Blake*

---

[2] Fernando Pessoa's private library, composed of 1,312 titles (1,419 volumes), has been fully digitized since 2010. The catalog and digital facsimiles are available at: http://bibliotecaparticular. casafernandopessoa.pt/index/bibParticular.htm See also Pizarro et al. 2010, and Pizarro 2009. Several scholars have been researching his marginalia and readings, including Maria do Céu Estibeira (2008, 2013), Rita Catania Marrone (2016, 2017), Patrícia Silva (2016, 2018), Teresa Filipe (2018), and Diego Giménez (2020).

[3] As part of an ongoing analysis of the philosophical ideas in the *Book of Disquiet*, a virtual edition annotates all passages within texts from the *Book of Disquiet* that can be linked to specific reading traces or reading sources in Fernando Pessoa's philosophical library. This is an example of the retroaction between the reading and editing functionalities in the platform, while demonstrating how creative writing processes involve generative retroactions between reading and writing acts. See the virtual edition prepared by Diego Giménez, "Intertextualidade Filosófica," *Arquivo LdoD*, 2020. https://ldod.uc.pt/edition/acronym/LdoD-InterFil.

together with a Life, published in 1906), and an edition of William Blake's poems organized by W.B. Yeats (*Poems of William Blake*, published after 1905), both containing many annotations by Pessoa. Most of Pessoa's annotations on those two books (such as underlining the line "Man has no body distinct from his soul" in Blake's *The Marriage of Heaven and Hell*) suggest that he is selecting passages related to his future articulation of sensationism as the literary expression of the embodied nature of thought and feeling in the form of sensations.[4]

Reading traces offer material evidence of the productive and transformative nature of reading as a subjective process of constructing further meaning out of writing traces. They also show how this process implies both immersion in the symbolic world of the text and emersion in the semiotic world of writing marks. Annotations by artists and writers (as opposed to scholarly annotations) are often made in order to appropriate an idea or verbal form and integrate them in their own artistic or literary imagination. This is especially marked during the formative years when they are defining their personality and their system of ideas. It is often an affective annotation, showing positive or negative affect, and it can function as a point of departure for their own creations. Their interest in what they read lies not in understanding the diverse elements and layers in their textual sources, as happens in the scholarly reading protocol, but above all in isolating moments of illumination and stimulation that feed their mental and creative processes.

Texts from the *Book of Disquiet* make multiple, and sometimes contradictory, references to various reading practices in the narrator's life. Reading is mentioned in relation to the daily work of the narrator as a bookkeeper in a commercial office in downtown Lisbon: "… I'm at peace with the numbers I write, as if I were reading while waiting to fall asleep" (Text 33)[5]. It is described in relation to different types of reading materials (books by modern and classic authors; plays, novels, newspapers): "These thoughts occurred to me after reading a newspaper article about the great and multifaceted life of a celebrity" (Text 145).[6] Sometimes reading becomes an image of the general tedium of life: "But

---

[4] In recent years, analyses of Pessoa's readings of other poets based on his private library have been published, including annotations and marginalia on books by the following authors: Dante Alighieri, William Shakespeare, John Milton, Goethe, William Blake, William Coleridge, William Wordsworth, Edgar Allan Poe, Charles Baudelaire, Walt Whitman, and W.B. Yeats. For studies on his relation to Anglo-American writers, see Santos 2003, and Ferrari 2012 and 2018.

[5] Full text available at https://ldod.uc.pt/fragments/fragment/Fr181/inter/Fr181_WIT_ED_CRIT_Z (BNP/E3, 3-22r; Coelho 107; Sobral Cunha 598; Zenith 33; Pizarro 224).

[6] Full text available at https://ldod.uc.pt/fragments/fragment/Fr241/inter/Fr241_WIT_ED_CRIT_Z (BNP/E3, 4-12; Coelho 436; Sobral Cunha 558; Zenith 145; Pizarro 311).

the very idea of reading vanishes as soon as I pick up a book from the table, the physical act of reading abolishing all desire to read" (Text 265).[7] It also features through the narrator's reflexive engagement with reading the book that he is writing: "Page by page I slowly and lucidly reread everything I've written, and I find that it's all worthless and should have been left unwritten" (Text 169).[8] It appears as an image of the strangeness of former self to current self: "But what am I confronting when I read myself as if reading a stranger?" (Text 215).[9] Or even as the anticipated effects of his writing on his readers: "I'd like the reading of this book to leave you with the impression that you've traversed a sensual nightmare" (Text 215).

The narrator portrays himself as a daily reader of all sorts of fictional and non-fictional books, but also as someone whose vivid imagination prevents him from becoming fully immersed in what he is reading. Reading morphs effortlessly into writing:

> I know no pleasure like that of books, and I read very little. Books are introductions to dreams, and no introductions are necessary for one who freely and naturally enters into conversation with them. I've never been able to lose myself in a book; as I'm reading, the commentary of my intellect or imagination has always hindered the narrative flow. After a few minutes it's I who am writing, and what I write is nowhere to be found.
>
> (Text 417)[10]

This move from reading into mental writing and, then, into actual writing dissolves the reality of reading in the mental space of thinking about what is being read and ponder alternatives. Reading functions as the trigger for dreaming, i.e., for the extension and transformation of what is being read by the projection of an act of writing. Since the narrator's strong imagination and critical faculties prevent him from fully immersing in the "narrative flow," this reading-writing tension becomes one of the rhetorical figures of the dialectics between transparency and opacity in the *Book of Disquiet*. Being immersed in the flow of reading means being "able to lose myself in a book," whereas seeing

---

[7] Full text available at https://ldod.uc.pt/fragments/fragment/Fr036/inter/Fr036_WIT_ED_CRIT_Z (BNP/E3, 1-41r; Coelho 400; Sobral Cunha 345; Zenith 265; Pizarro 218).

[8] Full text available at https://ldod.uc.pt/fragments/fragment/Fr136/inter/Fr136_WIT_ED_CRIT_Z (BNP/E3, 2-64r; Coelho 321; Sobral Cunha 518; Zenith 169; Pizarro 372).

[9] Full text available at https://ldod.uc.pt/fragments/fragment/Fr548a/inter/Fr548a_WIT_ED_CRIT_Z_1 (BNP/E3, 144D(2)-44v-45r; Sobral Cunha 110, 111; Zenith 215; Pizarro 53).

[10] Full text available at https://ldod.uc.pt/fragments/fragment/Fr040/inter/Fr040_WIT_ED_CRIT_Z (BNP/E3, 1-46r; Coelho 18; Sobral Cunha 694; Zenith 417; Pizarro 273).

the reading as writing implies the critical distance that comes from focusing on the signifier instead of the signified.

However, there are other moments in which this resistance to immersion takes on a different expression. It is not the narrative flow, the characters, or the emotions in the book that resist immersion, but rather the actual outside world which seems impenetrable for a perceiving self who can only see it from afar:

> I don't know the meaning of this journey I was forced to make, between one and another night, in the company of the whole universe. I know I can read to amuse myself. Reading seems to me the easiest way to pass the time on this as on other journeys. I occasionally lift my eyes from the book where I'm truly feeling and glance, as a foreigner, at the scenery slipping by—fields, cities, men and women, fond attachments, yearnings—and all this is no more to me than an incident in my repose, an idle distraction to rest my eyes from the pages I've been reading so intently.
>
> (Text 348)[11]

This passage from the *Book of Disquiet* comes from a text in which the narrator is describing his identification with fictional characters as a substitute for affective relations with real people, a process that he seems to have perfected into a method for living vicariously through his imagined dreams. Writing and reading are the material elements of his method for daydreaming life and abstracting emotions: "My ideal would be to live everything through novels and to use real life for resting up—to read my emotions and to live my disdain of them." Self-estrangement is mediated by this inversion between the intensity of external reality and the intensity of fictional reality. The reality of the outside world and of human feelings and desires ("fields, cities, men and women, fond attachments, yearnings") turns into a passing occasional scenery for a self who is "truly feeling" in the book he is reading. The truthfulness of life is lived in the fictionality of novels and theater plays, while the actuality of life becomes a passing landscape experienced in a journey.

Bernardo Soares's description of how reading immersion and emersion relate in his reading experience can been used as a metaphorical model for designing reading interfaces. As implied by the oscillation between focused attention on the text and lifting one's eyes from the text to pay attention to one's physical, social, and emotional environment, the cognitive process of making sense of

---

[11] Full text available at https://ldod.uc.pt/fragments/fragment/Fr222/inter/Fr222_WIT_ED_CRIT_Z (BNP/E3, 3-74r; Coelho 382; Sobral Cunha 665; Zenith 348; Pizarro 390).

writing traces can be described as a recursive motion of going into the verbal world of the text and coming out of that world. In the quoted passage, this reading process is physically embodied through the narrator's self-conscious description of the movement of his eyes on and off the pages: "I've been reading so intently," followed by "lift my eyes from the book" and "rest my eyes from the pages." In the section "Visualizing the Spacetime of Reading," these two motions as physical embodiments of reading are described as immersive and emersive.

Intertext as Hypertext: A Network of Quotations

Additional facets of social reading represented in the *LdoD Archive* relate to two different reading protocols, described as "expert reading" and "common reading." The first one refers to critical readings by literary scholars and literary critics, while the second refers to various types of written evidence of reading by general readers. One strategy for analyzing the relation between the *Book of Disquiet* and those two reading protocols is to look at passages selected from the work for sustaining particular interpretations or for highlighting certain constellations of meanings. This abstraction of reading as a network of quotations begs the following research questions: how can we encode the reception of the *Book of Disquiet* by making explicit the network of relationships among the different reception documents (critical reviews and essays), and between these and the texts of the *Book of Disquiet*? How can we extend this process to the ongoing reception in social media, integrating the two modes of reception (the "expert critical reception" and the "common reading reception" of the work) in the same textual platform?

This hypothesis of representing intertextual relations in hypertextual mode posits the interference between an "intertext" theory as an implicit or explicit textual presence of a given text in other texts, and a "hypertext" theory as a network of technically processable documentary relations through anchors and links. The *LdoD Archive* infrastructure has been used to explore the mapping of quotations between the sources of each of those reading protocols (print publications of the "expert critical reception" and online posts of the "common reading reception") and the actual text of the *Book of Disquiet*. The categorized inclusion of the critical reception (between 1982 and 2020) was made through the digitization and XML-TEI encoding of a representative sample of sixty essays and book reviews. This encoding is focused on clarifying the network of cross-references among the various reception documents and the network of references of these documents to the texts of the *Book* itself and to other works (Marques and Portela 2020). An effort has also been made to model what we describe as textual grafts, i.e, the recontextualizing of the quoted passages in each critical reading text. In addition, computer techniques have been used to collect, analyze, and represent the reception of the work that occurs in social digital media, focusing on Twitter citations (from 2018 to the present).

Besides the encoded and annotated critical reception documents and the automatic extraction of online reception instances, forms of collaborative manual collection will also be developed through crowdsourcing tools. Eventually, it will be possible for the interactors to collect and integrate further instances of reception documents, extending the network of readings around the *Book of Disquiet*. The encoded reception as a network of documentary relations is also used for producing visualizations of the intertextual networks. Furthermore, annotation tools will allow users to build their own annotated collections of reception documents. The various expressions of reception of the work in different media—from academic journals in print media to readers' blog entries—can be collected, analyzed, and studied in an integrated manner. From this overview of the reading history of the work, a more abstract critical understanding of literary reading as a series of social semiotic practices can emerge. As a study of reading practices that takes advantage of the relationship between computer science and literary studies, the critical reception and social reading modules of the platform can be replicated for other corpora of reception materials.

An outcome of this approach is that we can look at large-scale patterns of the reception of the *Book of Disquiet*, and develop didactic and critical tools for students and teachers to examine the history of expert and common readings of the *Book*. The *LdoD Archive* provides a resource for investigating reading protocols of diverse interpretative communities at different moments of the work's reception history, in order to understand the ways in which they have built the intelligibility conditions for the *Book of Disquiet*, by underlining its fragmentation or its unity based on specific editions or texts. Zenith's narrative reading of the *Book of Disquiet* as a quasi-novel about the inner life of Bernardo Soares, for instance, selects texts and quotations that contribute to this interpretative framework (Zenith 2013). Reading interventions create the semantic conditions for their own intelligibility.

Shared protocols and individual acts of meaning production through enacted readings demonstrate the general principle of imaginative deformation for inscribing the subjectivity of readers in the textual field. This concept is at the center of Stephen Ramsay's argument about the algorithmic nature of critical reading processes from which he derives the plausibility of reading machines. If reading proceeds through constrained and deformative procedures, computational procedurality further expands the field of interpretative possibilities: "All textual entities allow for deformation, and given that interpretation occurs amid a textual field that is by nature complex, polysemic, and multi-referential, one might say that most entities require it. Seen in this light, deformation is simply a part of our permanent capacity for sense-making" (Ramsay 2011: 48).

Intertextuality can be seen in the light of the productive and deformative forces of reading. The concept of "intertextuality" refers to the network of relationships among written texts (or among other media forms). Such relations are explicitly or implicitly produced by any new text and they may be said to be constitutive of textuality (Allen 2006). Although the concept can be restricted to cited textual elements that are activated as semiotic operators within the new text, it can also be extended to the general processes of citability of writing, i.e., dependent on layers of allusion and memory of other texts, even when not explicitly invoked by textual producers (Phillips 2016). The intertext must also be produced through reading acts that activate the chains of textual association required for interpretation (Ott and Walter 2000; Haberer 2007). Intertextuality is thus constitutive of writing-reading protocols as networks of socialized textual processes (Bloome and Hong 2012).

In dialog with work by Bakhtin, Kristeva (1986), Barthes (1977, 2002) and others, Genette developed a general theory of textual relations (transtextuality) which defines intertextuality, in a structuralist sense, as "a relation of co-presence between two or among several texts: that is to say, eidetically and typically, as the actual presence of one text within another" (Genette 1997: 1–2). Riffaterre (1994) has also insisted on intertextuality as a "linguistic network" and "a closed-circuit exchange between text and intertext" (796). On the other hand, poststructuralist emphasis on the reader and the free play of signifiers contributed to a performative understanding of reading as an iterative (Derrida 1988), socialized (Fish 2000), and probabilistic (Drucker 2013a) traversal of the textual field to which readers bring their own networks of associations. Intertextuality can thus be conceptualized as a general means of textual production both from the writers' and from the readers' perspective: the "tissue of quotations drawn from the innumerable centers of culture" (Barthes 1977: 146) can be identified in the written text but its intertextuality remains open to additional associations by readers.

If we apply this concept to the domain of the reception of a work, we can understand it in two different but related ways: on the one hand, the reception texts of a given work establish intertextual relations among themselves, insofar as they mention and refer each other, thus sustaining certain interpretative paradigms; on the other hand, these reception texts also establish intertextual relations with the texts of the work, since they support their interpretation through the selection of citations from the work. Our encoding of the critical reception assumes that explicit networks of intertextual references can be reconstituted hypertextually, thus providing an overview of the evolution of the reception of the work based on a representative textual corpus. The moving networks of allusion and quotations express the living process of sense-making.

This intertextual mapping shows patterns at two levels: with regard to the network of inter-references across the essays, it reveals the network of citations and interpretative paradigms that shape the different models and communities of interpretation over time; with regard to the network of inter-references between articles and texts from the *Book of Disquiet*, it shows the thematization of the work performed by specific models and communities and how such thematizations are based on diverse corpora of examples. In other words, this model of reception analysis allows us to reconstruct the history of critical reception and to understand how it contributed to the construction of ideas about the *Book of Disquiet*, therefore creating specific conditions of readability and intelligibility for the work. Besides the investigation of the *Book of Disquiet* as an authorial project and as an editorial project, this encoding of the critical readings makes it possible for the *LdoD Archive* to examine the *Book of Disquiet* as a set of discourses about the book, that is, its production as a social artifact.

The concept of "hypertext," as originally formulated by Ted Nelson (1965), assumes the possibility of explicit and open linking across multiple documents, which can be traversed associatively through a link map. The hyperlink designates both a pre-existing link embedded in the document structure and a link that can be added by the reader between any two discrete strings. Electronically processable hypertext links gave technical expression to Nelson's concept of literature as a network of documents (Nelson 1987). Documents are interconnected by writing, rewriting, reading, and rereading processes in an ongoing collective historical and social process. Hypertext, particularly in terms of Nelson's later definition of *transliterature*, can be described as a mode of marking traces of previous connections (making explicit the mosaic of written quotations) and creating new reading trails (making explicit the open-endedness of their associative nature as an ongoing process). In this sense, links would be at once historical traces and future trails, the register of trodden paths and the opening up of new connections.

Extending intertextual networks by establishing trails of connection through acts of reading becomes part of the interpretative protocols for making sense of the tissue of writing. Early hypertext theory tended to look at the electronic link as the technological embodiment of the associative process that made intertextuality the condition of all textuality as a social process of ongoing citations. Nelson (1995) modeled this textual weaving as "transclusion, or reuse with original context available, through embedded shared instancing" (30). Landow (2006) considered hypertext as a "fundamentally intertextual system" (55), suggesting that it demonstrated Derrida's notion of citability, i.e., the possibility of breaking any given context of writing through quotation, thus "engendering an infinity of new contexts" (Derrida 1988: 185). Whereas hypertext technologists were concerned with tracing quotations to their sources—and thus proclaiming the identity of any given textual string with itself—poststructuralist and deconstructive critical theory postulates recontextualizability as the defining condition of writing and of its ability to signify. The flexible tracing and retracing of connections (which implies the non-identity of the textual strings with themselves) characterizes the workings of reading-writing and writing-reading processes.

Moreover, electronic hypertext has been conceptualized within literary theory as the embodiment of the decentralization of the original text in favor of the association networks in which it participates in a process of endless iteration, citation, and branching (Bolter 2001; Landow 2006). Although only a part of intertextual relations can in fact be translated electronically—those expressed through quotations of larger or smaller alphanumeric strings (character names, phrases, sentences, paragraphs, text blocks, etc.)—the representation of networks of intertextual references as electronic hypertexts has made it possible to extend the complexity of the critical apparatus inherited from printed editions and to build large, decentralized, and variable networks of documents.

The socialized construction of hypertext by teachers and students—from the pioneering examples of Andries van Dam in the 1970s and George P. Landow in the 1980s,[12] both developed at Brown University—demonstrates not only the uncoincidence between hypertext and intertext as procedures for creating textual associations, but the impossibility of any exhaustive explicitation of textual relations, since associations among texts are a function of the open construction of reading and therefore inexhaustible (Allen 2006; Pisarski 2011; Portela 2013a). The problem of intertextuality as a general condition of textual meaning can be exemplified by a particular case: that of critical apparatuses as constructions of networks of textual relations. They demonstrate not only the insufficiency of any text as a self-contained semantic space, but also the semiotic productivity of chains of meaning produced by associative acts of reading.

Creating a network of relationships connecting text to apparatus (either through codex or website graphic conventions) has been one of the traditional tools of the critical apparatus for identifying citations and allusions or suggesting interpretations through notes and comments. Take, for example, the *Walt Whitman Archive* (Cohen et al. 1995–2021), in which, in addition to the hypertext linking the production documents of the various successive autograph versions of *Leaves of Grass*, we also find a large set of reception documents.[13] When digital archives bring together a collection of reception documents for a given body of literary works, we can systematically analyze the processes of citation and cross-reference that take place in these documents, and illuminate their discursive and historical context. This opens up a field of research for analyzing interpretative models and reading protocols.

The representation of this network of quotations in the *LdoD Archive* stems from the hypothesis that the marking up of intertextual relations among texts of the reception corpus of the *Book of Disquiet* and their processing in the form of a dynamic hypertext allows us to discover patterns about the critical reception of the work and generate new knowledge. The dynamic context of Web 2.0 and digital social networks is integrated into this model of reading not only as a source for gathering instances of the reception of the work on the web, but also as the possibility of using automated as well as crowdsourcing methodologies to collect evidence of electronic reception through algorithmic processes. Thus,

---

[12] Cf. Andries van Dam, "An Experiment in Computer-Based Education Using Hypertext," National Endowment for the Humanities. 1976; and George P. Landow, *The "In Memoriam" Web*. Storyspace version. Cambridge: Eastgate Systems, 1992.
[13] See Commentary Section (http://whitmanarchive.org/criticism/index.html), which contains Contemporary Reviews, Selected Essays, Bibliography, Disciples, and Interviews and Reminiscences.

the investigation of the critical reception since the first publication of the work in 1982 can be combined with the analysis of the reception processes sustained by digital media, including the selection and citation of texts from the *Book of Disquiet*.[14]

The use of crowdsourcing methods in digital critical editing—encouraging audiences to transcribe, correct, and validate documents—and in social and cultural history projects developed over the past decade and is now an established practice in the Digital Humanities (Terras 2016). The use of volunteer participants' specific interests (in relation to a particular author or historical event—local or national) contributed to the creation of significant digital resources, which are then made available for reading, analysis, and research in other social and institutional contexts. Take, for example, the crowdsourcing project *Letters 1916-1923*, coordinated by Susan Schreibman.[15] Its interface enables users to transcribe, edit, and label the letters, but also to verify the transcription and encoding of the texts (Schreibman et al. 2017).

Although the manual marking up of the critical reception documents and the automatic collection of online citations from the *Book of Disquiet* follow distinct methodologies, a number of theoretical assumptions about them as social expressions of reading acts have already been made when we decided to mark and collect them. The first assumption is that citations are appropriated in other discursive contexts as highly significant elements, either because they are perceived as fitting an existing interpretative framework (philosophical, ethical, literary, etc.), or because they seem to open up a new interpretative frame. This degree of semiotic investment of readers, particularly in the case of expert readers, means that citations are often used generatively, i.e., they are used for extending the textual field of a given work with emerging interpretations and new ideas. They expand what can be said about a particular work, thus changing its intelligibility and our perceptual patterns for making sense of what we read.

Citability—a property of all written discourse—functions as a general proof of the differential chain of meaning in its endless process of resignification. Citations belong to the "extractive" traces of reading and they are significant signs of the reception of any work. A critical analysis of citations is important for an

---

[14] The selected bibliography of the critical reception of the *Book of Disquiet* includes texts published between 1977 and the present. Some of the early texts appeared even before the first publication of the *Book* in 1982, and they are authored by researchers who had examined the work's archive.

[15] http://letters1916.maynoothuniversity.ie/

understanding of reading communities, i.e., shared interpretative assumptions and practices of reading. In the case of the expert critical reception, citations can be used to identify particular focuses of attention in texts from the *Book of Disquiet*, and how the quoted elements contribute to framing an interpretation of the work. If we are looking at a long period of reception, they will help us understand the changing history of the critical reading of the work.

Critical Reception as Reading Practice

Critical reading of literary works is a reading practice with shared interpretative protocols. One such protocol consists of producing intertextuality, that is, networks of allusions and quotations based on (1) their textual object, (2) other texts that are explicitly linked to their textual object, and (3) other critical readings of their textual object. Through the highlighting of elements in a given textual field, on the one hand, and the integration of those elements in a network of textual references and interpretations, on the other, critical readings contain evidence about the general processes of reading. This section describes how critical readings of the *Book of Disquiet* have been analyzed and modeled in the *LdoD Archive*.

References and quotations provide a textual probe to understanding reading communities. Citations can be used to identify particular focuses of attention in texts from the *Book of Disquiet*, through which a number of topics and themes are highlighted as meta-signifiers of the work, such as the fragmented consciousness of the modern self or the daily life of Lisbon as a modern city. When examined as textual grafts within the critical text, citations allow us to model the reading protocols through which quoted elements contribute to framing an interpretation of the work. Analyzed during the past four decades of reception, these networks of quotations and reading protocols also help us understand the changing history of the critical reading of the work as a function of their modes of production of intertextuality. Processes of de-contextualization and re-contextualization that support the dynamic feedback between writing and reading are being analyzed in a representative sample of the critical reception of this work.

The notion of "protocol" is often used in the social sciences to refer to an individual's verbal description of how a given task is carried out. These self-verbalizations are used as sources of information about cognitive processes through which a specific task is given meaning. "Protocol analysis" was formalized as a research methodology in several disciplinary fields, such as psychology, sociology, or anthropology (Ericsson and Simon 1993). In the field of reading and literacy studies, particularly in studies about reading comprehension, the concept of "verbal protocol" has been used to describe the ways in which readers make sense when verbalizing the relationships and inferences made from that they read (Pressley and Afflerbach 1995). Data generated by "thinking out loud" verbal protocols and by different questionnaire models—in the disciplinary fields of psychology, educational sciences, or applied linguistics—aim at both the analysis of cognitive processes and the development of strategies that improve understanding and reading ability, which can then be used in teaching and learning processes at different levels of education (Israel 2015).

Although the phrase "reading protocol" has been a productive concept in the field of literary studies at least since the 1970s, it has not yet been the subject of sustained theoretical discussion.[16] It is often used to characterize a set of reading practices (that is, ways of reading and interpreting) that are common to certain interpretative communities and specific reading frameworks, such as feminism, Marxism, deconstruction or postcolonial theory, for instance. An "interpretive community" is defined by the sharing of a set of protocols through which it produces meaning *from*, *with*, and *through* texts. These protocols are socialized and historical, reflecting modes of institutional regulation of writing and reading, including the constitution of gendered subject positions. Religious institutions, teaching and research institutions, publishing institutions, legal and political institutions are among the main regulators of reading protocols.

One of the assumptions of this theory (which emerges from the poststructuralist view that meaning is not in the texts per se but has to be performatively produced by readers at each reading, according to a set of heterogeneous conventions) is that the construction of meaning through reading follows certain patterns and it is these patterns that we can refer to as protocols. Any formalization of a reading protocol cannot be a universally valid description of reading as such, but only locally valid as a description of a socially

---

[16] Although the phrase appears in Robert Scholes's *Protocols of Reading* (Yale University Press, 1989), it is used for aggregating a collection of essays that express a certain ethics of critical reading rather than any theoretical discussion about the concept of "reading protocol."

and historically situated way of reading. We could claim that meaning is not in the writing (since it cannot be inferred exclusively from the artifact), and it is not in the reading either (because it cannot be determined by any "definitive" reading). Meaning emerges contingently and experientially from the encounter between readers and texts, mediated by specific practices and protocols of interpretation and validation of interpretation. It is a contingent form of social action in which individual improvisations depend on shared parameters.

In other words: reading does not extract meaning, it produces meaning, by making the text mean according to a process of recognition and transformation of intentions and forms that connects writers and readers. The theoretical problem addressed here (the analysis of critical reception as reading practice) is whether we can find in the critical texts markers of their protocols for the production of meaning, that is, elements that record the reading acts of their interpreters. Therefore, the objective of analyzing the critical reception as one dimension of reading in the *LdoD Archive* becomes meta-critical: it is not primarily focused on what the interpreters of the *Book of Disquiet* write, that is, the topics of their interpretations (although this is also an essential part of the data that is being constructed and analyzed, and which grounds the possibility of constructing a narrative of its reception history), but in the analysis of their shared ways of reading and in the critical texts themselves as manifestations of this process.

Describing the limitations of formalist and positivist approaches, while underlining the experiential and productive nature of reading as a condition for the production of meaning, Stanley Fish draws attention to the difficulty of apprehending the moving process constituted by interpretative acts insofar as any description of the process is also an interpretative act: "It will be a description of a moving field of concerns, at once wholly present (not waiting for meaning, but constituting meaning) and continually in the act of reconstituting itself" (Fish 1976: 474). Our attempt at simulating "a moving field of concerns" in the *LdoD Archive* tries to move away from neoformalist and neostructuralist approaches that have dominated the field of Digital Humanities.[17] The aim of the

---

[17] In effect, from the point of view of literary theory, Digital Humanities often represents a return to a formalist and structuralist past of the discipline (1920–70), which ignores poststructuralist theoretical advances of recent decades (1970–2020). This is due to the limitations of quantitative methods for modeling humanistic artifacts and practices, but it also originates in the epistemological anxiety of digital humanists for forms of knowledge validation that rely on strictly quantitative methodologies. For a critique of DH approaches, see Drucker 2009 and 2020, Fiormonte 2018, and Dobson 2019.

Ldod Archive is to capture that dynamic process of interpretation, and to develop a computational model of intertextuality that is capable of incorporating the poststructuralist theorization of the citability of writing as an infinite chain of resignification.

Insofar as interpretative strategies from different communities produce the meanings they read (the perception of forms being part of the shared process of interpretation), the very acts of writing are already invitations for the execution of a set of shared interpretive strategies:

> In my model, however, meanings are not extracted but made and made not by encoded forms but by interpretive strategies that call forms into being. It follows then that what utterers do is give hearers and readers the opportunity to make meanings (and texts) by inviting them to put into execution a set of strategies. It is presumed that the invitation will be recognized, and that presumption rests on a projection on the part of a speaker or author of the moves *he* would make if confronted by the sounds or marks he is uttering or setting down.
>
> (Fish 1976: 484–5)

The adaptation of this notion of interpretive communities (whose reading protocols are based on the production of intertextuality) implies three hypotheses whose articulation the modeling of critical reading of the *Book of Disquiet* in the *LdoD Archive* is trying to test. Firstly, interpretative strategies in critical texts are expressed through specific reading protocols. These reading protocols can be described in terms of two major sets of elements: *networks of citations* and *textual grafts* (Figure 2.4). Secondly, networks of citations can refer to the *sourcetext* (*Book of Disquiet*), to *extratexts* (other texts that the interpreter relates to the sourcetext) and to *intratexts* (other critical texts about the sourcetext). Thirdly, textual grafts, that is, the process of embedding a particular quotation or reference within an interpretative framework, can be analyzed in terms of three major features: *excerpt* (type of citation), *insert* (type of graft), and *dissert* (rhetorical function within the critical text).

Regarding *type of citation*, it can be merely an identifying reference, transcription of some words or sentences, or transcription of long passages. *Type of graft* refers to the ways in which the graft is syntactically, semantically, and discursively integrated into the new text. At the syntactic level, for instance, it can appear as an epigraph, within the body of a paragraph (beginning,

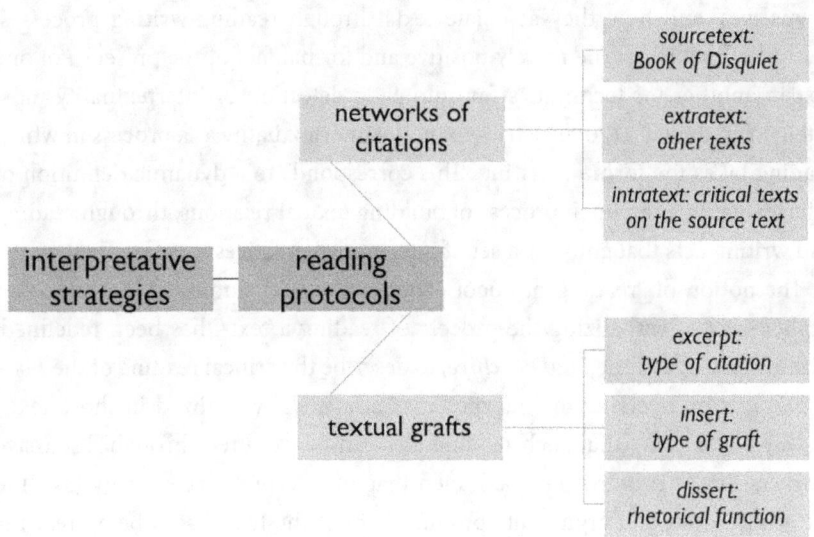

Figure 2.4 A diagram for the production of intertextuality as a writing-reading process based on the critical reception of the *Book of Disquiet*. © Manuel Portela, 2019.

middle, or end), or as detached text. At the semantic level, for instance, it may be expressed as the occurrence of a topic that has been enunciated before or after the quote, or as a recurring motif. At the discursive level, it participates in a larger discourse field related to interpretations of the work. In its turn, *rhetorical function* refers to its specific role in the argument constructed by the critical text, taking into account that the citations can be semantically constellated and also related to a constellation of topics in the critical text itself, allowing us to observe how the interpretative action is constructing meaning for the text that is being quoted and analyzed. Through this set of actions, which we have described as a reading protocol, an interpretative framework takes shape.

The *LdoD Archive* models critical reading protocols through integrated analyses of the network of citations, understood as interventions in the textual field of the work, and of the set of textual grafts, seen as evidence for the construction of arguments about the work through specific modes of excerpting and inserting those citations, and dissertating on and with them. When analyzed in conjunction, these reading protocols show that intertextuality (as a set of relations among texts) is an expression of the action of the interpretive communities themselves, and how they associate texts through reading-writing processes. Instead of looking at the merely positive and formal fact of the presence of one text in another (as techniques for automatic detection of intertextuality most often do),[18] the *LdoD Archive* tries to model intertextuality as a process in which reading takes the form of writing. This corresponds to a dynamic definition of intertextuality as an open process of building textual relations, through reading and writing acts that embody a set of interpretive practices.

The notion of "reading protocol"—understood, in studies of literacy, as an explicit way of verbalizing the process of reading a text—has been redefined, within the scope of the *LdoD Archive*, to describe the critical reading of the *Book of Disquiet* by referring to "interpretative strategies" verbalized in those texts, and by considering that such reading acts can be captured through discursive markers. In other words, it is assumed that an interpretative strategy (say, the set of meanings and arguments produced about the text that is being read) is based on reading protocols that can be identified and analyzed. A text about another text is characterized precisely by a set of verbal protocols through which the critical reader makes a particular reading explicit, that is, a set of meanings produced through the text s/he reads—in this case, not according to a rationale of merely understanding its words and inferences (as would be the case in a cognitive analysis of reading comprehension), but according to a highly complex practice of critical appropriation for the production of multiple inferences, resonances, and associative chains.

These multiple meanings are constructed according to an argument that is internal to the critical text (dependent on its own semantic chains of inferences and relations), but which is sustained, simultaneously, by successive iterations of the text being read (namely through the recurrent use of quotations).[19] Thus the relationship between iteration and interpretation is a manifestation of the intertextual action that is constitutive of the text itself, that is, as a composite written texture that emerges from a heterogeneous field of discourses. The intertextual nature of textuality can be evidenced not only through the evidence of one writing in another writing (the text of the *Book of Disquiet* quoted in the text about the *Book of Disquiet*), but also through this continuing

---

[18] See, for example, Trillini et al. 2010; Sula et al. 2014; Scheirer et al. 2014; Ganascia et al. 2014; Romanello 2016; Forstall et al. 2019.

[19] An insightful analysis of the use of italics as a mode of emphasis in writing through which this resignifying process of citation works can be seen in Wallen 2013.

presence of reading in writing (the framing of the text of the *Book of Disquiet* within an alien field of signifiers).

Although there is research in the field of verbal protocols of reading comprehension using computational formalizations of the problem,[20] there are no computational formalizations related to reading protocols in the critical reception of specific works as outlined here. In reception studies, many studies use the concepts of interpretive strategies and interpretive communities to characterize schools or paradigms of interpretation in the reception history of a given work or author. However, these studies are generally focused on the thematization of interpretations and ignore the material protocols through which such interpretations are textually and discursively constructed. The focus of analysis of the critical reception of the *Book Disquiet* in the *LdoD Archive* is to determine not only the *what* of the interpretive strategies—that is, the set of topics that have been defined about the various texts of the *Book of Disquiet* by the experts in the critical reading of the work—but also the *how* of those strategies. The notion of "reading protocol" adopted here is a way of articulating the relationship between the *what* and the *how* in the analysis of the reception corpus.

Reading Protocols

This section illustrates reading protocols by examining the relations between networks of quotations and textual grafts. The workings of textual grafts are described in excerpts from three critical essays about the *Book of Disquiet*. Quotations of the source text are briefly analyzed as textual grafts whose features (type of citation, type of graft, and rhetorical function) show *how* a specific interpretative framework is being constructed for each of the three topics highlighted in each case: the later *Book of Disquiet* as a book about Lisbon, according to Jerónimo Pizarro (2018); the relation between bookkeeping and literature as writing practices in the life of Bernardo Soares, according

---

[20] Research on verbal protocols of reading generally consist of collecting data produced by children and adolescents that show the ways of assigning meaning to reading (cf. Mills et al. 2009). Analysis of this cognitive component in relation to other interpretative frameworks would probably open up interesting research hypotheses for a theory of reading protocols. In *Scripting Reading Motions* (Portela 2013a), I have explored literary works in print and digital media that prime the cognitive and interpretative processes in their material surface, highlighting the performative dimension of reading. For empirical studies on reading across media, see Mangen et al. 2016, 2019.

to Fernando Martinho (2014); and Bernardo Soares as character rather than heteronym, according to Fernando Cabral Martins (2014).

> Not only because both books are individualizable, but because, by separating the *Book* made between "In the Forest of Estrangement" (1913) and the "Funeral March of Ludwig II, King of Bavaria" (1916)—to name two famous fragments of first phase—from the later *Book* composed of untitled texts, such as those that begin "I love the stillness of early summer evenings downtown" (1929) and "For some reason or other, I'm alone in the office" (1933), by separating the two books, I say, we clearly realize that Pessoa's great discovery, when he resumed the project that he abandoned for almost ten years, was Lisbon.
>
> (Pizarro 2018: 141–2; *my translation, except for the quotes from Pessoa*[21])

In this case citations (titles, dates, incipits) are used to identify texts that can be related to a chronology of composition. Although they seem to have mainly a referential function, they also serve to establish the contrast between the two periods of composition and the topics of the two books. The topic Lisbon, mentioned at the end of the sentence, will then serve to guide the selection of the excerpts that follow:

> That famous phrase from the *Book*, "Oh Lisbon, my home!" (Pessoa, 2014a, p. 322), is the exclamation of someone who has appropriated a city and who has become part of its urban fabric in an almost imperceptible way. The *Book of Disquiet* is a great portrait of Lisbon, and also of Pessoa, that is to say, of the office clerk inseparable from the streets, the electric cars, the buildings, the squares, the viewpoints of the Portuguese capital.
>
> (Pizarro 2018: 142; *my translation, except for the quotes from Pessoa*)

Quotations in the following paragraphs (of different types—phrases, short sentences, long passages), all from the first phase of the *Book*'s writing, are used to show the absence of concrete references to the city, even when the words seem to refer to an urban space. It is a strategy of exemplification by enumeration that serves to establish the starting point of the argument and to reinforce by contrast the analysis of the second part of the *Book* in the remainder of the essay as a book about the city of Lisbon. Notice how the inclusion of brief quotations within the sentences of the critical text shows a type of textual graft in which the quoted text is semantically resignified also by the effect of

---

[21] Except when noted otherwise, all translations of titles and quotations from the *Book of Disquiet* embedded in the quoted critical texts are by Richard Zenith.

this strict syntactic embedding, turning those phrases into signifiers of a set of topics listed in each sentence or sentence segment, but which are subordinate to the larger topic of the opening paragraphs which is the "absence of Lisbon" in the earlier book. The recontextualizing process is evident in the fact that the quotations are read symptomatically as an expression of the "absence of Lisbon."

> The *Book of Disquiet* can be considered, somewhat loosely, as a work of urban literature, but if we study the first 18 fragments, those that constitute the first nucleus of the work, we notice that there are prayers, invocations, glorifications, apotheosis, maxims, breaks and even a "Peristyle" (which starts: "It was in the silence of my disquiet, at the hour of day when the landscape is a halo of Life and dreaming is mere dreaming, my love, that I raised up this strange book like the open gates at the end of an abandoned boulevard."[22]), but the city of Lisbon shines through its absence, since that "boulevard," for example, can be any street with trees of any kind. And if we move forward, nothing really changes.
>
> (Pizarro 2018: 144; *my translation, except for the quotes from Pessoa*)

In the second example (Martinho 2014), it is possible to notice two different types of textual grafts: the embedded quote within the body of the interpreter's sentence, including parenthetical references, and the long quote, which functions with greater autonomy. The text also uses "brief excerpts," in its initial sentences, as micro-representations of the "long excerpt" transcribed after them: the structuring of the argument about the manifestations of writing (bookkeeping entries in the ledger and literary writing) is announced in this initial opposition and later corroborated by the long excerpt. The quotation serves a documentary function, that is, it serves to prove the interpretative argument and to illustrate that argument. The phrases that had been highlighted initially appear later within the integral passage functioning as anchors of the proposed interpretation. The text can now be interpreted on the basis of those two structuring axes. This citation practice is also frequent in the reception corpus: a set of phrases are highlighted to draw attention to a structure of meaning in the text, and then the text in which they appear is transcribed in full. A response to the textual force

---

[22] Richard Zenith's translation reads "open doors of an abandoned house" as he has chosen the earlier textual variant ("portões abertos numa casa abandonada"). Pizarro chooses the later variant "portões abertos ao fim d'uma alameda abandonada" ("open gates at the end of an abandoned boulevard"). Given that Pizarro's interpretation is based on the word "alameda," I have modified Zenith's translation to accommodate this reading.

field which abstracts elements from that field in order to frame an interpretation is materially manifested through the relationship between those two types of textual graft.

> A little further on, in the passage we have been analyzing, Soares refers to the two types of writing that occupied him, "literature" and the "ledger entries" that he is writing, as an "assistant bookkeeper," in the "ledger." With the same attitude ("carefully and indifferently") he writes one and the other, as he insists by underlining, "equally confined to the Rua dos Douradores." However, while granting the two writings identical dignity, he nevertheless points out that literature is written on the "paper of the soul":[23] "I write my literature as I write my ledger entries—carefully and indifferently. Next to the vast starry sky and the enigma of so many souls, the night of the unknown abyss and the chaos of nothing making sense—next to all this, what I write in the ledger and what I write on this paper that tells my soul are equally confined to the Rua dos Douradores, woefully little in the face of the universe's millionaire expanses.// All of this is dream and phantasmagoria, and it matters little whether the dream be of ledger entries or of well-crafted prose. Does dreaming of princesses serve a better purpose than dreaming of the front door to the office? All that we know is our own impression, and all that we are is an exterior impression, a melodrama in which we, the self-aware actors, are also our own spectators, our own gods by permission of some department or other at City Hall."
>
> (Martinho 2014: 34; *my translation, except for the quotes from Pessoa*)

In the third example (Martins 2014), quotations are deeply embedded and subordinated to the essay's argument. They work metonymically to represent the document known as the *Bibliographic Table*,[24] but their meaning is redefined by their function in the argument, which consists of proving the non-heteronymic nature of the figures of Bernardo Soares and Fernando Pessoa. It is interesting to see how all the quotes and references in this essay are strongly re-contextualized in the arguments related to the nature of Pessoa's heteronymic system and the place of Bernardo Soares and the *Book* inside or outside of that system. This type of surgical excerpting—from different sources and sparsely distributed throughout

---

[23] The *Book of Disquiet* text reads "o que escrevo neste papel da alma." Zenith renders this passage as "what I write on this paper that tells my soul." This particular quote from the *Book of Disquiet* in the essay—"paper of the soul"—is my translation.

[24] Published in December 1928, in the modernist magazine *Presença*, no. 17, this text provides a general overview of Pessoa's published and unpublished works up to that moment. It is generally seen as a significant statement in the definition of the relative place of his constellation of heteronyms in his system of writing.

the essay—suggests that the rhetorical force of recontextualization is greater than that in which only a restricted set of topics are identified (in this article, the set of selected excerpts revolve around the topics of person, character, individuality, and author). We may argue that the production of a general theory of heteronymy and the place of the *Book of Disquiet* in this theory has rhetorical expression in the type of citations and the type of graft that is being produced to sustain that claim.

> That is why a clarity of system can be found in the *Bibliographic Table*. At a certain point, it reads: "These individualities must be considered distinct from the author of them." There is no confusion, the clear autonomy of the figures is complete. Curiously, Bernardo Soares is not mentioned in the *Bibliographic Table*, although he already exists, that is, despite having already established himself in 1928 as the author of the *Book of Disquiet*. But it is as if he did not exist. Or rather, it is as if the problem he poses could not be articulated in the light of that system.
>
> 1929 is the year in which Bernardo Soares and Fernando Pessoa appear together in *Livro do Desassossego*, one as a narrator, or "composer" (the book is subtitled "Composed by Bernardo Soares, assistant bookkeeper in the city of Lisbon"), the other as author. This double bibliographic condition should have been obvious enough to make it impossible for the first edition of Jacinto do Prado Coelho's *Livro do Desassossego*, in 1982, as well as António Quadros's edition, for example, to have been able to write on the frontispiece: "*Book of Disquiet*, by Bernardo Soares." In fact, Bernardo Soares and Fernando Pessoa, since the first fragments of the *Book* come to light, place themselves outside the system that is organized in the *Bibliographic Table*, in which there is an author "in his person" and other authors "out of his person." Bernardo Soares, although he is, as much as the heteronyms are, a "complete individuality," is outside the drama they constitute. The *Book of Disquiet* is not written "outside of his person," as his author signs it "in his person." There is no heteronymic unfolding. Bernardo Soares's case goes beyond the authoring system that had just been built and exposes it as a construction. Bernardo Soares is, strictly, a character. Even if it is far from being a simple character.
>
> (Martins 2014: 44; *my translation including the quoted excerpts by Pessoa*)

Regarding the computational analysis of verbal protocols, one of the methods used consists of Latent Semantic Analysis (LSA). This method makes it possible to calculate, for example, the semantic similarity between the readers' verbal protocols and the relationship between the current sentence and the previous causal sentences of the text being read. As mentioned in Millis et al. (2006), in reading comprehension, low-level processes (that is, syntactic and lexical comprehension) are combined with high-level processes (that is, discursive comprehension): "One important discourse skill is being able to establish causal and bridging inferences between units of text, and another is being able to establish the text's theme. Indeed, establishing causal relations among sentences that span several sentences is crucial for understanding many text genres" (225).

An adaptation of this methodology to the critical reception of the *Book of Disquiet* consists of analyzing the semantic relationship between a certain amount of textual context immediately before and immediately after a section of quoted text in order to verify their semantic similarity. With this method it is possible to highlight those elements in the textual field of the excerpt that become significant in the textual field of insertion. The relation between excerpt and insert, including its rhetorical function, is described in this model as a textual graft. Reading protocols in the critical reception documents can be analyzed through textual grafts. Insofar as our own analyses create their own textual grafts we can show our own mode of analysis as partaking in the semiotic process of interpreting an interpretation.

In the case of critical reception texts, automatic text classification would not be important, since texts have been previously classified. However, even at that level it would be possible to create an automatic procedure to be applied to other *corpora* for automatic classification of critical texts by calculating the number of quotations originating in the same source and the distribution and relative frequency of those quotations in the same text as markers of the textual genre known as "critical essay" or "critical review." The topic modeling methodology, on the other hand, could be applied to the corpus to identify and calculate relative similarity among interpretative topics in the entire set of critical reception texts. This identification of topics and the proximity of the topics could then be combined with the encoded information regarding the sources of citations from the *Book of Disquiet* and the publication dates of the critical texts. Finally, the analysis of textual coherence could be adapted to the microanalysis of the reading protocol, that is, of the linguistic markers (connectors and entities, for example) that establish both the internal coherence of the reading argument or a set of relations between the place of the graft (understood as the context outside the quote that justifies the appearance of the quote) and the excerpt itself (understood as the internal context of the quote, which establishes its connection to the source).

Figure 2.5 contains a tentative description of our intertextuality model in the critical reception of the work. The literary component hypothesizes that the construction of intertextuality is made by acts of writing and by acts of reading. In the first case, this includes textual relations (explicit references) linking (1a) critical texts and the *Book of Disquiet*; (1b) critical texts and other works; (1c) critical texts and other critical texts. These links are computationally modeled through XML-TEI encoding of those three sets of relations in order to provide multiple perspectives on textual relationships, presented in the form of visualizations (1d) and textual excerpts (1e). In the second case, it includes the network of reading protocols, defined according to (2a) type of quotation; (2b) type of textual graft; and (2c) rhetorical function of the explicit references within the critical text. These links are computationally modeled through XML-TEI encoding of those three sets of elements of the reading protocol in order to provide multiple perspectives on the reading protocols, presented in the form of (2d) visualizations and (2e) textual excerpts.

Intertextuality is thus conceptualized as an open textual network. It is (3a) produced by pieces of writing that quote, refer to, and echo other pieces of writing; it is also (3b) produced by reading processes that associate pieces of writing. Intertextuality is ultimately the general condition of textuality as both a possibility of writing and a possibility of reading. Citability, that is, the fact that any piece of writing is decontextualizable and recontextualizable, can be demonstrated through the analysis of these open textual networks and the reading protocols that sustain them. In other words: a quote is a material evidence of the presence of one text in another (an intertext as an act of writing), but also evidence of an interpretative process by means of textual association (an intertext as an act of reading).

A computational formalization of this "intertextual algorithm" would need to be sensitive to the network of textual relations and also to the network of reading protocols. It would need to meet the following conditions: (3c) the algorithm should be able to locate and identify citations and references to other texts and, at the same time, (3d) identify types of citations, their modes of grafting and their rhetorical function, by semi-automatically analyzing the immediate context in which references appear. For the first feature, it would be enough to program the recognition of graphical markers in the text (such as quotation marks, person names, and titles). For the second feature, it would be necessary to identify discursive markers of the reading protocols, based on natural language processing and user-generated ontologies for the rhetorical analysis of

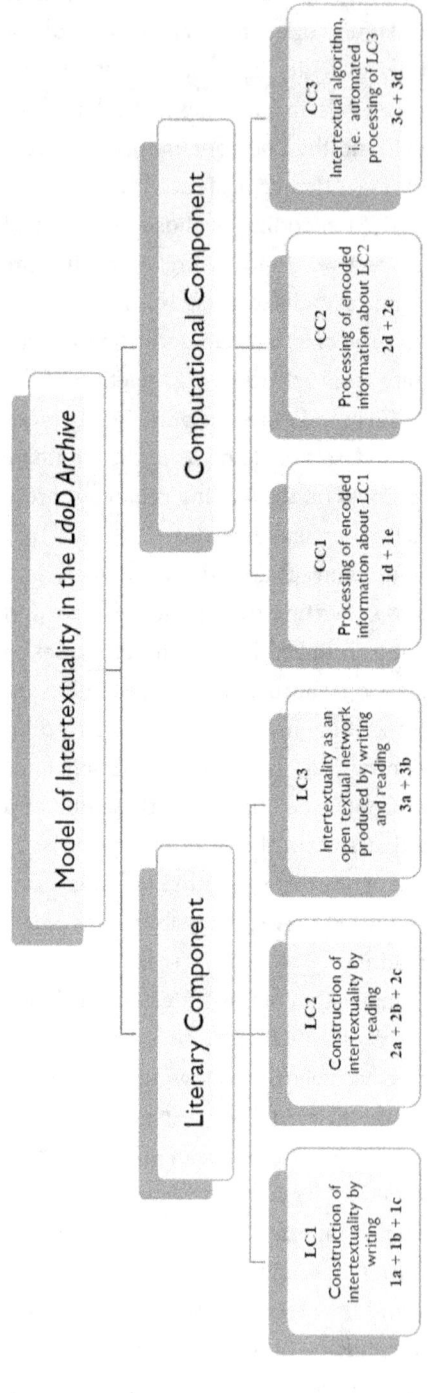

Figure 2.5 A literary and computational model for analyzing intertextuality in the critical reception of the *Book of Disquiet*.

reading protocols. Unlike processing of marked-up text (1 and 2 above), at this level of formalization the "intertextual algorithm" should enable the analysis of unmarked text.

The critical reception hypothesis embodied in the *LdoD Archive* is that "interpretative strategies" are manifested through verbal reading protocols that leave their marks in the text and that these marks can be analyzed and encoded for automatic processing. This is an attempt to both represent and simulate the movement of reading as a process of interweaving textual relations between the text I write and the text I read, showing intertextuality as an interpretative practice, the motion of meaning in production. As an open ongoing action, intertextuality simultaneously creates the interpretability conditions for the text that is being read and the interpretability conditions for the text that is being written.

Our aim is to show critical texts as intertexts in which the production of intertextuality as an act of writing and the production of intertextuality as an act of reading can be observed in parallel. Insofar as the critical text reading protocol allows one to follow the production of juxtapositions of fragments from its textual object and the weaving of relations among those fragments in the process of constituting itself as text, it can be used (1) to characterize particular interpretative strategies of a text or group of texts or particular interpretative communities through their reading protocols, and (2) to model intertextuality itself as the general foundation for semiosis, that is, for the processes of production and transformation of meaning through acts of writing and reading.

This model has greater complexity than models currently used in data mining and distant reading projects, since in these latter cases intertextuality is mostly conceived as the degree of relationship between some texts and others in terms of textual similarity (via quotation, allusion, or paraphrase). The *LdoD Archive* critical reception component offers a computational model which looks at all texts as intertexts, that is, as networks of open relationships that are being socially and historically produced and transformed through the performative processes with which their meaning is being produced in multiple institutional contexts. To the extent that the selected textual corpus is restricted to the community of specialized readers of the *Book of Disquiet*, our method of analysis, encoding, and processing allows us to model and visualize very precisely the complexity of the intertextual process within a specific discourse community.

Critical readings show how texts remain open to further networks of textual association. Textual networks, in turn, are constructed according to specific practices:

> The set of texts that might be juxtaposed and the ways meaning might be derived from their juxtaposition is constrained by the discourse community within which the text is being used and its intertextual practices.
>
> (Bloome and Hong 2012: 5)

The analysis of the juxtapositions and textual montages made by the critical readers of the *Book of Disquiet* offers us a history of the reception of the work based on the chosen corpus, but also a testing ground for a theoretical and computational model of the intertextual dynamics that manifests itself in the co-production of texts by authors and readers. Let us say that the corpus of the critical reception is being used to test the poststructuralist theory of textuality, trying to formalize certain aspects of that theory, namely the notion that any piece of writing is infinitely citable and resignifiable, either by acts of writing or by acts of reading in their iterative cycles of feedback and feedforward.

Social Media Reception as Reading Practice

When considering the automatic collection of online citations in the *LdoD Archive*, several computational problems have to be addressed before we can analyze the collection. For instance, quotes are of varying length according to the specific media channel: in social media feeds, brief quotes (often epigraphic or aphoristic in their intention) predominate, whereas in websites and blogs longer citations (one or several paragraphs; sometimes a full text) are more frequent. There is also the related issue of false positives or false negatives in automated collected citations to be considered. In blogs they will probably be lower (given that the sample to be analyzed is larger), while in the case of social media platforms it will be higher.

How can we optimize the criterion for citation length (five words? ten words? twenty words?) to increase the accuracy of collected instances? What is the minimum length of a citation to be recognized as a citation? On the other hand, when it comes to weighting citation frequency for ranking purposes, will there be any factor that also takes into account the length of the citation? For example, is the quotation of a single sentence from text A equivalent to the full quotation of text B, or should one of them have more relative weight? How can we use the keywords referring to the author ("Fernando Pessoa") or the heteronym ("Bernardo Soares"; "Vicente Guedes"), or the source ("Book of Disquiet") as a disambiguating element of false positives or false negatives when the quoted text does not contain enough textual information for authorship attribution?

The automatic collection of citations in Portuguese from the *Book of Disquiet* posted on the social network Twitter provides an interesting case study not only about its online reception, but also about the nature of reading practices sustained by the affordances of current social media platforms (Oliveira 2018; Oliveira et al. 2019).[25] The algorithm for collection of citations has been running since March 6, 2018. On June 30, 2020, it had harvested a total 6,550 quotes (monthly average of 164; daily average of 5.4). As expected, most publications were made from locations in Brazil (above 80 percent), with the second most representative group coming from posts originating from Portugal, and then quotes from several other countries. If the system had been programmed for harvesting citations in translation, results for languages such as Spanish, Italian, French, and English would allow us to examine social reading expression in other parts of the world. The fact that several translations and several editions (including recent publications) circulate in those and in several other languages would probably identify significant patterns of citation of this work. This confirms the online popularity of this work: the *Book of Disquiet* is one of the most quoted works by Pessoa, who probably is the most frequently cited twentieth-century Portuguese literary author.

Twitter citations from the *Book of Disquiet* reveal a number of extracting and appropriation patterns. Such patterns are interesting from the point of view of reading behaviors, including the mediation of reading behavior by the communication platform, and also in terms of what those patterns suggest about the work itself. Citations come from many texts: the aggregated result of 1,100 days of collection comes from 365 different texts (*c.* 60 percent of the main corpus of the *Book*). On average, quotes originate from fifty to sixty different texts every month. This suggests the aphoristic or axiomatic character of many sentences, since they resonate with readers as highly meaningful when decontextualized or provided with minimum context from the source. Constellations of topics in the Twitter accounts further demonstrate the deformative nature of interpretation as the subjective inscription of the reading self in the directly or indirectly

---

[25] For an overview of the collection, see https://ldod.uc.pt/citations.

quoted text. From the point of view of Pessoa's writing practice, this indicates that the expressive and self-contained intensity of a significant number of sentences is stronger than the narrative or logical flow of discourse, a feature which correlates with the self-conscious reflexive writing processes described below (cf. Chapter 4).

From the perspective of reading, this shows how the character-constraint imposed by this social media platform encourages readers to fragment the source text in search of meaningful quotes. Furthermore, given that the platform is designed to increase the sharing of short strings of writing, the repetition of the same quote implies that *most readers are quoting from text that has been already quoted and shared.* The majority of quotes are thus mediated by other quotes. They are rarely selected directly from the source text, as demonstrated by the fact that when a text is quoted multiple times, tweets always quote the same single excerpt or, in very few cases, the same two excerpts. The reading and writing mechanism enforced by the platform is highly efficient in creating synchronous temporary reading-writing communities around shared strings of language.

For instance, the most frequently quoted passage from the *Book* comes from the text beginning "I experience a feeling of inspiration and liberation as I passively reread" (Text 46).[26] Most Twitter extractor-readers, however, will not have read the source text. Only the tweeted excerpt (and a few other quotes from his prose or poetry) will be familiar to them. A continuous stream of tweets and retweets for eighteen months (March 2018–August 2019) has kept a single quote from this text in circulation. It has been tweeted or retweeted 434 times (Figure 2.6). The quoted text is actually a text by Alberto Caeiro (a poet who is another heteronym of Pessoa) which is being quoted and commented upon by Bernardo Soares (the semi-heteronym who is the writer-narrator of the second phase of composition of the *Book of Disquiet*): "Because I'm the size of what I see / And not the size of my stature" (Text 46).[27] It is of course significant that, in this particular text, Bernardo Soares is behaving as reader and showing the deep effect that that particular sentence has on him. Its emotional, cognitive, existential, and metaphysical truthfulness for the reading self is, in many respects, similar to the ways in which online readers try to invest quoted texts with personal and universal meaning.

---

[26] "Releio passivamente, recebendo o que sinto." Cf. https://ldod.uc.pt/fragments/fragment/Fr256/inter/Fr256_WIT_ED_VIRT_LdoD-Twitter_1.
[27] "Porque eu sou do tamanho do que vejo/ E não do tamanho da minha altura." Cf. https://ldod.uc.pt/fragments/fragment/Fr256/inter/Fr256_WIT_ED_VIRT_LdoD-Twitter_1.

Reading as Simulation 91

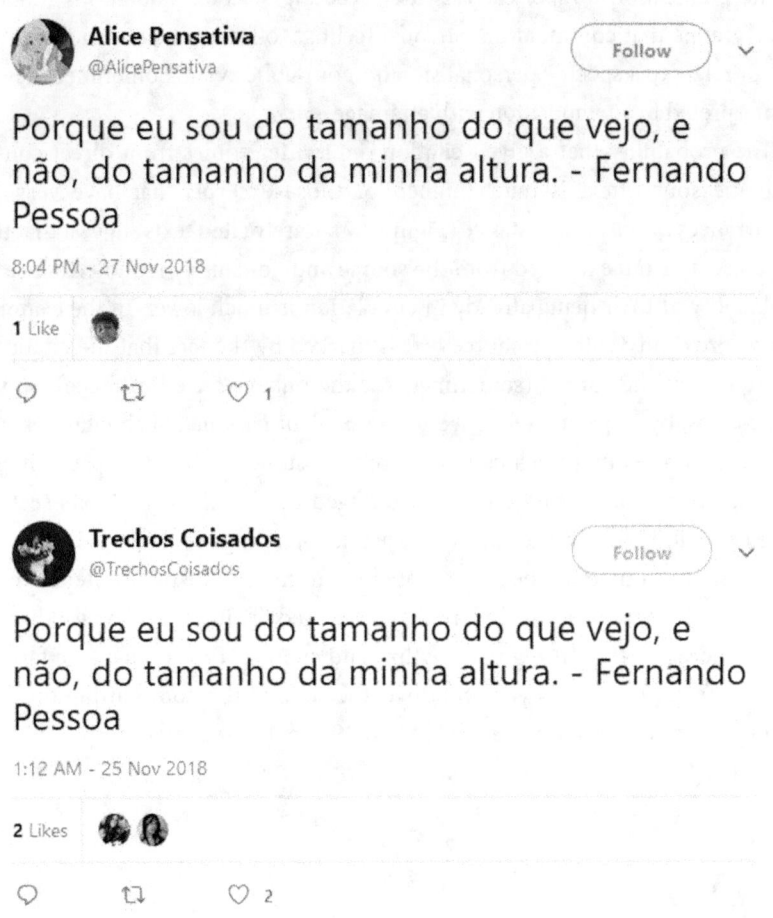

Figure 2.6 The most quoted extract from the *Book of Disquiet* on Twitter for the period March 2018–August 2019. Examples dated November 25 and 27, 2018.

The automatic collection of citations clearly shows how the socio-technological principles of the platform and its regime of hyper-reading and hyper-attention are far more powerful than the continuous close reading practice of literary reading. Readers are compelled to repost the same quote over and over again without reference to or any direct knowledge of its source text. Quoted passages are appropriated for their intrinsic meaning but also, very often, as an indirect comment on the readers' inner life, on ongoing activities (such as travels or work, for instance) or on their general outlook on the world. When read in the context of the publication flow of each Twitter account, selected quotations function as epigraphs that comment on personal feelings, offer some general maxim on life, or relate to a specific personal situation or public event. Sometimes they are reinterpreted by juxtaposition with an image.

The probability that a given citation on Twitter comes from direct contact with the source text is much higher for those excerpts that have very few occurrences or only one instance (Figure 2.7). Rarely cited texts suggest that they were selected and extracted from the source and not simply requoted, since the probability of their being already in circulation is much lower. In the examples below, proximity with the source text is marked by the fact that the citation is infrequent in the corpus (sometimes it is the only collected instance), and, in some cases, by a specific reference to the *Book of Disquiet*. Such citations offer evidence of a reading practice not entirely subsumed by the fast-paced hyper-reading stream of sharing quotes encouraged by the platform. Texts seem to have been individually selected and transcribed, not merely requoted.

The first example has been excerpted from the middle of a sentence in the middle of the text. It seems to have been selected for its power in visualizing a very concrete scene through its rhythm and syntax: "the boots of the family's son, who's going out and yells goodbye, the slam of the door cutting the echo of the *later* that follows the *see you*" (Text 393).[28] The second example contains

Zémar
@josemarsehnem

Follow

os passos de bota do filho de casa que sai e se despede alto, com o bater da porta cortando o eco do logo que vem depois do até
Fernando Pessoa

1:20 PM - 17 May 2018

---

[28] "os passos de bota do filho de casa que sai e se despede alto, com o bater da porta cortando o eco do logo que vem depois do até." Cf. https://ldod.uc.pt/fragments/fragment/Fr061/inter/Fr061_WIT_ED_CRIT_Z.

Reading as Simulation 93

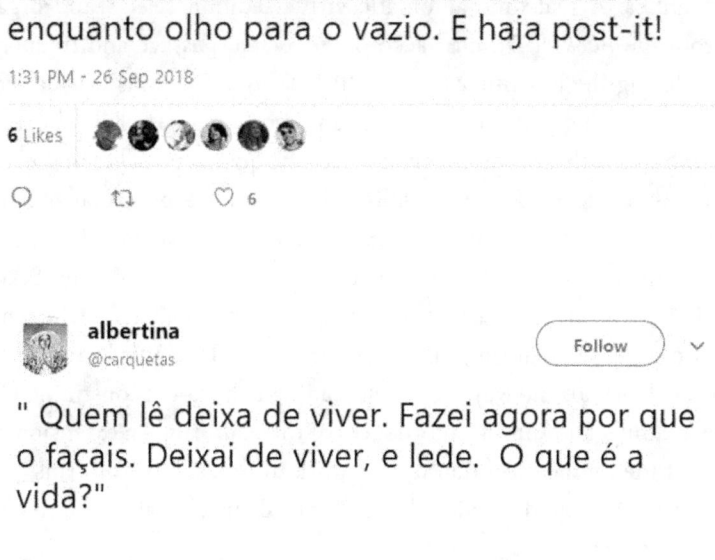

Figure 2.7 Three instances of unique quotes from the *Book of Disquiet* on Twitter for the period March 2018–August 2019. Examples dated May 17, September 26, and December 10, 2018.

a comment implying that the device is being used to transcribe text while reading: "It has been very difficult to advance in my reading of the *Book of Disquiet*, each paragraph takes half an hour of reflection on Pessoa's sentences just staring at the void. And let there be post-it!" (*my translation*). The third example adds a translation of the quoted text into Spanish. The topic of reading (or writing or dreaming) as a substitute for living—recurrent in the work—is reflexively appropriated by this particular reader: "Whoever reads ceases to live. Do it now just because. Stop living, and read. What is life?" (*my translation*).

Automatic collection of citations has been integrated with the virtual editing functionalities. A real-time automatic virtual edition selects and organizes texts from the *Book of Disquiet* according to cited passage and frequency of citation during the last thirty days.[29] This "Twitter Citations" virtual edition captures the sharing patterns of quoting and requoting described above. It is a useful resource at three levels. First, it places the quoted passages in the context of their source texts. Recontextualization of the decontextualized textual strings gives readers the ability to plunge into the full text, and also of moving back from the full text to the social media stream of quoted strings. Secondly, selected quotes let us analyze the patterns of extraction and define the semantic network of topics that are appealing for current readers. Thirdly, they provide specific evidence for the ways in which reading behavior is constrained by the writing, reading, and sharing affordances of the platform. An extension of this analysis of the online reception of this work to other web platforms, such as blogs and wikis, would provide further critical insights about the nature of online reading practices.

Visualizing the Spacetime of Reading

Besides the presentation of the multicursal readings of the *Book of Disquiet* according to the critical editors and to the algorithmic recommendation sequence, the *LdoD Archive* offers additional ways of constructing and registering reading paths, including visualizations of multiple textual

---

[29] Available at "Virtual Edition: Citações no Twitter": https://ldod.uc.pt/edition/acronym/LdoD-Twitter.

constellations and the ability for each reader to track his or her own reading trail. Reading is thus reflexively engaged at three levels: (1) as an actual set of expert critical readings and online common readings presented as an intertextual network of quotations mapped onto the *Book of Disquiet*; (2) as a user-defined sequence that responds dynamically to a range of possibilities, such as reading sequences defined by the expert critical editors, algorithmic sequences based on similarity analysis, and diagrammatic sequences dependent on meta-information produced either by the expert or virtual editors (heteronyms, dates, taxonomies) or by text similarity algorithms; (3) as a mapped reading trail whose timeline offers readers an overview of their trajectory and the possibility of tracing back their own personal reading sequence.

The overall logic of turning the acts and processes of reading into an explicit element of the interaction is the conceptual equivalent to the virtualization of editing and writing. By means of these interactive graphical interfaces the construction of reading as a series of movements within the constrained semiotic space of the *LdoD Archive* is abstracted in the textual encoding and in the visualizations, and it is also scripted back into the simulatory system. The simulation of reading results from the multiplicity of navigation and mapping tools which foster an engagement of readers with their own unique processes as they explore the *Book of Disquiet*. Texts always reorganize themselves in response to such exploratory processes without defining a single or preferred reading trajectory.

This exploratory process has been metaphorically translated into two features of the reading interface that attempt to model reading as the recursive process of going into the text and coming out of the text. The "Visual Book" is a specific component of this interface in which that double cognitive movement has been used for structuring the interaction with the texts.[30] The immersive reading movement is graphically represented by a reading interface in which the text becomes the only element on display. The emersive reading movement is graphically embodied by a series of diagrammatic visualizations that offer various global maps for creating and exploring reading sequences. While the zoom in of the first movement is designed for engaging with the word-by-word

---

[30] The code for this component was developed by José Raposo in 2018–19. See also Raposo 2019. The concept of "in-phase" and "out-phase" as reading behaviors equated with specific display modes in the Graphical User Interface is developed in Raposo et al. (2021).

reality of the verbal strings, the zoom out of the second movement shifts the focus to overall patterns of relations among texts. The possibility of moving back and forth between the close and distant reading scales is another expression of the simulation rationale.[31]

Figure 2.8 shows the "immersive" or "in"-phase display mode of the reading process. The top menus allow users to select other visualization activities, and there are two navigation buttons for "previous" and "next," respectively on the left- and right-hand side of the text. Black arrows enable users to navigate according to this virtual edition's sequence, while yellow arrows will lead readers only through the subset of texts that have been marked with the current tag (i.e., the meta-information element selected for constellating a subset of texts). Highlighted words in the text (blue color) represent the four most relevant words. After five seconds all menus and navigation aids and buttons are hidden, leaving only the text for the reader. Readers are expected to engage with the uncluttered display of words on the screen.

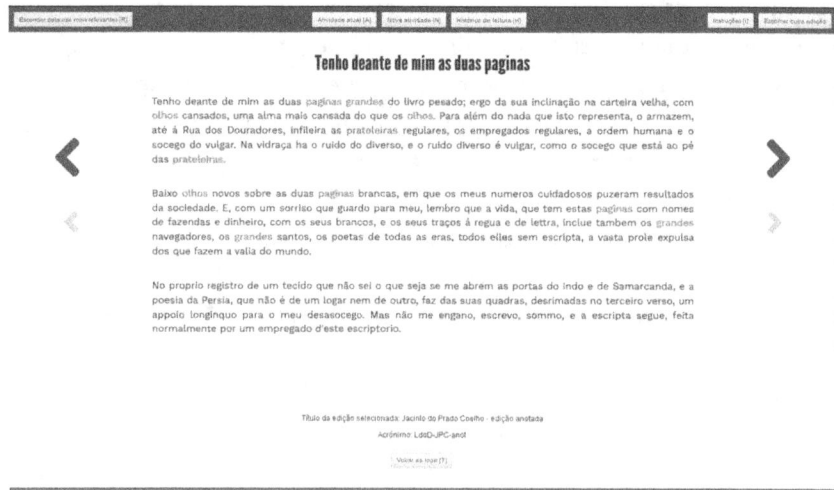

Figure 2.8 One of the texts with the tag "escritório" ("office") as presented in the reading interface of the "Visual Book" application. Display mode designed according to the "immersive" or "in"-phase of the reading process.

---

[31] For a discussion of information visualization, see Manovich 2011; for experiments in the integration of close and distant reading tools, see Cheema et al. 2016, Jänicke et al. 2017, and Eve 2019; for a discussion of non-representational generative forms of visualization, see Drucker 2014b, 2020.

Figures 2.9, 2.10, and 2.11 show the "emersive" or "out"-phase display mode of the reading process. In the emersive mode, readers engage only with visualizations that offer macro-representations based on the meta-information of the selected virtual editions. In Figure 2.9 texts are visualized according to the chronology of their composition. In Figure 2.10 texts are visualized as a word cloud according to the taxonomy of a specific virtual edition. Each word represents a category of the taxonomy that has been associated with a subset of texts by the virtual editors. There can be as many word clouds as taxonomies freely created in the system. Reading sequences can be defined on the basis of the semantic tags associated with groups of textual units. Figure 2.11 presents one example of a reading sequence (highlighted squares) that is determined by the tag "escritório" ("office").

Since thematic visualizations are always relative to the classification system of a given virtual edition, they are always variable and dependent on virtual editions, which are themselves open and subject to change. This "emersive" distant reading is thus responsive to the evolving nature of this technosocial system. Visualizations are experienced as variable perspectives on the textual data that respond to subjective inquiries and inflected analyses.

One of the ways in which reading activities become reading traces is through the visualization of one's reading trajectory within the "Visual Book" interface, as shown in Figure 2.12. Given the aleatoric and serendipitous nature of reading

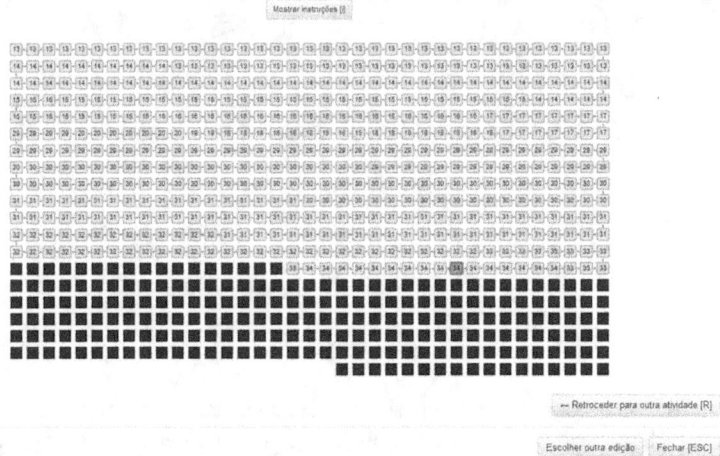

Figure 2.9 Diagrammatic representation of a virtual edition of the *Book of Disquiet* in which the sequence is determined by the chronology of composition of each text. Each square represents a textual unit. Display mode designed according to the "emersive" or "out"-phase of the reading process.

98   *Literary Simulation and the Digital Humanities*

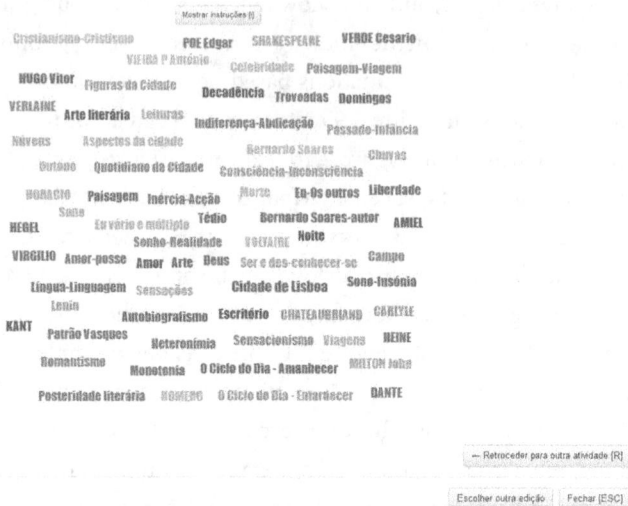

Figure 2.10 Word cloud representing the taxonomy of a particular virtual edition of the *Book of Disquiet*. Display mode designed according to the "emersive" or "out"-phase of the reading process.

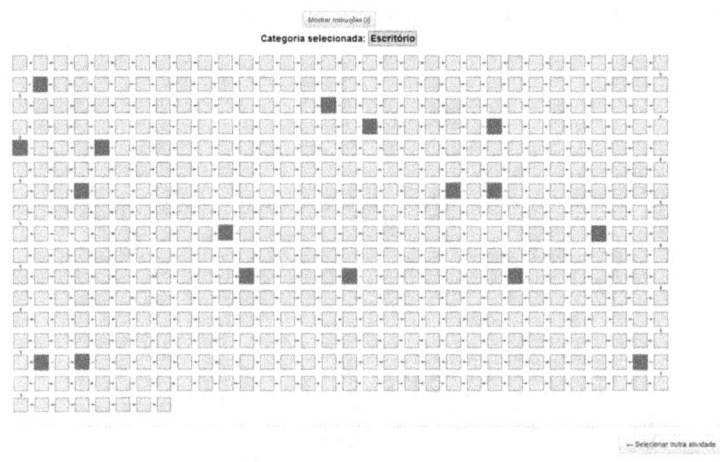

Figure 2.11 Diagrammatic representation of a virtual edition of the *Book of Disquiet* in which the reading sequence (highlighted squares) is determined by the tag "escritório" ("office"). Each square represents a textual unit. Display mode designed according to the "emersive" or "out"-phase of the reading process.

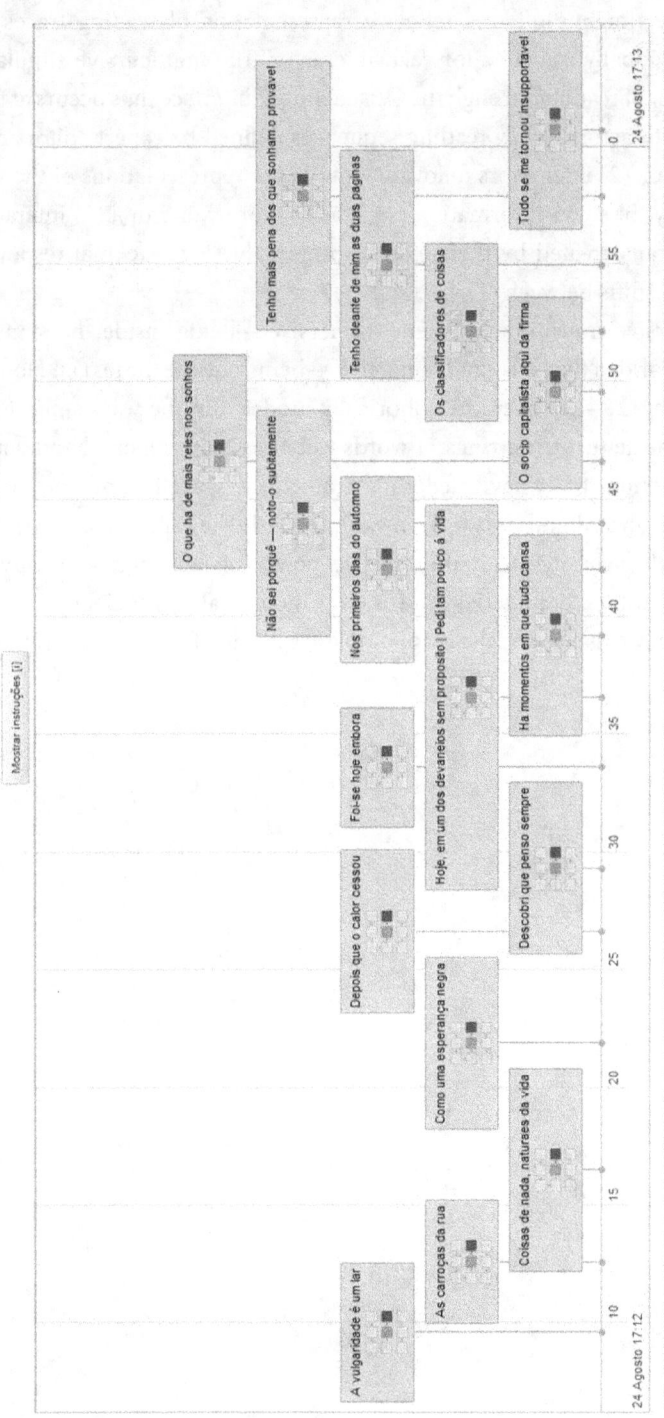

Figure 2.12 Timeline representing an interactor's reading history during one reading session.

motions, the timeline offers a reflexive representation of reading traces that is only individually available for each interactor. The multicursive simulatory enhancement of reading through the "Visual Book" interface thus occurs at three levels: (1) interactors follow reading sequences defined by expert editors or by virtual editors; (2) interactors follow diagrammatic representations of the work as defined by the meta-information (such as date or taxonomy); (3) interactors follow the trails created by their own reading paths. Hypertextual responsive reading thus shifts between (1), (2), and (3).

The recursive transition between "immersive"—being inside the symbolic imaginary world of the text—and "emersive"—being outside the text and looking at the text as text—has been metaphorically modeled in the ways subjects can interact with the text. As strings of words to be read, on the one hand, and as visual abstractions to be navigated, on the other, the spacetime of reading thus enfolds both inward and outward. Inward, towards the rapturous, mysterious, and personal encounter with the creative power of language; and outward, towards a multitude of material traces of our individual and social processes of reading as they engage with the diagrammatic spacing of written inscriptions.

3

Editing as Simulation

This chapter addresses the editorial component of the *LdoD Archive*. First, I will show how its representational dimension takes the form of a meta-edition, i.e., an edition that has been designed as a comparative micro- and macro-representation of other editions. Secondly, I will show how this representational dimension is turned into a simulation when the encoded textual units from the various expert editions are freely used as building blocks of the virtual editions. Finally, I will argue that this dynamic computer-assisted simulation space is an attempt to embody the performativity of the editorial act itself. The editorial focus of the *LdoD Archive* thus shifts retroactively (1) from each particular expert edition to the archive of the *Book of Disquiet* as a series of autograph documents; (2) from each particular expert edition to other expert editions as possible and actual versions of the *Book of Disquiet*; and (3) from those two documentary focuses to any number of potential textual arrangements. The continuous un-editing and re-editing through the programmed functionalities of the platform instantiates the very processuality of editing.

From Edition to Meta-Edition

One of the goals of the *LdoD Archive* is to show Pessoa's *Book of Disquiet* as a network of potential authorial intentions and a conjectural construction of its successive editors (Figure 3.1). Our digital representation of the dynamics of textual and bibliographical variation depends on both XML encoding of variation sites (deletions, additions, substitutions, variants, paragraph and text divisions, etc.), metatextual information concerning authorial and editorial witnesses (date, order, heteronym, etc.), and a data model that fosters multiple perspectives and exploratory interactions with the textual materials at different scales. While

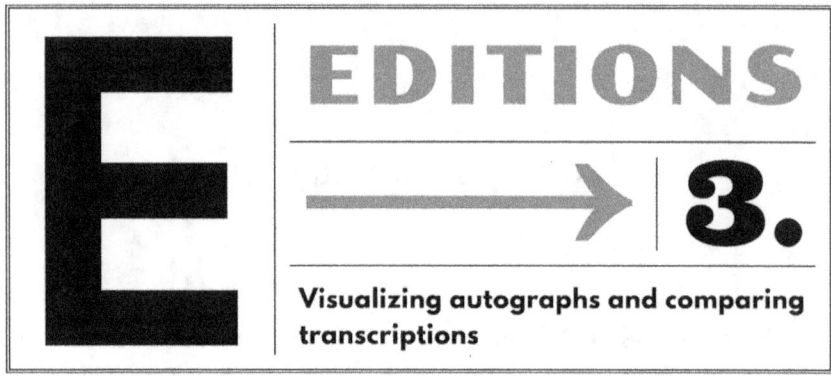

Figure 3.1 Graphic representation of the editions interface. This interface takes readers directly to tools for comparing editions at the textual and bibliographic levels.

XML-TEI markup may be considered as a critical apparatus on its own, it is through algorithmic analysis, visualization tools, and graphical interface that users are able to critically engage with the evidence of variation in authorial and editorial witnesses.

Besides representation of textual and bibliographical variation in the work's genetic and editorial history, the *LdoD Archive* enables interactors to generate new virtual editorial forms of the work, as described in the next section. This section discusses the theoretical and technical aspects of the strategies adopted for encoding, visualizing, and generating variation in the *LdoD Archive*. The data model for the textual archive and the strategies adopted for encoding all the authorial and editorial witnesses were aimed at providing comparability between all the authorial or editorial versions of the same text, including their relative position within the book. Instead of following a digital scholarly editing model based on the bibliographic practice of the "definitive" critical edition that subsumes and transcends earlier editions, the *LdoD Archive* is designed according to meta-editorial principles. The purpose of the meta-edition is to offer a critical probe into four editions as actual forms of the *Book of Disquiet* whose textual embodiment results from four distinct sets of editorial principles and criteria. Through comparison and manipulation, the editorial interface has been designed to emphasize the hypothetical constructedness of the *Book of Disquiet* rather than a single version of the work. Thus each historical version is seen as the contingent result of specific editorial interventions among a network of versions.

Fernando Pessoa's *Livro do Desassossego* (*Book of Disquiet*) is an unfinished book project. During his lifetime Pessoa only published twelve pieces from this ongoing project in literary magazines (1913, 1929, 1930, 1931, and 1932).[1] Currently, the National Library has cataloged 722 sheets as belonging to the *Livro do Desassossego*, of which 374 are typescripts, while 348 are manuscripts. Some of the documents are written only on recto, others on recto and verso. Witnesses show multiple stages of composition and revision: short annotations; brief paragraphs; multiple-page first drafts; clean corrected typescripts. Texts explicitly assigned by Pessoa to *Livro do Desassossego* contain the annotation "L. do D." However, there are more than two hundred texts without the "L. do D." annotation that also belong (or have been ascribed by editors as belonging) to the *Livro*.

The first edition of this book was published only in 1982. This first edition (2 vols.; reprinted only once, 1997), was edited by Jacinto do Prado Coelho, with textual transcriptions by Maria Aliete Galhoz and Teresa Sobral Cunha.[2] Three major editions have been published since then. These were edited, respectively, by Teresa Sobral Cunha in 1990–1 (2 vols.; 7th rev. ed., 2013), by Richard Zenith in 1998 (11th rev. ed., 2014), and by Jerónimo Pizarro in 2010 (2 vols.; 3rd rev. ed., 2014). Thus the expert editions included in the *LdoD Archive* are the main critical editions published between 1982 and 2012: Coelho 1982; Sobral Cunha 2008; Zenith 2012; and Pizarro 2010. Those particular editions were selected because they were the latest editions when we began encoding the files for the *LdoD Archive* in the year 2012.

With the exception of the first edition, the remaining three critical editions have continued to undergo revision and change. For the past forty years, editors have rarely managed to publish the work twice under the exact same textual form. Every reprint becomes an opportunity for revision: new readings are offered for particular passages, additional fragments are included or excluded, fragments are fused or divided, and a few pieces change place. The number of texts in the editions that we have encoded for the *LdoD Archive* is as follows: the edition by

---

[1] "Trechos" (which can be translated as *excerpts* or *passages*, but also *texts*) from the *Book of Disquiet* were published in the following periodicals: *A Águia*, no. 20 (August 1913, pp. 38–42), *A Revista*, no. 1 (1932, p. 8), *A Revista*, no. 2 (1929, p. 25), *A Revista*, no. 4 (1929, p. 42), *Presença*, no. 27 (June–July, 1930, p. 9), *Descobrimento*, no. 3 (1931, pp. 405–15; 5 texts), *Presença*, no. 34 (1931–2, p. 8), and *Revolução*, no. 74 (June 7, 1932, p. 3).

[2] Jorge de Sena had started working on the preparation of an edition of the *Book of Disquiet* in the 1960s, but this work was never finished. Sena wrote an introduction for the *Book* in 1964, which was published posthumously in *Persona*, no. 3, July 1979 (Sena 1984). For current editorial views on the *Livro do Desassossego*, see Pizarro 2016a and 2018; Zenith 2016; and Lopes 2016.

Prado Coelho, 520; by Sobral Cunha, 748; by Zenith, 541; and by Pizarro, 586. All editions include additional fragments to the main corpus, transcribed either as annexes, appendices, or preliminary materials.

Those four editions (of which Sobral Cunha, Zenith, and Pizarro remain in circulation) have been the basis for most other editions in circulation both in Portuguese and in translation. To these, we could add many trade editions in Portugal and Brazil, particularly those published after 2005 when Fernando Pessoa's works came definitively into the public domain. If we further add the translations of the *Book of Disquiet*, some of which are based on a particular selection and arrangement of fragments by the translators themselves, we could argue that multiform bibliographic structure and unstable textual form have become defining features of the work in its myriad incarnations. There are now several versions of the book in circulation in languages such as Spanish, French, Italian, English, and German, for instance. Pessoa's mental and verbal disquiet has materialized in the posthumous variability of his textual legacy.

As it exists today, the *Livro do Desassossego* may be characterized as (1) a set of autograph (manuscript and typescript) fragments, (2) mostly unpublished at the time of Pessoa's death, which have been (3) transcribed, selected, and organized into four different editions, implying (4) various critical and genetic interpretations of what constitutes this book. Editions show four major types of variation: variation in readings of particular passages, in selection of fragments, in their ordering, and also in heteronym attribution. The first authorial persona for the *Livro* was Vicente Guedes, but the work was later reassigned by Pessoa to Bernardo Soares, a persona described by Pessoa as a "semi-heteronym."[3] Although the authorial personae behind *Livro do Desassossego* tend not to be viewed as full heteronyms, heteronym attribution has been an important function in structuring the work.[4]

Those editorial instantiations have given material expression to four different models of constructing the *Livro*. We could summarize these models

---

[3] In 2015 Teresa Rita Lopes edited a new version of the work titled *Book(s) of Disquiet*, in which she added thirty-five texts by Barão de Teive (another heteronym by Pessoa) to the corpus of texts assigned to Vicente Guedes and Bernardo Soares. Although most scholars will disagree with the addition of the textual corpus by Barão de Teive, who appears linked to the *Book of Disquiet* in very few witnesses, the edition by Teresa Rita Lopes is yet another demonstration of the projectual nature of the authorial and editorial forms of the work, reinforcing, to a certain extent, the theoretical justification for the virtual editing dynamic functionalities in the *LdoD Archive* (cf. Pessoa 2015, edited by Teresa Rita Lopes).

[4] Fernando Cabral Martins (2014) and others have argued that Bernardo Soares, the narrator of the *Book of Disquiet*, is a character and thus not part of Pessoa's system of heteronyms as authorial personae.

as follows: the first orders fragments according to a combination of thematic and chronological proximity (edition by Jacinto do Prado Coelho); the second distinguishes between two periods of composition and their respective heteronyms (Vicente Guedes and Bernardo Soares), while strengthening the discursive unity of the fragments within each part, for example, by removing text numbering and by rearranging the internal structure of a certain number of more fragmentary texts (edition by Teresa Sobral Cunha); the third considers the production of Bernardo Soares as the main axis of the work and anchors the remaining fragments so that Soares's voice and style become predominant, relegating the set of early large texts by Vicente Guedes to a final section (edition by Richard Zenith); finally, the fourth model produces a critical and genetic reconstruction based on the documented or inferred chronology of the composition of fragments, thus bringing the order of the *Livro* closer to its archival order (edition by Jerónimo Pizarro).[5]

The long and convoluted editorial history of Pessoa's works—most of which have been posthumously published since the 1940s until now—has been summarized by Pizarro (2012: 29-92). However, the detailed social history of the production of the *Book of Disquiet* has yet to be told. Signs of ongoing struggles for defining text and structure of the *Book of Disquiet* are more or less evident in each of the editorial prefaces. The fact that there have been two teams in competition to produce his complete works, in critical editions using different criteria (see, for instance, Castro 1993), reflects not only academic struggles for power over Pessoa's texts, but also market competition.[6] A particularly significant moment in this history happened when copyright was extended from fifty to seventy years after the death of the author. Pessoa's works were in the public domain for a few years after 1985, but they were repossessed by a major publisher when the new copyright law came into force in the early 1990s. It was only in 2005 that Pessoa's works fell again in the public domain, but each new textual organization generates its own exclusive rights for publishers and editors. During the last decade, a new generation of scholars has been editing and releasing unpublished texts and inventing all sorts of new books by Pessoa,

---

[5] For an analysis of the editions of *Livro do Desassossego* focused on the return to the archive fostered by digital media, see Silvestre 2014. Pessoa's editorial plans for the *Livro* have been closely examined by Sepúlveda 2013. For Pessoa's book projects, see Sepúlveda 2014, and Sepúlveda and Henny-Krahmer 2017.

[6] Each edition belongs to a different publisher: Ática (for Coelho 1982), Relógio d'Água (for Sobral Cunha 2008), Assírio & Alvim (for Zenith 2012), Imprensa Nacional Casa da Moeda (for Pizarro 2010), and Tinta-da-china (for Pessoa 2013b).

in a frenzy of editorial activity that cannot be explained without taking into account the institutional and economic competition in the academic and literary markets.

Analysis of editorial introductions and diachrony of publication demonstrates how editions compete against each other in order to legitimize their particular ways of constructing the *Book of Disquiet* from Pessoa's textual archive. In other words, variations in the *Book of Disquiet*'s internal textual form depend not only on the explicit criteria and literary models invoked by the editors of each edition, but also on a set of implicit socioliterary factors. The almost immediate publication of new revised editions for each of the three major editions whenever a new version of the book appears on the market highlights this dynamic of competition for cultural and financial capital. With regard to the explicit criteria, editorial intentionality on the transcription, selection, and organization strongly mediates access to authorial intentionality. This means that the transition from the transcriptional scale of the documents to the macro-scale of their textual form and bibliographic structure is also produced through a specific intersection of the ideas of "book," "Book of Disquiet," "work," and "Pessoa."

Editorial interpretations concerning the nature of the *Book of Disquiet* as a work, including notions about its place in the literary economy of Pessoa's entire oeuvre, function as organizing principles for each version of the *Book*. Jerónimo Pizarro, for instance, highlights its protean dimension, referring both to the double origin of autograph texts, which correspond to two moments of distinct intentionality and style, associated, first, to the heteronym Vicente Guedes and, later, to the semi-heteronym Bernardo Soares. He also refers to the polyphony of Pessoa's other heteronymic voices, many of which seem to converge within the *Book of Disquiet* in its later moment of composition. The metamorphic character of the work is further testified by the incommensurability between the four major editions published since 1982 (Pizarro 2016a). Richard Zenith, on the other hand, considers the fragment as a literary form, and not as a mere contingency of the incompleteness of the writing process. For Zenith, the fragment as literary form is adequate to the internal logic of the *Book of Disquiet*, and his edition explores the hypothesis of presenting the work as a novel narrating the inner life of Bernardo Soares (Zenith 2013). Different ways of conceiving the work thus correspond to different models of editorial construction.

Document, Text, Book, Work

The meta-editorial perspective described above is a way of modeling the textual dynamics that determines the transformation of documents into books. The *Book of Disquiet* takes shape through interpretative acts that have selected, transcribed, and organized the text according to specific conceptions of the work. Understood as a particular textual form based on autograph witnesses, the *Book* becomes the expression of an editorial project that has inscribed itself into the work's archive. The encoding of the network of variations across the editions, on the one hand, and the relations between them and the autograph witnesses, on the other, makes the textual form of each edition available for algorithmic processing. Editions become machine-readable *qua* editions, i.e., as specific interventions in the work's documentary and textual archive. The editorial process itself is primed through a series of analytical and comparative tools. Critical editions in print are electronically edited according to a digital rationale of a second-order representation of a first-order representation. Editions are material instantiations of editorial performativeness. By representing how Pessoa's text is mediated through these particular editions, a certain number of acts and processes of mediation can be foregrounded.

Hans Walter Gabler (2010), Elena Pierazzo (2011, 2015), and other editors see in the digital edition the possibility of returning the work and the text to the document, which suggests an identification between text and document that would suspend the interpretative intervention of the editor. This theoretical perspective is encouraged by the feasibility of high-resolution facsimile images of autograph witnesses, which can thus be objectified without the mediation of a transcription. The growing number of documentary digital editions during the past two decades is a consequence of this technical production context. This general return to the sources enabled by digital reproduction across all areas of culture tends to proceed according to the logic of photographic transparency, effacing interpretative layers implied in processes of remediation and visualization.

However, as Peter Robinson (2013) claims, the separation between text and document is inherent in the act of reading itself, since marks inscribed onto a surface only become legible forms through an interpretive act. It is the performance of reading that transforms the marks of the document (that is, inscriptions on a given surface) into the text (that is, into a set of signifiers that imply questions of intentionality, agency, authority, and meaning), and it is also through the act of reading that text is projected into the unstable and changing horizon of the work. Robinson proposes the following principle to describe the dynamic relationship between text and document, on the one hand, and between text and work, on the other: "text is the site of meaning which links the document and the work" (123).

Printed editions have traditionally focused on the relationship of text to work, while digital editions have been more focused on the relationship of text to document. Robinson suggests that "a scholarly edition must, so far as it can, illuminate both aspects of the text, both text-as-work and text-as-document" (123). The movement from document to text and from text to work contains an inverse movement (from work back to document) through which a certain idea of the work inscribes itself in the form and organization of the text as inferred from the documents. Textual semiosis involves self and object in a continuous and co-dependent process of meaning production through acts of reading. Editing Pessoa's centrifugal and reticular body of unpublished work is an especially acute experience of the productive function of reading in activating the force fields that allow you to move back and forth from document to text to book to work.

From a theoretical standpoint, the concept "document" is used to describe the object containing the original inscriptions. In the *LdoD Archive*, the document is represented by the digital image of manuscripts, typescripts, and printed autographs. The concept "text" refers to the document after an act of reading takes place. To the extent that transcription is also a reading act, the result of any transcription would be a "text." In the *LdoD Archive* the text is represented by the topographic transcription of autograph documents and by the textual transcription of the four selected editions. Finally, the concept of "book" refers to the diverse forms of the *Book of Disquiet*, that is, to a particular selection and organization of texts into a bibliographic whole.

Expert editions thus correspond to historically existing forms of the book, each of which transcribes, selects, and orders texts according to certain criteria that aim to produce a book as an instantiation of the "work." Virtual editions, on the other hand, are other possible (temporary or persistent) ways of producing the *Book of Disquiet* (or simply a particular collection of texts) in the context of the collaborative and dynamic functionalities offered by the *LdoD Archive*. Each expert version of the *Book of Disquiet* is the historical embodiment of a particular idea about the work, while each virtual editing of the *Book of Disquiet* is a way of experiencing the process of moving from text to book to work. The fact that most virtual editions by non-experts will only engage with a small sample of the fragments is in itself a reiteration of the *LdoD Archive*'s procedural and unfinished dimension. The process of editing rather than the edited object have become the center of the system.

The *Editions* interface contains a complex representation that brings together the micro-scale of genetic transcription, based on the document, and the macro-scale of editorial arrangement, based on each expert's editorial interventions (Figure 3.2). On the right-hand side column, a bibliographic visualization of the relative position of this text in each expert edition is provided: "Minha alma é uma orchestra occulta" has been divided into five different texts in Jacinto do Prado Coelho (27, 78, 259, 357, and 437), corresponds to text 15 in Teresa Sobral Cunha, text 310 in Richard Zenith, and text 1 in Jerónimo Pizarro.[7] Textual transcriptions can also be compared against each other, and all points of variation (orthography, choice of variants, divergent readings, punctuation, paragraph division, text division) are highlighted (Figure 3.3).

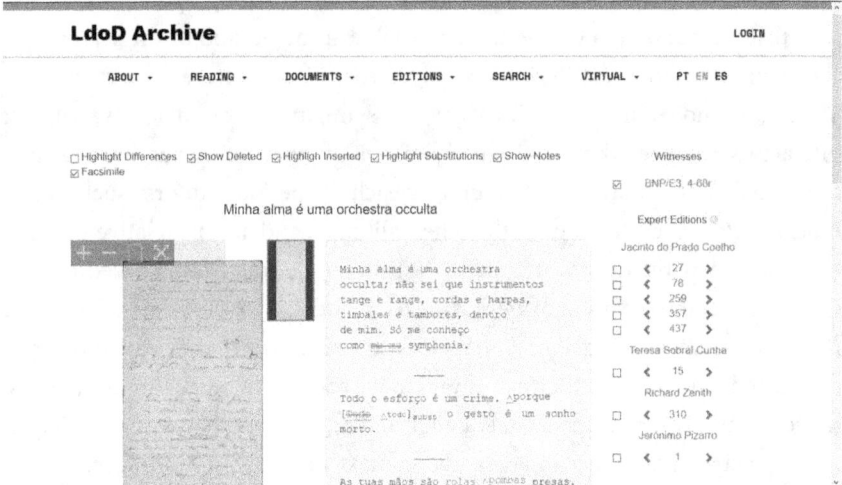

Figure 3.2 Screen capture of the *Editions* interface. Display of the topographic genetic transcription against the digital facsimile image, and display of the relative structure and relative position of this text in four expert book sequences (macro-variations).

---

[7] Full text available at https://ldod.uc.pt/fragments/fragment/Fr279/inter/Fr279_WIT_ED_CRIT_Z (BNP/E3, 4-68r; Coelho 27, 78, 259, 357, 437; Sobral Cunha 15; Zenith 310; Pizarro 1).

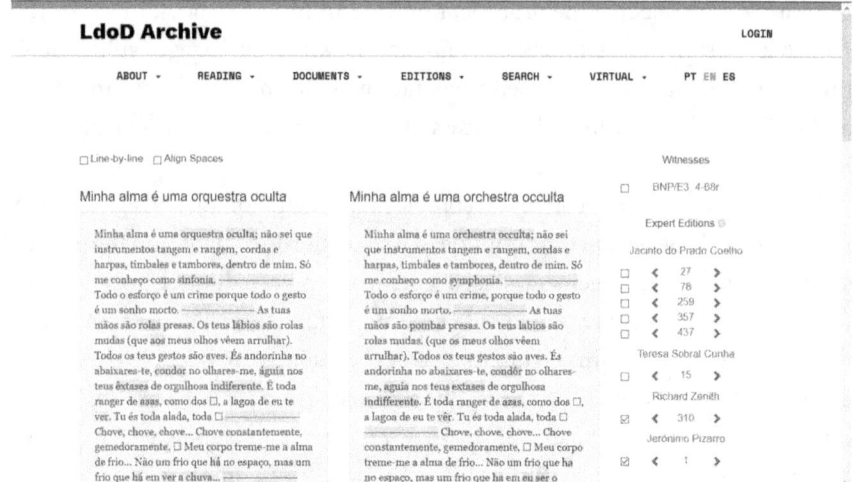

Figure 3.3 Screen capture of the *Editions* interface. Display of the comparison of the textual transcription in Richard Zenith and Jerónimo Pizarro for witness BNP/E3, 4-68r.

Highlighted elements indicate points of variation (orthographic, substantive, punctuation, paragraph division, etc.). A table at the bottom of the screen (not shown in the figure) identifies all textual micro-variations across expert editions. The right-hand column provides a synoptic synthetic view of macro-variations: interactors can see whether a particular autograph witness has been treated as one unit or as more than one unit by each of the four editors (such as five units in JPC versus one unit in the other editions), and also its relative position (represented by the fragment number) within the *Book of Disquiet* according to each editor. From the point of view of the data model, editorial witnesses become part of a network of versions. Interactors can move from each edited book to another edited book and they can always move back to the work's archive, that is, the text can be represented as unedited or re-edited in another version of itself.

By placing digital facsimiles in the context of topographic transcriptions, the *LdoD Archive* enables users to experiment with the transit from document to text and from text to document. Situating both facsimile and topographic transcription in the context of the experts' editions, the *LdoD Archive* shows several possible transitions from text to book and from book to text. To the extent that each text of each edition is contextualizable in an archive of authorial and editorial witnesses, it is the very process of construction of text from document and book from text that the genetic and social dimensions of the

LdoD Archive place in evidence. The construction of the book—as the product either of a projected first-person self-editing authorial act, or a series of third-person editorial acts—becomes an instantiation of the conceptual and material process of identity and difference that enables text and book to emerge from a series of inscriptional marks and metamarks and from the acts of reading and interpreting those marks and metamarks.

The electronic edition of modern manuscripts that are unfinished book projects can be conceived according to different principles. The principle used in the *LdoD Archive* is based on the unit "trecho" (literally, "stretch" or "passage," i.e., a continuous piece of completed writing) or fragment (a continuous piece of writing in progress), understood as a certain textual extension with thematic or material evidence of textual unity, which can be further marked (or not) by graphical markers: for example, a larger space or a larger number of blank lines between two handwritten textual sequences suggests an interruption; or by genetic and editorial events, for example, a piece that has been typed or published in a magazine.

The *LdoD Archive* uses the notion "fragment" to refer to all texts from the *Livro*. Although a significant number of texts can be considered fragmentary because they may have not been finished or revised, there are also several hundred texts that are finished and revised pieces ("trechos"), including a set of twelve published texts. Pessoa seems to have conceived the book as some kind of arrangement of brief and long "trechos." Regardless of their stage of completion and revision, all textual pieces may be considered textual fragments of the projected book. In the *LdoD Archive*, each fragment can be represented by a minimum of two and a maximum of seven interpretations (transcriptions): there will be two if there is only one authorial witness and the text was included only in one edition (i.e., a topographic transcription of the authorial source plus a transcription of the editorial source); there will be seven in those rare cases in which there are three authorial witnesses (one handwritten, one typewritten, and one published version; or, sometimes, two typewritten and one published version) and four editorial transcriptions. For most texts, there are five interpretations (transcriptions): one from the authorial witness and four from the editorial transcriptions.[8]

The units of composition included in the *LdoD Archive* are based on either the set of four critical editions, or the ensemble of digital facsimiles

---

[8] An overview of the encoded fragments included in the *LdoD Archive* is available at https://ldod.uc.pt/fragments.

of authorial witnesses that correspond to that set. On the other hand, it is possible to think of the act of writing as a speech act, that is, as a certain temporal unit of writing that does not always coincide with the documentary material unit (recto and verso of a loose leaf, or a set of contiguous pages in a notebook, for example) or with units of written discourse, such as the paragraph, or other units of bibliographical structure, such as the chapter. Pessoa's writing practice for the *Livro* seems to emphasize this act of scripting as a unit of composition of the work itself. This notion can be related to Peter Shillingsburg's "script act" (2006), although what I want to emphasize here is the fact that most textual units in the *Livro* seem to coincide with one temporal unit of writing, i.e., one sustained period of continuous writing, as discussed in Chapter 4.

The existence of very short fragments, almost aphoristic in scale, along with fragments of varying length (one paragraph to one page to a few pages), written at very different moments in time, suggests precisely this noncoincidence between the temporal unit of writing and the cumulative and retrospective process of accretion and rewriting that produces semantic coherence and syntactic cohesion. Each moment of writing (which is also a moment of self-consciousness of writing) originates a new self-contained thematic and stylistic unit. These units proliferate as fragments of a book in progress but they resist the material order of the book. Edward Vanhoutte (2006) characterizes the modern manuscript as a complex network of those temporal units of writing. Marta L. Werner (2011), in her turn, describes the modern manuscript as a record of the dynamics of text in the process of creating itself. She places it in a liminal space of private inscription which becomes physically reflected in its undisciplined textual condition.

By using the notion "trecho" to refer to the units of composition of the *Book of Disquiet*, Fernando Pessoa is aware of this dimension of aggregation and sequencing of small textual units as one of its compositional principles. The revision process that he imagines toward the bibliographical horizon seems to imply the simultaneous production of psychological coherence and stylistic consistency:

B. of D.
(NOTE)
The organization of the book should be based on a highly rigorous selection from among the various kinds of texts written, adapting the older ones—which lack the psychology of Bernardo Soares—to that true psychology as it has

now emerged. In addition, an overall revision of the style needs to be made, but without giving up the dreaminess and logical disjointedness of its intimate expression.

It must also be decided whether to include the large texts with grandiose titles, such as the 'Funeral March for Ludwig II, King of Bavaria' or 'Symphony of the Restless Night'. The 'Funeral March' could be left as it is, or it could be made part of another book, one that would gather together all the Large Texts.

(Pessoa 2002: appendix III; translation by Zenith)[9]

Fernando Pessoa is thinking about subsuming the fragments of the *Livro* to the conceptual and material coherence of the book form. He is recognizing both the disjointed dreamlike introspective style of Bernardo Soares, and also textual affinities among the large texts. One of the difficulties alluded to by Pessoa in the quoted passage (written *c*. 1931) derives from the fact that during the first stage of composition (1913-20), he assigned the *Livro* to Vicente Guedes, whose style and psychology are significantly different from the book's later heteronym, Bernardo Soares, responsible for the second stage of composition (1928-34). Vicente Guedes authored many of the "large texts" in the *Livro*. The stylistic and psychological unity of these large texts leads Pessoa to envision the possibility of collecting those in a second book.

Editors have tried to solve the dilemma arising from those compositional differences in four different ways: Jacinto do Prado Coelho arranges the texts according to a combination of chronology and thematic affinities, assigning the whole book to Bernardo Soares; Teresa Sobral Cunha divides the texts into two groups and assigns each of them to Vicente Guedes or to Bernardo Soares, while defining an internal textual order for each part based on thematic proximity, an editorial intervention that she emphasizes by carefully balancing spaces in between texts instead of numbering the texts as all other editors do; Richard Zenith makes Bernardo Soares's pieces the structural axis of the book and relegates all the earlier large texts by Vicente Guedes to a final section in his edition (somehow following the suggestion containing in Pessoa's organization note); finally, after determining a likely date for all undated fragments, Jerónimo Pizarro decides to follow a strictly chronological and genetic sequence, assigning all texts to Fernando Pessoa, dispensing altogether with the mediation of the heteronymic fictional authors.

---

[9] Full text available at https://ldod.uc.pt/fragments/fragment/Fr132/inter/Fr132_WIT_ED_CRIT_Z_A_4_B (BNP/E3, 2-60r; Coelho 8; Sobral Cunha 747; Zenith 539; Pizarro 459).

It is also interesting to observe that editors establish specific relations with the internal and external dimensions of the textual experience. In an interview to the author (recorded on November 2015), Teresa Sobral Cunha refers to her arrangement of texts as based on their discursive unity, thus suggesting that she sequenced them based on textual similarity in terms of topics and style.[10] Her arrangement of the texts is perhaps the one in which the affective and subjective identification of the editor with the narrative and semantic flow of the texts is stronger. The emotional and intellectual resonances of the act of reading rather than a strictly philological criterion determined how she decided to arrange the texts in each part. In the case of Jerónimo Pizarro, given his genetic-critical approach, the external documentary dimensions of the text (including types of paper, watermarks, and pens) tend to predominate. Jacinto do Prado Coelho and Richard Zenith, on the other hand, seem to have adopted a more balanced combination of reading for meaning and reading for marks when deciding how to sequence the texts.

Bibliographical coherence seems to depend simultaneously on two separate logics: an external logic of organization that sequences and articulates its elements according to the syntactic structure and the horizon of codex totalization, which creates unity through its discrete and finite character; and an internal logic of organization that selects and associates fragments because of semantic and stylistic affinities, producing bibliographical unity through the cumulative effect of discursive and narrative coherence between associated brief and lengthy pieces. The difficulty in matching the material and discursive space of writing to the material and conceptual space of the book results in a process of incompleteness and deferment, and in a variable and open conformation between writing space and book space. The editorial horizon of the book—as a final textual arrangement—remains open.

Pessoa's heteronymic split is not only the result of a retroactive effect of subjectivity produced by a given writing mode. It results also from the noncoincidence between the order of writing and the order of the book, which unfolds in an authorial self-consciousness as a product of the rules of writing and in an authorial self-consciousness as a product of the rules of the book. "Bernardo Soares" appears as a psychological entity that manifests itself in a given style and as the name of the potential author of a book, an author who is retroactively produced by the book he wants to produce, and not only by the psychography of his writing mode. The implication is that the writing rules that

---

[10] The relevant excerpt from the interview is available at: https://ldod.uc.pt/about/videos#V4.

define him as a semi-heteronymic author are also a device for the production of a bibliographical coherence through which the heteronym edits himself as an author, thus determining the texts that are part of his book in progress and, through this joint production of writing and codex, the subject of writing produces its self as the author of the book.

Exploding the Book: Editing as Process

Critical editing approaches to the *Book of Disquiet* have attempted to reconstruct the unity of authorial intention based on textual and documentary evidence. Their unstated aim is to turn the projective and conjectural unity of the edition into a continuation of the authorial project, as inferred from the "L. do D." texts and from its metatexts, i.e., Pessoa's notes and plans for the *Book of Disquiet*. Acknowledging the changing nature of authorial intentionality at different moments, and the necessarily open-endedness resulting from its unrevised and unstructured incompleteness, editions have to make their own intentionality stand in as a surrogate for an elusive final textual form. The problem of organizing the *Book* thus becomes a problem of dealing with the unruly and undisciplined material manifestations of acts of writing for a work in progress whose major feature is the multiplication of texts in various stages of completion, many of which are also relatively self-contained and finalized units.

By definition, editing the *Book of Disquiet* is this obsessive process of suturing textual pieces in ways that minimize their constitutive fragmentariness, even if many texts and documents in the corpus are bound to resist any seamless integration. Acts of editorial surgery cannot but fail to efface themselves, since text, book, and work (and, to a certain extent, some of the documents themselves) have always to be post-produced. The purpose of the meta-editing perspective in the *LdoD Archive* is to redirect our focus to the seams and sutures in order to see how each edition is sewing its own version of the book into some coherent form. An opposite heuristics to the integrative mode of print editions becomes imaginable: the text can be exploded even more radically so that all textual pieces are nothing more than a constellation of fragments. This explosion became a critical tool for the textual simulation experiment.

Literary materiality can be remade according to the modularity of digital materiality. Texts can be factorialized in their permutations. Not only loose sheets collected in envelopes or strung together in the autograph archive can be subject to further disintegration, but the posthumous print editions themselves can be torn apart and critically fragmented. Once autographs and expert editions have been exploded in this way, then the processuality through which an editorial act begins to take shape can perhaps be simulated and enacted. Each transcription and each book emerge within a series of possible instantiations of their form. Neither the edited text nor the edited book, but the process through which the act of editing performs itself as a choreography of readings and interpretations that inscribe themselves in the work's archive and in its socialized forms.

So what is a fragment in the *LdoD Archive*? A fragment is a modular textual sequence and it constitutes the basic unit of composition of the *LdoD Archive*. Most textual sequences of the *Book of Disquiet* are also independent material units, since they are written in single loose sheets (or small groups of loose sheets) without a defined relative ordering. The fragments encoded in the *LdoD Archive* correspond to the sum of all texts that were considered as belonging to or associated with the *Book of Disquiet* by the four critical editions, including those texts that are published as appendix or annex to the main text. All fragments of the *LdoD Archive* are also textual units of the *Book of Disquiet* according to at least one of the editions. As they metamorphose into digital objects, textual units meant for the *Book of Disquiet* turn into computational fragments whose modularity also reflects their new medium.

The structure of the *LdoD Archive* places all the fragments at the same relative distance from one another, that is, with the same modularity index. However, in the editions, not all textual units have the same degree of relative independence, since there are groups of texts that are closer to each other, either because they are part of a larger textual unit, or because of thematic or chronological proximity. The textual units of the editions have different indexes of modularity, as there are groups of texts which are closer to one another. This is the main difference between a text as a unit within a given edition (or in the authorial archive) and a fragment as a unit within the *LdoD Archive*.

The modular organization of the fragments (i.e., the fact that they are at the same relative distance from each other) in the *LdoD Archive* is a precondition for the comparison and virtualization of the editions to be processed in the open way envisioned by our model. This stressing of the modular fragmentariness of the *Book* in the *LdoD Archive* is a critical tool for opening up this work's potential for reading, editing, and writing to new interventions. The critical distortion introduced by our data model—which is the major support of the dynamic features of the *LdoD Archive*—gives technical expression to a digital rematerialization of documents, texts, and work beyond bibliographic models. The *Book of Disquiet* is not an entirely freely remixable assemblage of loose fragments, but the radial and heterarchical configuration of its units in the *LdoD Archive* allows us to simulate authorial projectuality and editorial projectuality as processes for imagining the work as book and the document as text. By using the modularity of the digital medium as a critical probe into the modularity of the *Book of Disquiet*, the *LdoD Archive* becomes a computer-assisted simulation of the processuality of editing.

Encoding and Visualizing Variation

As mentioned above, representation of the dynamics of variation in the *LdoD Archive* involves the consideration of two distinct levels. One is the level of micro-variations, i.e., variations that are internal to the fragments, such as authorial revisions, editorial readings of particular passages, or orthographic variants that resulted from reforms in spelling conventions.[11] The other is the level of macro-variations, i.e., variations that are external to the fragments, such as inclusion and sequencing of fragments, as well as heteronym attribution. In other words, the first type of variations results in a given textual form for each fragment or piece of writing, while the second type results in a given book structure for the entire corpus (Figure 3.4). How are these micro- and macro-variations represented in the *LdoD Archive*? How are authorial revisions and editorial variants marked and visualized in ways that enable readers to understand the writing and editorial processes at the scale of both textual form and book structure? (Portela and Rito Silva 2016b) The *Editions* interface gives readers the ability to visualize authorial and editorial variations in terms of both textual form and book structure.

Transcription of the authorial and editorial textual forms are treated as variants for encoding purposes (Figure 3.5). The <rdg>TEI element stands for reading and is used to represent both authorial and editorial micro-variations (within the TEI body) and macro-variations (within the TEI header). The editions

---

[11] A reformed orthography was introduced in Portugal in 1911, but Pessoa continued to write according to the earlier spelling conventions. In their editions of the *Livro do Desassossego*, Coelho (Pessoa 1982) and Pizarro (Pessoa 2010) follow Pessoa's orthography, while Sobral Cunha (Pessoa 2008) and Zenith (Pessoa 2012) have modernized Pessoa's spelling according to contemporary Portuguese orthography, i.e., the spelling agreement of the 1970s (the convention that has been used until 2015). In 2015 a new reformed orthography of the Portuguese language was officially adopted, which means that further spelling variations will be added to forthcoming editions of the *Livro*. In the *LdoD Archive* all spelling variations in both authorial sources and editorial transcriptions have been marked up.

118 *Literary Simulation and the Digital Humanities*

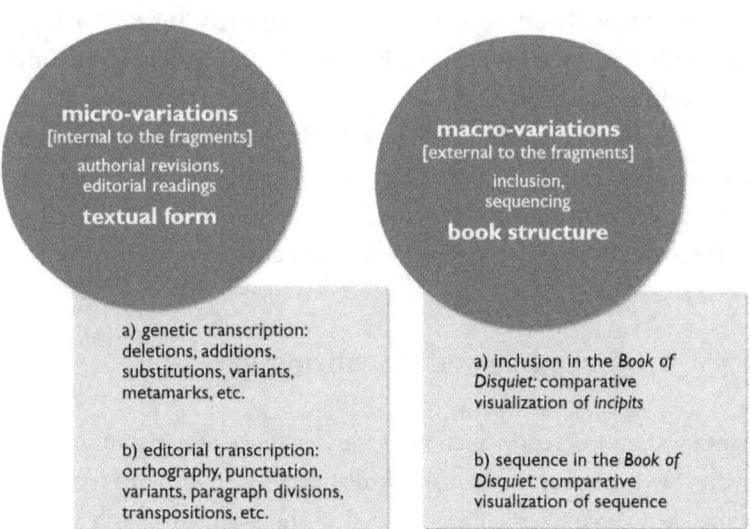

Figure 3.4 Authorial and editorial texts are encoded as a network of variations, both at the micro-scale of the scripting acts that constitute each fragment and at the macro-scale of codex sequence.

```
<p>
 <app>
  <rdg wit="#Fr279.WIT.MS.Fr279a.338 #Fr279.WIT.ED.CRIT.C1 #Fr279.WIT.ED.CRIT.Z #Fr279.WIT.ED.CRIT.SC #Fr279.WIT.ED.CRIT.P">Minha alma é uma
   <app type="orthographic">
    <rdg wit="#Fr279.WIT.MS.Fr279a.338 #Fr279.WIT.ED.CRIT.P #Fr279.WIT.ED.CRIT.C1">orchestra</rdg>
    <rdg wit="#Fr279.WIT.ED.CRIT.SC #Fr279.WIT.ED.CRIT.Z">orquestra</rdg>
   </app> <lb ed="#Fr279.WIT.MS.Fr279a.338"/>
   <app type="orthographic">
    <rdg wit="#Fr279.WIT.MS.Fr279a.338 #Fr279.WIT.ED.CRIT.P #Fr279.WIT.ED.CRIT.C1">occulta;</rdg>
    <rdg wit="#Fr279.WIT.ED.CRIT.SC #Fr279.WIT.ED.CRIT.Z">oculta;</rdg>
   </app> não sei que instrumentos <lb ed="#Fr279.WIT.MS.Fr279a.338"/>
   <app type="substantive">
    <rdg wit="#Fr279.WIT.MS.Fr279a.338 #Fr279.WIT.ED.CRIT.C1">tange e range,</rdg>
    <rdg wit="#Fr279.WIT.ED.CRIT.Z #Fr279.WIT.ED.CRIT.P #Fr279.WIT.ED.CRIT.SC">tangem e rangem,</rdg>
   </app> cordas e harpas, <lb ed="#Fr279.WIT.MS.Fr279a.338"/>
   timbales e tambores, dentro <lb ed="#Fr279.WIT.MS.Fr279a.338"/>
   de mim. Só me conheço <lb ed="#Fr279.WIT.MS.Fr279a.338"/>como
  <app>
   <rdg wit="#Fr279.WIT.MS.Fr279a.338"><del rend="overstrike">mu mu</del></rdg>
  </app>
  <app>
   <rdg wit="#Fr279.WIT.MS.Fr279a.338 #Fr279.WIT.ED.CRIT.C1 #Fr279.WIT.ED.CRIT.P">symphonia.</rdg>
   <rdg wit="#Fr279.WIT.ED.CRIT.Z #Fr279.WIT.ED.CRIT.SC">sinfonia.</rdg>
  </app>
  <app>
   <rdg wit="#Fr279.WIT.MS.Fr279a.338 #Fr279.WIT.ED.CRIT.Z #Fr279.WIT.ED.CRIT.SC">
    <space dim="vertical" quantity="1" unit="minims"/>
   </rdg>
   <rdg wit="#Fr279.WIT.MS.Fr279a.338"><space dim="horizontal" quantity="6" unit="minims"/>————</rdg>
   <rdg wit="#Fr279.WIT.ED.CRIT.P"><seg rendition="#center">————</seg><lb/></rdg>
```

Figure 3.5 Excerpt from the XML-TEI encoding of the fragment "Minha alma é uma orchestra occulta" (BNP/E3, 4-68r).

and authorial sources are referred through the "wit" attribute. Additionally, a structured hierarchical nomenclature is used to identify witnesses, for instance, the value "#Fr279.WIT.MS.Fr279a.338" denotes an authorial source (MS) witness (WIT) identified by "Fr279a.338" of fragment "279" (Fr279), where 279 is an arbitrary number that identifies a particular XML file within the *LdoD Archive* system. This same identifier is used for referring to the textual transcriptions in the four expert editions ("#Fr279.WIT.ED.CRIT.C," "#Fr279.WIT.ED.CRIT.Z," "#Fr279.WIT.ED.CRIT.SC," "#Fr279.WIT.ED.CRIT.P"). Thus, in this instance, the same abstract entity (Fr279) can have five textual expressions, one of which is a topographic transcription of the autograph witness and the other four are transcriptions of the editorial transcriptions of the autograph witness.[12] Transcription of authorial source and transcription of transcription of authorial source (editorial transcription) become part of a constellation of variations.

We may say that the representation of the genetic dimension takes place in the context of the work's socialized dimension, while the work's several editorial forms can be perceived in the context of its genetic history. Revision processes in the autograph materials as well as variants and variations in editorial readings are encoded in the same XML file in a way that allows for both a single view of each autograph or editorial witness and comparative views of multiple witnesses (Figure 3.4). At the level of the header each TEI file contains the metatextual information required for comparing bibliographical features, such as "L. do D." markers in Pessoa's papers, numerical sequence of fragments in each edition, date of composition, or other metatextual attributes.

In the *LdoD Archive*, visualization of variations takes place at the general level of the graphical user interface and within textual transcriptions. The user is allowed to move within each (authorial or editorial) textual witness and across different textual witnesses. This navigational strategy allows readers to see revision sites within authorial witnesses, but also to generate comparisons between any 2, 3, 4, 5, 6, or 7 witnesses, that is, up to three authorial witnesses and up to four editorial witnesses.[13] Authorial witnesses can be compared against each other but also against their editorial versions, and vice

---

[12] For a detailed discussion of the encoding template, see Rito Silva and Portela 2015. This article explains how the software architecture supports the standard XML-TEI encoding with the added function of dynamically extending the versions of the *Book of Disquiet* on top of a TEI representation: "To do this we had to we had to implement TEI import and export functionalities to allow the manipulation of the TEI-encoded information in an object-oriented database. Additionally, the export functionality allows backup in a safe repository in a human-readable format. On the other hand, there is information in the object-oriented database that is specific to a Web 2.0 environment, like the information required to support access control policies, and which is not explicitly encoded using TEI because it depends on the dynamic aspects of the Web 2.0 tools" (§10).

[13] For most fragments there is only one extant witness for the autograph text, either a manuscript or a typescript. However, there are twenty-two instances in which there are two or three autograph versions. See, for example, the following texts with multiple authorial witnesses: "Amo, pelas tardes demoradas de verão" (one typescript, one printed version); "Ás vezes, em sonhos distrahidos" (two typescript versions); "Na perfeição nitida do dia" (two typescript versions, one printed version); and "Durei horas incognitas" (one manuscript, one typescript, one printed version).

versa: editorial witnesses can be compared against each other but also against their source documents. Our topographic transcription represents four types of spatial marks in the autographs: line breaks (<lb>element), spacing between paragraphs (<space>element), dividing rulers (<space dim> element), page breaks (<pb>element), and revision sites (@place attribute on). The main goal of the topographic transcription is to facilitate the side-by-side reading of the facsimile and its transcription.

This ability of examining the micro-variations in the textual form of each fragment across the database of witnesses is further contextualized, at the level of macro-variations, by the possibility of navigating within the bibliographical sequence offered by each scholarly edition. Buttons for showing revision sites (deletions, additions, and substitutions) and buttons for comparing transcriptions against the digital facsimiles of authorial witnesses allow users to move across all layers of variation from within a single screen. The right-hand menu provides immediate visualization of the relative position of each fragment within any given expert edition of the *Book*, while the bottom of the page note provides other metatextual information concerning heteronym attribution or "L. do D." mark, for instance. One-to-one or one-to-many comparisons between the archive's transcription and the four editions are also supported. This principle also applies to each and all expert editions.

The *LdoD Archive* combines a genetic edition with a social text edition. Readers will engage with the genetic edition when they see Pessoa's acts of revision in each fragment as well as his various partial plans for the *Book of Disquiet*. Annotations in specific virtual editions also mark intertextual relations of fragments to Pessoa's readings, including references to passages, authors, and marginalia in his own personal library. Readers engage with the social text edition in two ways: first, by seeing actual historical instances of the *Book of Disquiet* as it has been edited in the four versions included in the archive, and in our own XML-encoded topographic transcription of the autographs; and second, by creating new virtual instances of the *Book of Disquiet* understood as a particular selection and organization of fragments. Tools for textual analysis, collation, and annotation intend to explore the dynamics of the acts of editing in the production and reproduction of the *Book of Disquiet*.

Micro-variations across textual transcriptions and macro-variations across bibliographical structures in the work's genetic and editorial archive are displayed through a network of shifting perspectives. This network of shifting perspectives allow users of the archive to see Pessoa's writing process and his changing and variable plans for the *Livro*. At the same time, readers become aware of the conjectural nature of the editorial solutions of the expert critical editions for producing a structured textual and bibliographical form out of a half-finished and fragmentary work. Further micro- and macro-variations will result from the archive's socialization of editorial and authorial acts of production at the virtual level, opening up the work's existing archive to future appropriations and transformations (Portela and Rito Silva 2016a).

Using the editions comparison interface screen, and *just by clicking once*, the multiple-entry navigation structure enables three navigation paths: users can navigate sequentially within each edition, starting from any point of entry; users can navigate sequentially within each edition, by going back to the ordered list of texts of each edition; and users can navigate across the editions and across the authorial archive by going to another transcription of the same text in another edition or to the topographic transcription and digital facsimile of the autographs. The modeling of all authorial witnesses and editorial transcriptions at the same hierarchical level has made it possible to completely decenter all textual versions for purposes of navigation, comparison, analysis, reading, editing, and writing. Any text can become the center of this exploratory navigation: the hierarchical representation of the structure of each version of the *Book of Disquiet* has been critically dissolved in ways that maximize the associative possibilities of algorithmic processing of textual representation.

From Meta-Edition to Virtual Edition

The processes of transcribing documents and organizing texts to produce a literary and bibliographic form become visible both in the historicity of the modeled editions and, equally important, in the interpretative action explicitly embodied in the ways interactors are asked to perform the actions they have been observing and analyzing. Textual form and bibliographic structure are shown as actual properties of the ways in which author and expert editors collaborated, but also as emergent properties of each reader's interpretative traversal and transformation of the *Book of Disquiet*. Given the fact that, as virtual editors, readers can have a certain level of editorial responsibility through textual selections, arrangements, and annotations, their interventions become part of the textual environment. The virtual editing interface (Figure 3.6) opens up the editorial role to further bibliographic transformations.

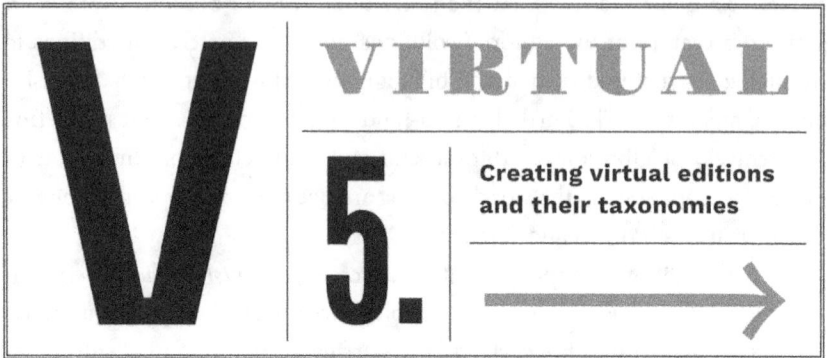

Figure 3.6 Graphic representation of the virtual editing interface. This interface has been designed to take readers directly to virtual editing tools.

Besides using XML-TEI encoding and programming to recreate the history of the editorial dynamics, the *LdoD Archive* also explores the simulative potential of the digital medium as a space for virtualizing the *Book of Disquiet* in ways that enable users to experiment with the processes of editing. Expert and non-expert collaborate by making and annotating their own editions. Editorial interventions can take two forms: selecting and ordering fragments as part of a user-defined virtual edition; and annotating selected fragments through tags and glosses, including the development of taxonomies. This interactive feature of the archive is further enhanced by search and navigation functions that allow a strong integration between the closed set of scholarly materials and the open set of virtual editing additions.

Users of the archive are able to register in the system and collaborate in the creation of virtual editions. This collaboration can take place informally but also in institutional contexts, particularly within schools and universities. We have set up several virtual communities of students and teachers who work with the *Book of Disquiet* at different locations, with the aim of supporting their use of the dynamic features of the *LdoD Archive*. Usability tests were made to assist us in graphical interface design, and also for developing guidelines and tutorials that explain the archive's collaborative functions. We have also analyzed actual pedagogic, scholarly, and creative uses of the *LdoD Archive* (Portela and Magalhães 2020; Portela 2022).

Virtual editing results in the creation of a persistent virtual edition (Figure 3.7). A group of users can create and work together on a virtual edition; they are the virtual edition members. Virtual editions can be either private

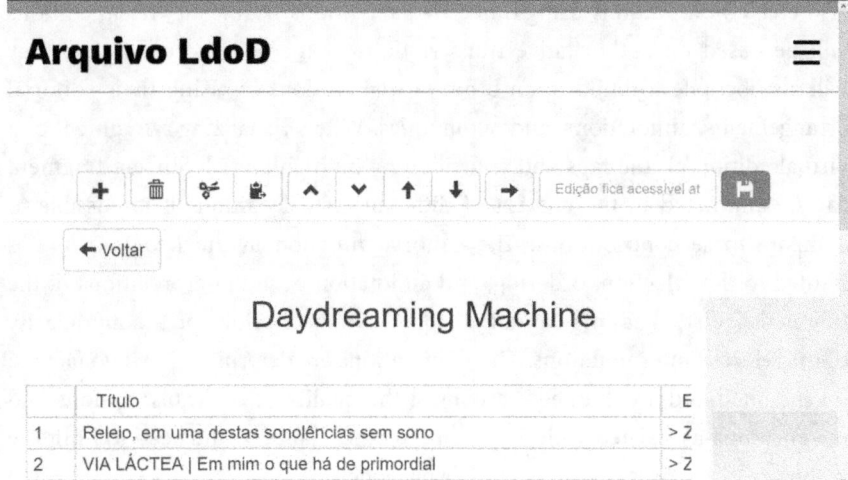

Figure 3.7 Virtual editing interface: editing tools. The top row contains tools for searching, selecting, adding, deleting, cutting, pasting, saving, and moving texts.

or public. Private virtual editions can only be visualized by their members. A virtual edition contains a set of fragments selected and ordered by its members. Virtual edition fragments use the archive's topographic transcription and/or the expert's editorial transcription and they can be enriched by annotations made by virtual edition members. An annotation can contain a comment and one or more tags, and it is associated to a part of the fragment transcription, the quote, or to the entire text. The system also allows a virtual edition fragment to use annotations from another virtual edition fragment. The use of annotations and tags preserves the authorship of the original contributions. Therefore, when a virtual edition is built on top of another virtual edition, the source tags and annotations are inherited but cannot be changed in the context of the new virtual edition. This means that an inherited tag can be used in the new virtual edition to categorize a fragment or a part of a fragment, but if it is changed or deleted in the source edition the change is reflected in the new virtual edition by, respectively, changing it or deleting all its uses. Obviously, inherited tags and annotations cannot be changed or deleted in the context of the new virtual edition, though it is possible to create new tags and annotations.

The virtual editing process has been designed as an open and recursive process of selection, organization, and annotation of the database elements. Virtual editors can use as their working materials both the expert editions and the topographic transcriptions of autograph documents, but they can also create new editions using other virtual editions. While all virtual editions will be based on authoritative transcriptions of the source documents, they will also be able to build upon other virtual editions by using their editorial arrangements, annotations, and taxonomies. When visualizing a fragment of a virtual edition all the tags and contributors are highlighted. Since a fragment can be annotated in the context of different virtual editions it is possible to compare these contributions. The editorial function in the *LdoD Archive* is limited to the selection, ordering, and annotation of the interpretations of the fragments. Virtual editors cannot change the transcriptions or the modularity of the selected interpretations. These limitations are determined by two factors: on the one hand, by the need to control the quality of the transcriptions and the encoding associated with them; on the other hand, by the need to limit the complexity of processing the materials produced by users.[14]

Virtual editions can be assembled manually by searching and adding selected fragments to a given edition, but they can also be assisted by automated processes, such as topic modeling. "Mallet," for instance, is a virtual edition based on the corpus of the Jerónimo Pizarro edition, whose taxonomy has been algorithmically generated.[15] The topic generation software Mallet (MAchine Learning for LanguagE Toolkit) was used for generating 30 categories after performing 1500 iterations on the corpus. Each category was named with the three most relevant words of the generated topic, resulting in topics such as "nevoa leve frio" ["mist light cold"], "noite dia luz" ["night day light"], "sonho cousas sonhos" ["dream things dreams"] or "vida ser alma" ["life being soul"].

Fragments were associating to their category if the percentage was higher than 11 percent. Given that Pizarro's edition has sequenced the texts according to their dates of composition, the way those categories are attached to particular texts provides a glimpse into the persistence or emergence of topics over time. They could become the basis of another virtual edition in which the topic modeling of the fragments might be used for defining theme-based clusters or sequences. They could also be used as the source for defining a more complex

---

[14] The inclusion of a transcription and encoding module, with its own validation system—which would be particularly useful in the context of specialized learning of digital critical editing—may be considered in the future, depending on the available resources. One feature that we have considered for this module is to provide a collection of magnified facsimiles of particularly difficult passages and invite virtual editors (1) to select between divergent readings, and (2) to offer their own conjectures for those passages.

[15] https://ldod.uc.pt/edition/acronym/LdoD-Mallet.

and refined taxonomy. Both operations—sequencing texts or re-categorizing texts based on automated analyses—are examples of the range of interactions provided by the platform: from the machine-assisted human edition to the human-assisted machine edition.

An example of a fully automated edition is the "Twitter Citations" virtual edition.[16] This edition captures the online sharing of quotes from the *Book of Disquiet* in the Twitter social network (Oliveira 2018; Oliveira et al. 2019). It is based on the corpus of the Richard Zenith edition, and contains the fragments cited on Twitter in the last thirty days, ordered in descending order of number of citations. This edition, which generally hosts between fifty and sixty texts, is updated daily to reflect the tweets and retweets from the *Book of Disquiet*. It brings together the machine reading and machine editing tools of the platform, and it illustrates the programmed and networked nature of the *LdoD Archive* as a space that is sensitive to its online textual environment. This social media-aware virtual edition is another expression of the simulation rationale of the *LdoD Archive* as an open and evolving textual environment that is responsive to actual reading, editing, and writing interactions of its users. By opening itself up to the ecology of social media networks, this virtual edition provides a snapshot of reading as a social practice.

A different example is provided by the "Jacinto do Prado Coelho—Annotated Edition."[17] The production of this edition was used as our initial test of the virtual editing tools of the platform, including both the strictly textual—selecting, adding, deleting, rearranging, tagging, glossing—as well as the collaborative and administrative tools (Figure 3.8). This virtual edition is based on the edition organized by Jacinto do Prado Coelho. It is a virtual edition with the same selection and ordering of texts as the printed edition of 1982, to which a taxonomy was added based on the two indexes of the original print edition: "Ideographic Index" (volume II: 275–7) and "Index of Cited Authors" (volume II: 279–80). This virtual edition was developed by nine virtual editors, under the coordination of Rita Catania Marrone, in May 2017. The taxonomic associations resulting from the original indexing provide us with a global visualization of the thematic rationale of that first critical edition, which grouped most of the texts according to fifty-six constellations of topics and subtopics.

---

[16] https://ldod.uc.pt/edition/acronym/LdoD-Twitter.
[17] https://ldod.uc.pt/edition/acronym/LdoD-JPC-anot.

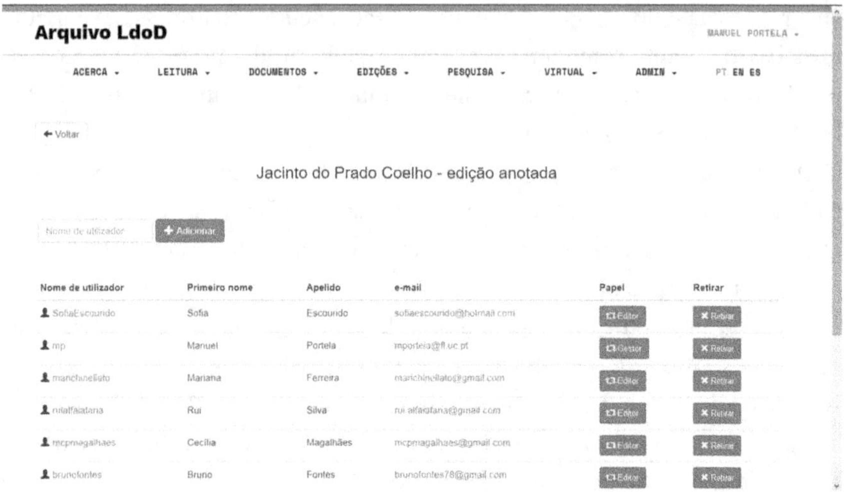

Figure 3.8 Virtual editing interface: administrative tools. Managing functionalities provided include adding editors to a virtual edition and granting them editorial or administrative permissions.

Additional examples include theme-based anthologies of selected texts, such as the "Daydreaming Machine" virtual edition,[18] which is presented as follows:

> This edition contains selected texts from the *Book of Disquiet*. All texts include references to different types of media technologies (typewriter, printing, lithography, gramophone, photography, film, radio) either in relation to the practice of writing or in relation to sensation and perception. "Those who can write are those who know how to see their dreams with sharp clarity (and do so) and to see life as they see dreams, to see life immaterially, taking pictures of it with reverie's camera, which is insensible to the rays of what's heavy, useful and circumscribed, such things yielding nothing but a black blur on the photographic plate of the soul" (BNP/E3, 7-35-36). "I'm an ultrasensitive photographic plate. All details are engraved in me out of all proportion to any possible whole. The plate fills up with nothing but me. The outer world that I see is pure sensation. I never forget that I feel" (BNP/E3, 9-49). "And it is then, in the middle of life's bustle, that my dream becomes a marvellous film" (BNP/E3, 2-79r). "On rainy days his talking never became mournful, and he would cry out—sure of his shelter—a constant sentiment that hovered in the sadness like a phonograph before its time" (BNP/E3, 2-89 3-2).
>
> (Synopsis of the virtual edition "Daydreaming Machine")

[18] https://ldod.uc.pt/edition/acronym/LdoD-Medial.

One of the most interesting features of the virtual edition layer is the possibility of tagging the selected texts. Tags can be linked to the entire text or to specific passages within the text. The outcome of tagging, in the context of the *LdoD Archive*, is the creation of a taxonomy. Taxonomies can result from a controlled vocabulary predefined by a virtual edition editor and then applied by his/her virtual coeditors to their textual selections. Vocabularies can also be entirely open and evolve according to folksonomic processes. Once texts in a given edition have been categorized—for instance, according to topics and subtopics, material features of the autograph, date of composition, and many other criteria—the resulting taxonomies offer additional forms of clustering and navigating the annotated texts. Each virtual edition is thus defined by a specific selection and taxonomic categorization. Taxonomies have been turned into a multifaceted editorial filter, providing interactors with a tool for seeing the emergence of semantic relations that justify certain editorial decisions. The action of trying to encapsulate the text in a limited number of keywords demonstrates the role of categorization in general processes of interpretation. Such annotations are also meant to make interactors aware of the ways in which computational text processing and retrieval are deeply dependent on the categories encoded in their operations.

The latest addition to the virtual editing functionalities is the gamification and crowdsourcing of the creation of taxonomies, by means of the "LdoD Classification Game" (Marques 2018).[19] The goal of the game is to classify texts from specific virtual editions of the *Book of Disquiet*, and encourage collaboration in the process of finding adequate categories. The analysis of the set of tags created by players in the game shows two strategies of semantic text analysis: on the one hand, the identification of keywords (or key phrases) in the text itself, turning the quotation of a word or phrase from the text into its descriptor; on the other, the abstraction of a general topic understood as a dominant semantic thread but expressed in words other than those that appear in the text. Most voted tags tend towards an abstract thematization of the text that loses reference to the concrete experiential context of the narrator's reflection. This feature is one of the difficulties that the texts of the *Book of Disquiet* pose to any descriptor of its topics, as most texts always oscillate between a metaphysical and abstract reflection of the narrator and a concrete observation anchored on his daily life and on ongoing perception of the passage of time.

[19] https://ldod.uc.pt/classificationGames.

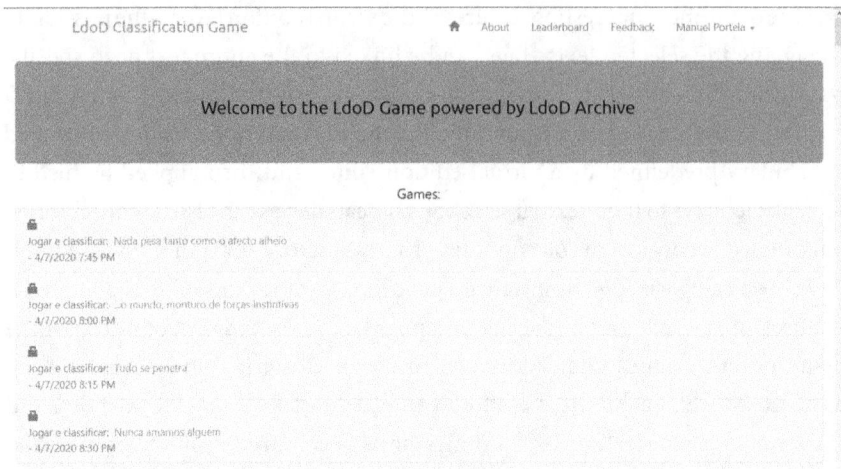

Figure 3.9 "LdoD Classification Game": play and classify.

Figure 3.9 shows the "LdoD Classification Game" interface. Each multiplayer online game consists of tagging one text from the *Book of Disquiet*. In successive rounds, players are asked (round 1) to associate a category with the first paragraph of the text; (round 2) once a tag has been associated and the time is up, all players are able to see the set of categories created by all the participants and they have to vote on the category they consider most adequate for that paragraph; (round 3) after repeating rounds 1 and 2 for all paragraphs of the chosen text, all players have access to the entire text and to the most voted categories, at which point they have to vote on the category they consider most adequate for the entire text. The author of the most voted category receives the most points. After every game participants will have their points added to the general scoreboard.

A future strategy to make the "play and classify" principle of this game more adequate may consist of asking each player to enter two tags for each paragraph—one with an abstract reference to the narrator's feelings, emotions, or thoughts and another with a concrete reference to the observations, situations, and spaces described. A game that could induce this double attention to the text would also help to avoid assigning overly generic tags, which is one of the dominant trends in the ways topics and themes are indexed. Thus, instead of using only meta-categories such as "sadness," "joy," "boredom," or "dream," readers would be moved to qualify the particular nature of "sadness," "joy," "boredom," or "dream" by a concrete reference in each text. In this case the game would also contribute to a pedagogy of reading, in the sense that readers would be asked to frame the topic as formulated by the narrator and not just as a generic and abstract concept independent of that particular text. Instead of voting for only one category, each player would have to vote for two—let's say, one in the "narrator's thoughts" group, another in the "narrator's observations" group.

The taxonomy of each text would thus have categories of both types: some that point to the inner world of the narrator and others that point to his external observations. This would be more accurate in relation to the nature of this particular text and also to the general practices of abstracting textual experience through limited semantic categories. The inclusion of indexing processes in the virtual editing rationale provides virtual editors with a critical lens on processes of clustering texts through these mediating tools. Interactors are able to explicitly engage with processes of textual classification used for structuring the bibliographic sequences. Despite their role in guiding editorial arrangements of textual sequences, such classification processes are rarely detailed. Furthermore, the ability to manipulate texts through their associated taxonomies makes visible the classificatory nature of text-processing operations, which contributes to a critical understanding of the metadata layers that constrain our interaction with digital objects.

The participatory affordance of the digital medium is expressed in two major ways: an environment for collaboration and social interaction, on the one hand, and the possibility of marking material changes at the level of code, on the other. Material changes can be marked up in the XML encoding, but also as new data and metadata generated by the users' interaction with the archive, which are stored in the database. These features of networked computational media have been used to redesign the digital archive as a dynamic environment for editorial experimentation. A scholarly remediation of the *Book of Disquiet* according to tested principles of electronic philology becomes part of a larger interactive environment where editing practices are playfully socialized within the digital medium itself. Aggregation of genetic and editorial witnesses according to criteria defined by readers occurs within a virtual space that allows users to make their own selections and annotations. Representation of textual form and textual transmission is complemented by simulatory experiments with editing processes and bibliographic structures.

4

Writing as Simulation

This chapter interrogates the representation and simulation of acts of writing in the *LdoD Archive*. What answer can we give to the question *what is an act of writing* when this question is asked through the affordances of this machine? How can we model a writing space for experimenting with the processuality of writing? The act of writing will be described from three related perspectives: as thematized in several passages from the *Book of Disquiet* itself; in its material manifestations in Pessoa's manuscripts and typescripts; and as an open process of exploration of our extended consciousness as it becomes externalized in the recursive process of thinking and writing. Textual witnesses are analyzed as records of the temporal and kinetic dynamics of writing and rewriting, but also as textual units of a work in progress. Self-consciousness of writing emerges both in autograph textual marks, and in the concept of fragment as a piece of text meant for an imaginary bibliographic whole. Finally, the writing process itself is engaged in its processuality through a range of experimental acts of writing, from human-authored variations to computer-assisted permutations (Figure 4.1).

Writing Acts in the *Book of Disquiet*

One of the recurring topics in the *Book of Disquiet* concerns the relationship between writing and feeling and, in particular, the implication of writing in the consciousness of the sentient self. The description of the act of writing as an expression of the process of consciousness recurs in the *Book*, and is thematized by both narrators—Vicente Guedes and Bernardo Soares. The act of *feeling oneself feeling*, which mirrors the infinite regression of a self who is absorbed in his/her own sensations, turns into the act of *feeling oneself writing*. In the copy of a letter sent to Paris addressed to Mário de Sá-Carneiro, dated March 14, 1916,

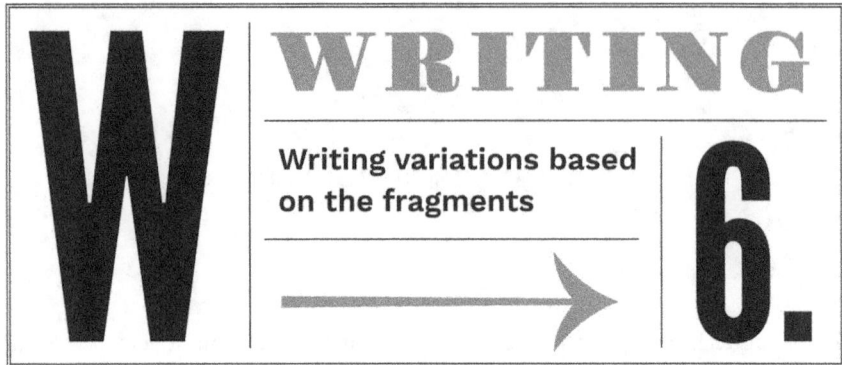

Figure 4.1 Graphic representation of the virtual writing interface. This interface has been designed to take readers directly to virtual writing tools.

we find references describing this internal and external processuality of the acts of writing (Figures 4.2, 4.3, and 4.4). Three layers seem to be involved in this cognitive, symbolic, and material processuality of writing as a defining aspect of the *Book of Disquiet*. In a first layer, through powerful evocative images, we encounter a representation of the conscious self in which the mind is aware of its own emotions and feelings:

> In the garden I glimpse through the shuttered windows of my kidnapping, they threw all the swings at the branches from which they hang; they are rolled up too high; and so even the idea of my escape cannot have, in my imagination, swings to forget the hour.
>
> (BNP/E3, 114³-35, *LdoD Archive*; my translation[1])

In a second layer, the moment of writing is presentified as the textual experience of the impossibility of intersecting the enunciating self and the enunciated self, that is, of the impossibility of coincidence between *being myself* and *writing myself*. The memory of past feeling filters the present feeling and that particular form of past-present imagination, superimposed on the ongoing consciousness of the body, coincides with the moment in which the self writes itself:

> On days of the soul like today I really feel, in all my consciousness of my body, that I am the sad child whom Life has beaten. They put me in a corner where one can hear play. I feel in my hands the broken toy they gave me as an irony of tin. Today, on the fourteenth of March, at ten past nine in the evening, my life tastes at knowing this.
>
> (BNP/E3, 114³-35, *LdoD Archive*; my translation)

---

[1] Full text available at https://ldod.uc.pt/fragments/fragment/Fr614/inter/Fr614_WIT_ED_CRIT_C (BNP/E3, 114(3)-35; Coelho—prefatory material; Sobral Cunha 170; Pizarro 650).

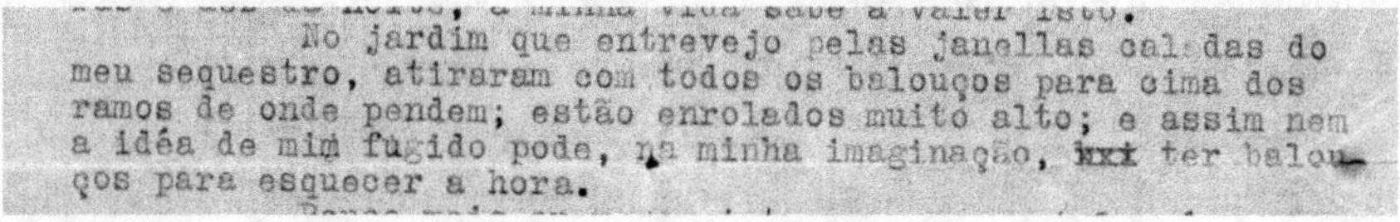

Writing as Simulation 133

> No jardim que entrevejo pelas janellas cal das do
> meu sequestro, atiraram com todos os baloiços para cima dos
> ramos de onde pendem; estão enrolados muito alto; e assim nem
> a idéa de mim fugido pode, na minha imaginação, uxi ter balou-
> ços para esquecer a hora.

Figure 4.2 Facsimile BNP/E3, 114³-35 (detail), *LdoD Archive*. © National Library of Portugal. Reproduced with permission.

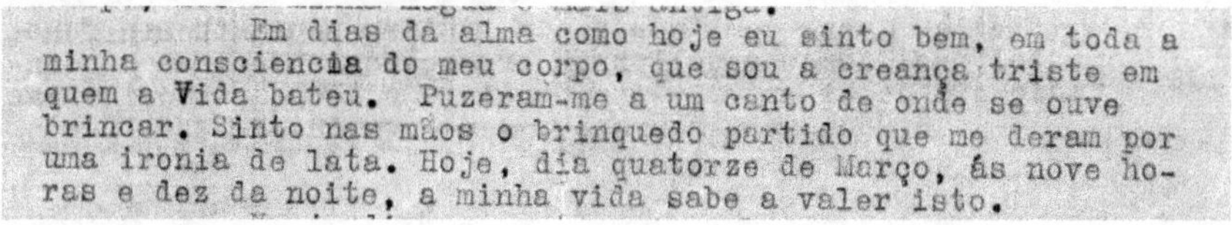

> Em dias da alma como hoje eu sinto bem, em toda a
> minha consciencia do meu corpo, que sou a creança triste em
> quem a Vida bateu. Puzeram-me a um canto de onde se ouve
> brincar. Sinto nas mãos o brinquedo partido que me deram por
> uma ironia de lata. Hoje, dia quatorze de Março, ás nove ho-
> ras e dez da noite, a minha vida sabe a valer isto.

Figure 4.3 Facsimile BNP/E3, 114³-35 (detail), *LdoD Archive*. © National Library of Portugal. Reproduced with permission.

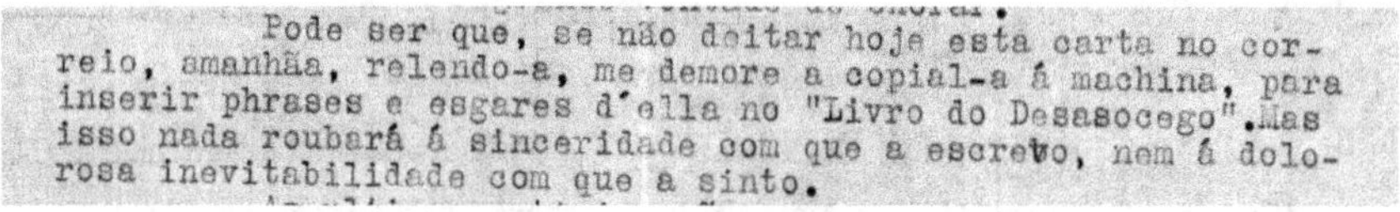

> Pode ser que, se não deitar hoje esta carta no cor-
> reio, amanhãa, relendo-a, me demore a copial-a á machina, para
> inserir phrases e esgares d'ella no "Livro do Desasocego". Mas
> isso nada roubará á sinceridade com que a escrevo, nem á dolo-
> rosa inevitabilidade com que a sinto.

Figure 4.4 Facsimile BNP/E3, 114³-35 (detail), *LdoD Archive*. © National Library of Portugal. Reproduced with permission.

Finally, in a third layer, the integrated consciousness of those two processes—that is, of self-awareness and of the consciousness of writing as part of self-awareness—becomes evident to the writer as a significant content of the *Book of Disquiet*:

> It may happen that if I do not put this letter in the mail today, on rereading it tomorrow, I will take the time to typewrite it, in order to insert phrases and twists from it in the *Book of Disquiet*. But this will steal nothing from the sincerity with which I write it, nor from the painful inevitability with which I feel it.
> (BNP/E3, 114³-35, *LdoD Archive*; my translation)

A phrase such as "on rereading it tomorrow, I will take the time to typewrite it, in order to insert phrases and twists from it in the *Book of Disquiet*" indicates that Pessoa worked with a specific concept of the *Book of Disquiet* in mind—in which certain twists of phrase, sentences, and paragraphs from that letter would fit. Additionally, it also allows us to characterize the physical and technical labor of writing. Writing by hand, rereading, and copying at the typewriter are part of the material and instrumental morphology of the modes of writing production, as witnessed by Pessoa's own autograph materials. On the other hand, the implication of feeling and writing—"with what I write it"/"with which I feel it"—suggests the anchoring of the meaning of writing in the feedback system between writing and emotion. The "phrases and twists" to be inserted in the *Book of Disquiet* would be sincere expressions of felt emotions and not mere retroactive effects of emotions post-produced by writing, although copying them using the typewriter also implies the critical distance created by the recognition of a writing effect. Feeling is an oscillating loop between pre-written and post-written.

The *Book of Disquiet* can also be described as a book of the consciousness of writing, that is, a book that peers into the cognitive, perceptual, and verbal processes that allow the self to feel and think itself through writing. If we admit, with António Damásio (2010), that autobiographical consciousness is a complex emergent process that requires the levels of visceral proto-consciousness, which maintains the homeostasis of the organism, and of core consciousness, which maps the modifications of the organism in its interaction with objects, we could describe the *Book of Disquiet* as a particular phenomenology of the emergence of that level of complexity that we call autobiographical consciousness—not only a self that has a memory and a wide feeling of itself, but a self that emerges in and through the process of writing. Writing is an instantiation of consciousness as an emergent property of neural networks.

The coming of the self to the mind—that is, the neurological possibility of consciousness—is rehearsed and replicated thorough the act of writing. Instead of electromagnetic imaging techniques that trace oxygen flows in certain brain areas, the observability of the production of consciousness is guaranteed by writing as an expanded cognitive system that externalizes in marks on paper a feeling and thinking self. This reflexive structure would be the linguistic expression of a neurological and psychic process, and the act of writing an intensifier of language as a phenomenon of consciousness. The retroaction that closes the neurological circuit and makes consciousness possible, and therefore also the consciousness of consciousness, appears mediated and amplified by the process of autographic inscription and by the system of enunciation that, through this autographic process, is constitutive of subjectivity.

The effect of consciousness—the effect through which consciousness emerges as consciousness of itself—takes the form of biographicality, that is, of the life of a self that becomes self through the act of writing itself and of whom writing is both a signal (an index) and a sign. Writing the act of writing would therefore be one way of showing the emergent nature of the processes of consciousness and their connection to the unique perception of the individual self that these processes instantiate. The memory that sustains the sense of self, and which is available through those recollections of childhood, is linked to ongoing conscious processes and to the emergent cognition made possible by very act of writing. This act is based on the memory of lived experience, and on the invention of the life of the self as a writing self, sometimes taking the form of an attempt to synchronize perceiving self and writing self, while placing both selves in the continuous present of being in the world (Figure 4.5).

> I don't know what subtle effect of light, or vague noise, or memory of a fragrance or melody, intoned by some inscrutable external influence, prompted these divagations when I was walking down the street and which now, seated in a café, I leisurely and distractedly record. I don't know where I was going with my thoughts, nor where I would wish to go. Today there's a light, warm and humid fog, sad with no threats, monotonous for no reason. I'm grieved by a

```
Não sei que effeito subtil da luz, ou ruido vago,
ou memoria de perfume ou musica, tangida por não sei
que influencia externa, me trouxe de repente, em pleno
ir pela rua, estas divagações que registro sem pressa,
ao sentar-me, no café, distrahidamente. Não sei onde ia
conduzir os pensamentos, ou onde prefeririaa conduzil-
os. O dia é de um leve nevoeiro humido e quente, triste
sem ameaças, monotono sem razão. Doe-me qualquer senti-
mento que desconheço; falta-me qualquer argumento não
sei sobre quê; não tenho vontade nos nervos. Estou tris-
te abaixo da consciencia. E escrevo estas linhas, real-
mente mal-notadas, não para dizer isto, nem para dizer
qualquer coisa, mas para dar uma occupação á minha des-
attenção. Vou enchendo lentamente, a traços mol-
les de lapis rombo, que não tenho sentimentalidade para
aparar, o papel branco de embrulho de sandwiches, que
me forneceram no café, porque eu não precisava de me-
lhor e qualquer servia, desde que fôsse branco. E dou-
me por satisfeito. A tarde cahe monotona e sem chuva,
num tom de luz desalentado e incerto. E deixo de escre-
ver porque deixo de escrever.
               Reclino-me.
```

Figure 4.5 Facsimile BNP/E3, 1-57r (detail), *LdoD Archive*. © National Library of Portugal. Reproduced with permission.

feeling that I can't place; I'm lacking an argument apropos I don't know what; I have no willpower in my nerves. Beneath my consciousness I'm sad. And I write these carelessly written lines not to say this and not to say anything, but to give my distraction something to do. I slowly cover, with the soft strokes of a dull pencil (I'm not sentimental enough to sharpen it), the white sandwich paper that they gave me in this café, for it suits me just fine, as would any other paper, as long as it was white. And I feel satisfied. I lean back. The afternoon comes to a monotonous and rainless close, in an uncertain and despondent tone of light. And I stop writing because I stop writing.

(Text 66[2])

In this paragraph, participant-observation about the act of writing invokes the randomness of the chain of sensations and perceptions that triggered the action of writing as an effect of the sensuous reverberation of the immediate world on consciousness. At the same time, the notation of the material and embodied task of writing describes, almost ethnographically, the scene of writing—"And I write these carelessly written lines not to say this and not to say anything, but to give my distraction something to do. I slowly cover, with the soft strokes of a dull pencil (I'm not sentimental enough to sharpen it), the white sandwich paper that they gave me in this café." It is true that the text no longer reaches us in "the white sandwich paper," but in the typewritten sheet of paper to which the initial text has been copied. Even if this reference could be an entirely fictional account not indexically related to this particular act of writing while siting in the café, there is an attempt to notate the process through which a vivid sense of one's perceptions and sensations produce the desire of writing the perceiving and feeling self. The presentness of the whole process is stressed by bringing the moment of writing into the content of writing, not without a sense of self-irony—"with the soft strokes of a dull pencil (I'm not sentimental enough to sharpen it)."

The passage from an initial handwritten autograph (described as taking place in the café under the scribbling automatism of a given moment) to the revised typescript shows us the technological nature of the mode of production of writing, which allows the acts of inscription and reinscription to explore the creative recursivity of language, making it possible to increase the complexity of the thinkable and the sayable. The particular form of

---

[2] Full text available at https://ldod.uc.pt/fragments/fragment/Fr050/inter/Fr050_WIT_ED_CRIT_Z (BNP/E3, 1-57r; Coelho 39; Sobral Cunha 391; Zenith 66; Pizarro 280).

inscriptions, the intimate disposition and rhythm of the body, the instrument and writing medium, the physical and social place where it takes place, are given very concrete descriptors. Finally, the repeated oscillation between the present of observation/perception and the present of writing shows that the consciousness of being writing becomes one of the major contents of writing. The sentence "And I stop writing just because I stop writing" is not mere self-description marking the end of the text, it is above all the evidence of the text as a record of the temporality of a presentified act of writing that has to be interrupted, and in whose interruption signifier and signified seem to be briefly synchronized.

When we consider textual witnesses as acts of writing, that is, self-documenting testimonies of actions that create what they write, two hypotheses arise to characterize the *Book of Disquiet*. First, witnesses are *signals of a particular writing act*, that is, signals of a biological (bio-graphical) duration of a concrete act of writing, which allows the self to focus his/her attention for a certain amount of time and move his/her hand holding pen or pencil over paper or over typewriter keyboard. Textual witnesses are autographic records of a writing body. Indexes of body movements, they are the written evidence of writing. Secondly, witnesses are *signs of acts of writing*, that is, representations of sensations and perceptions coincident with the moment of writing and which, therefore, enhance that moment. Considered in this double sense, many texts from the *Book of Disquiet* would be signs of the intensified access of the self to his/her own consciousness of self and signals of the acts of writing through which this process is autographed.

The physical presence of the writing act, through the inscription and the awareness of the inscription, becomes determinant in instituting a fragmentary logic in the work: every time I begin to write, that is, every time a self or a voice instantiates itself through writing, it is the very act of writing as both signal and sign that is inscribed on paper. The presentification of a moment of sensation and perception which is coextensive with the moment of writing, that is, the existence of an unfolding that transforms consciousness (including the consciousness of writing) into the content of writing, would determine the linguistic and documentary materiality of the text: *a limited set of paragraphs that can be physically produced in a continuous action* according to the circadian rhythms of a body that writes. This set of sentences and paragraphs generally fills up a short section of a page, half a page, one page, or one or two leaves, or a limited sequence of small leaves, and its extension corresponds in most cases to

> Nos primeiros dias do automno subitamente
> entrado, quando o escurecer toma uma evidencia de qual-
> quer cousa prematura, e parece que tardámos muito no
> que fazemos de dia, góso, mesmo entre o trabalho quoti-
> diano, esta antícipação de não trabalhar que a propria
> sombra traz comsigo, porisso que é noite e a noite é
> somno, lar, livramento. Quando as luzes se accendem no
> escriptorio amplo e escuro, e fazemos serão sem que ces-
> sassemos de trabalhar de dia, sinto um comforto absurdo
> como uma lembrança de outrem, e estou socegado com o
> que escrevo como se estivesse lendo até sentir que irei
> dormir.

> E tam suave é a sensação que me alheia do
> debito e do credito que, se acaso uma pergunta me é fei-
> ta, respondo suavemente, como se tivesse o meu ser ôco,
> como se não fôsse mais que a machina de escrever que
> trago commigo, portetil de mim mesmo aberto. Não me cho-
> ca a interrupção dos meus sonhos: de tam suaves que são,
> continuo sonhando-os por traz de fallar, escrever, res-
> ponder, conversar até. E atravez de tudo o chá perdido
> finda, e o escriptorio vae fechar... Ergo do livro, que
> cerro lentamente, olhos cançados do choro que não tive-
> ram, e, numa mixtura de sensações, soffro que ao fechar
> o escriptorio de me feche o sonho tambem; que no gesto de
> mão com que cerro o livro encubra o passado irreparavel;
> que vá para a cama de vida sem somno, sem companhia nem
> socego, no fluxo e refluxo da minha consciencia misturada,
> como duas xxxxxxx marés na noite

Figure 4.6 Facsimile BNP/E3, 3-22r (details), *LdoD Archive*. © National Library of Portugal. Reproduced with permission.

a single act of writing, although it may be subject to a number of later revisions, particularly in the case of the typewritten drafts.

> During the first days of Autumn when nightfall arrives suddenly, as if prematurely, and it seems we took longer to do our day's work, I enjoy, while still working, the thought of not working which the darkness brings, for the darkness is night, and night means sleep, home, freedom. When the lights come on, dispelling darkness from the large office, and we continue our day's work in the beginning of night, I feel a comfort that's absurd, like a remembrance belonging to someone else, and I'm at peace with the numbers I write, as if I were reading while waiting to fall asleep …

> And so gentle is the sensation that estranges me from debits and credits that if by chance I'm asked a question, I answer in a soft voice, as if my being were hollow, as if it were nothing more than a typewriter I carry around with me— portable, opened and ready. It doesn't faze me when my dreams are interrupted; they're so gentle that I keep dreaming them as I speak, write, answer, or even

discuss. And through it all the long-lost tea finishes, the office is going to close ... From the ledger which I slowly shut I raise my eyes, sore from the tears they didn't shed, and with confused feelings I accept, because I must, that with the closing of my office my dream also closes; that as my hand shuts the ledger it also pulls a veil over my irretrievable past; that I'm going to life's bed wide awake, unaccompanied and without peace, in the ebb and flow of my confused consciousness, like two tides in the black night where the destinies of nostalgia and desolation meet.

(Text 33[3])

In these two paragraphs of typewritten text, the priming of present sensation, unleashed by the anticipation of the end of work in the office when night falls, overlapped with other feelings of remembered tranquility, serves to stress the "mixed consciousness" of a self that sees itself as devoid of being—"as if it were nothing more than a typewriter I carry around with me— portable, opened and ready" (Figure 4.6). The feeling of this "hollow" being, whose emergence as a feeling of itself is merely a function of writing and its processes of imagination, depends, as in other texts of the *Book*, on the deep saliency of the sensation of the present as the content of writing. The reverse of the signifying void of the written self would be the full presence of the present of the writing self. But because the self can only be a signifier, its being must be shaped by the open potentiality of the typewriter.

The semi-structured and fragmented nature of the *Book of Disquiet* derives from the material and biological presence of the act of writing, that is, of an

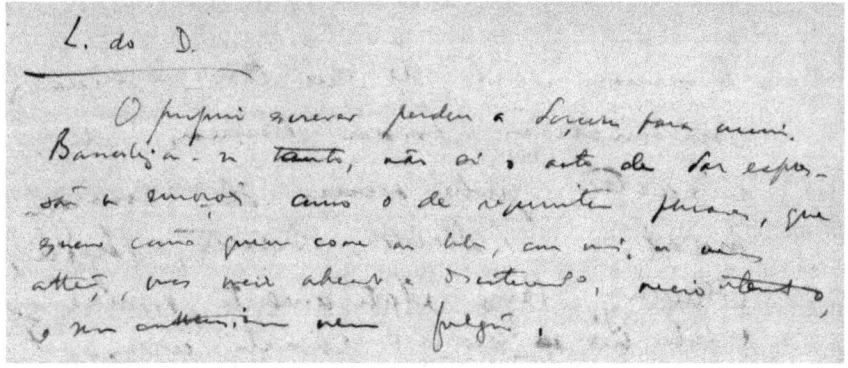

Figure 4.7 Facsimile BNP/E3, 9-11 (detail), *LdoD Archive*. © National Library of Portugal. Reproduced with permission.

---

[3] Full text available at https://ldod.uc.pt/fragments/fragment/Fr181/inter/Fr181_WIT_ED_CRIT_Z (BNP/E3, 3-22r; Coelho 107; Sobral Cunha 598; Zenith 33; Pizarro 224).

action of a living organism with a certain duration and etiology, dependent on the physicality of a set of bodily actions. Each time the self is willing to write, the sensation and perception of the topics of writing blend with the sensation and perception of the act of writing, making each piece of writing also a record of the act of writing it. The fragmentation of the *Book* results from this process of presentifying writing. By restarting over and over again, it brings into the text the biographicality that makes it possible for a self to write and to write itself: to write the self, to write the world, to write the writing. This awareness of being-in-writing becomes a determining content of the *Book*, even when that reflexivity is diluted or dispersed in other thoughts or when writing has become an almost automatic and unconscious habit (Figure 4.7).

> Even writing has lost its appeal. To express emotions in words and to produce well-wrought sentences has become so banal it's like eating or drinking, something I do with greater or lesser interest but always with a certain detachment, and without real enthusiasm or brilliance.
>
> (Text 469[4])

The action of writing is a bodily action, "like eating or drinking," whose circadian rhythm results in the fragmentary accretion of pieces for the *Book*, since the acts of writing that it contains resist integration into a textual or narrative macro-structure that would completely erase their evidence as records of the acts of writing that gave them material existence. It is as if, each time he writes, Pessoa-Guedes-Soares is dominated by the awareness of being in the process of writing and by the physical conditions that allow an act of writing to have only a certain duration, determined by the limits of attention and effort of the body that writes the moment in which it writes. Each text is a reiteration and a restarting of the process, resulting in dispersion and proliferation, once we look at its documentary, semantic, and narrative result. The fragment would then be the graphic evidence of writing as biographical action, that is to say, of the possibility of life writing itself through a conscious organism. Writing expands the homeostasis of the organism to the system formed by its body and the inscriptions produced by its body, as if the sensation of itself came from the instrument of writing (Figure 4.8):

> I write with a strange sorrow, slave to an intellectual suffocation, which comes to me from the perfection of the afternoon. This sky of precious blue, fainting to

---

[4] Full text available at https://ldod.uc.pt/fragments/fragment/Fr428/inter/Fr428_WIT_ED_CRIT_Z (BNP/E3, 9-11; Coelho 201; Sobral Cunha 696; Zenith 469; Pizarro 148).

pale pink tones under an equal and gentle breeze, gives to my consciousness of me a desire to scream. I am writing, after all, for escape and shelter. I avoid ideas. I forget the exact words, and they shine before me in the physical act of writing, as if the pen itself were producing them.

(Text 22,[5] *my translation*)

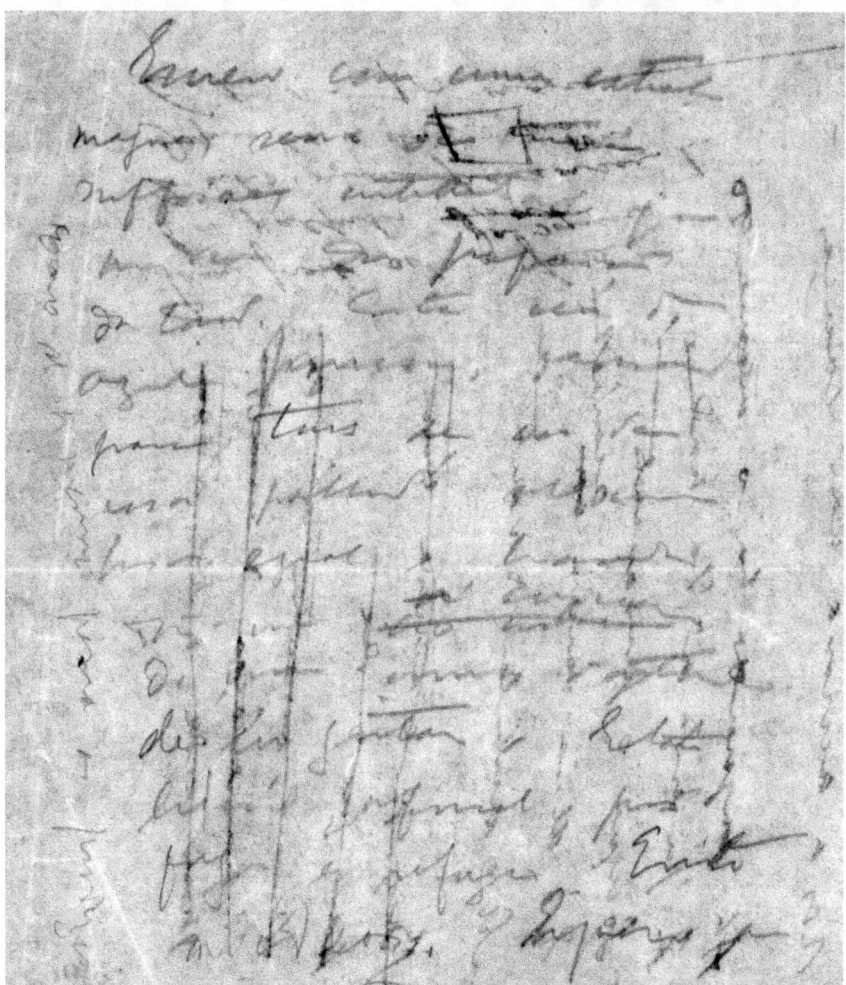

Figure 4.8 Facsimile BNP/E3, 60A-22v (detail), *LdoD Archive*. © National Library of Portugal. Reproduced with permission.

---

[5] Full text available at https://ldod.uc.pt/fragments/fragment/Fr491/inter/Fr491_WIT_ED_CRIT_Z (BNP/E3, 60A-22; Zenith 22; Pizarro 263). This text (which is no. 22 in Zenith 2012) is a late addition to the corpus. It was not yet included in the 2002 English edition and translation by Zenith.

The referential description of the outside world ("perfection of the afternoon," "sky of precious blue," etc.) is given through the sensation of its perception, bringing it closer to the feeling of subjectivity itself—one (world) and other (sensation of the world) always filtered through consciousness ("consciousness of me"). The exactness of the phrases thus appears to have been produced by the pure exteriority of the act of writing, revealing the act of writing as an element of the expanded cognitive system which supplements the processes of feedback from which a sentient consciousness emerges: "I forget the exact words, and they shine me in the physical act of writing, as if the pen itself were producing them." It is this powerful presence of the physical act of writing and the millimetric images, produced from the outside towards the inside, that allow us to see the acts of writing in the *Book* as a model of the recursive processes of consciousness.

To the extent that each moment of writing is the iteration of this process, that is, of a physical act of writing that registers itself in the autographic event of its enunciation, the *Book of Disquiet* would be a collection of acts of writing, definable by their action as writing that is self-absorbed in its own present. For this reason the presentification of the sensation accompanying the act of writing becomes so frequent: the coincidence of sensation with the consciousness of sensation and both with the action of writing stage the scripting act as a phenomenological manifestation of consciousness. Acts of writing enable me to observe and feel the feedback that allows me to see, feel, think, and write in the second degree, that is, to see myself seeing, to feel myself feeling, to think myself thinking, to write myself writing (Figure 4.9).

> On the afternoon in which I write, the rain has finally let up. A gladness in the air feels almost too cool against the skin. The day is ending not in grey but in pale blue. A hazy blue is even reflecting off the stones of the street. It hurts to live, but the pain is remote. Feeling doesn't matter. One or another shop window lights up. In a window higher up, there are people looking down at the workers who are finishing up for the day. The beggar who brushes my shoulder would be shocked if he knew me.
>
> (Text 191[6])

---

[6] Full text available at https://ldod.uc.pt/fragments/fragment/Fr095/inter/Fr095_WIT_ED_CRIT_Z (BNP/E3, 2-20; Coelho 189; Sobral Cunha 716; Zenith 191; Pizarro 162).

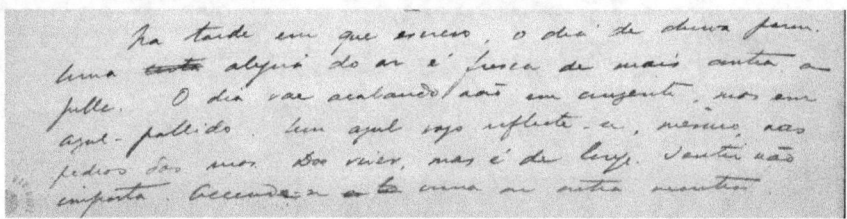

Figure 4.9 Facsimile BNP/E3, 2-20 (detail), *LdoD Archive*. © National Library of Portugal. Reproduced with permission.

The Kinetics of Writing

Peter L. Shillingsburg (2006) proposed a general theory of script acts in the processes of textual transmission to underline the singularity of each instantiation of a work, whether in its authorial versions or in its editorial versions. Any material instantiation of a work subsumes a chain of script acts that configure the particular historicity of its form as it is produced and reproduced over time. In other words: each textual form bears witness to a set of specific script acts, "each leaving its record in manuscripts, proofs, books, revisions, reprintings, and translations" (50). From this theoretical standpoint, the *LdoD Archive* can be described as a script act of its own containing a representation of two types of script acts: authorial script acts, such as those described in the previous two sections; and editorial script acts, that is, the particular editorial interventions that are registered in the four editions selected for inclusion in the *Archive*. Besides the interventions made by the editors on the script acts recorded in the author's witnesses, we could add the acts of type and page setting that originated the actual printed forms of the book in its various editions. It is this multiple system of inscriptions and its social conditions of production that allow for the instantiation of the work under a specific textual and bibliographic form.

By placing facsimiles of authorial witnesses, new transcriptions of these documents and transcriptions of four editorial versions of the documents at the same comparative level, the *LdoD Archive* constellates them as representations of writing (cf. Figure 4.10). New transcriptions and the four editions are considered in the *LdoD Archive* as modes of production of the *Book of Disquiet*, that is, textual versions that re-materialize a certain idea of the work. The menu for comparing autograph witnesses and transcriptions allows interactors to relate those two layers of textual

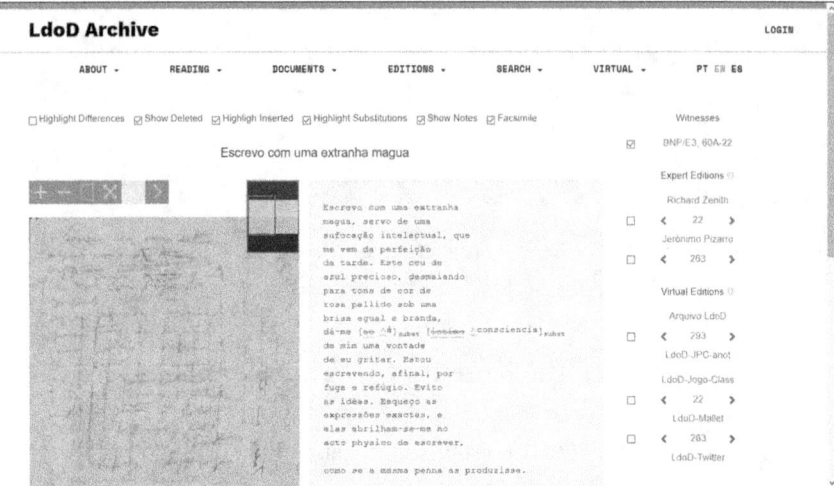

Figure 4.10 *LdoD Archive*: interface for viewing autograph witnesses and comparing transcriptions. Facsimile BNP/E3, 60A-22, next to its topographic transcription by the *LdoD Archive*. This text is no. 22 in Richard Zenith's edition and no. 263 in Jerónimo Pizarro's edition.

production—the authorial and the editorial—either at micro-textual level, that is, in the granularity of the internal variations of each textual unit, or at macro-textual level, that is, in the division and relative position of each textual unit in the *Book* as a whole, as we have seen in the previous chapter. The editors' interpretation of Pessoa's writing processes—for example, in cases where there are several witnesses belonging to the same sequence, or when some of these witnesses are partially identical versions of the same text—becomes observable through this meta-representation of selection and editorial organization, revealing the performativity of the editorial process as a specific way of re-scripting an earlier writing act.

To the question *what is an act of writing in the Book of Disquiet*, the *LdoD Archive* offers three distinct but correlated answers. The first answer says that an act of writing is a self-documenting inscription of which digital facsimiles and topographic transcription constitute two types of representation. The genetic component of the *LdoD Archive* seeks to model the topography and the temporality of these inscriptions through a transcription that re-represents the witnesses in their writing flow (cancellations, substitutions, additions, variants, etc.). The second response states that an act of writing, understood as a certain duration of a continuous and uninterrupted process of writing, is one of the compositional units of the *Book of Disquiet*. To the extent that the consciousness of being-in-the-process-of-writing is narratively constituted as a manifestation of a sentient writing self (thematized in several texts of the *Book of Disquiet*), and insofar as many texts attempt to presentify the perceptual content of consciousness at the time of writing, each act of writing is conditioned by the reenactment and reiteration of this process rather than by any narrative continuation of the content of previous texts. The fragmentation of the set of texts registers the processuality of acts of writing (through the weaving of immediate spatial and temporal perception with memory) as a major content of writing. Extreme modularization of the fragments in the *LdoD Archive* models this relation between textual form and writing events. The third answer says that an act of writing, in the broad sense of *script act* referred to above, is the particular intervention that, in each edition, results in a certain transcription and sequencing of texts. From this perspective, acts of editing involve a certain degree of overwriting through which autographs are collaboratively post-produced by editorial intentions. By moving back and forth between post-edited writing and pre-edited archived writing, the scriptive layer of editing is shown as a specific component of a system of writings.

Thus, it is the processuality of the act of writing as autograph and introspective evidence of the processes of consciousness that the witnesses self-document *also in their specific material and textual form*: a large set of loose sheets containing sequences of paragraphs that form texts with a significant degree of modularity, even though several nuclei, written at different moments, are semantically related to each other and obey other autographic motifs and topics. The broad space of intervention in the editing and re-editing of the text of the work depends on those documentary and textual features which make it possible to continue to constellate those texts in networks of variable and only semi-determinable relations.

Bernardo Soares's semi-heteronimity would be another figuration of *writing as action*: in the hollow space of language, the fictional being of Bernardo Soares maintains a bond with the perceptual and sensorial system of the organism that writes it and whose feeling itself writing is given by the presentification of consciousness as writing. As if, in this semi-heteronymization, the distance between being the actual enunciating self (Pessoa) and the fictional enunciated self (Soares) could be crossed, moment by moment, through the circadian and embodied repetition of acts of writing. The fact that, in the second stage of composition of the *Book*, Pessoa has chosen to define this semi-heteronym as assistant bookkeeper and set many of his writings and observations in an office in downtown Lisbon—a setting similar to the actual workplace of Pessoa's clerical job—is a further sign of such an enunciative and deictic system.

Textual units of the *Book of Disquiet* fall into three groups: (1) a few hundred manuscripts, most of which date to the first period of composition, are constituted by a few paragraphs (sometimes extending to several small sheets), generally first drafts with several emendations; (2) a few hundred typescripts (of less than ten paragraphs, many between three and six paragraphs), most of which date to the second period of composition and fit into a single typewriter page (*c.* 27 × 21 cm)—many of these contain handwritten emendations and a few of them also contain additional handwritten paragraphs; (3) twelve published texts, one of which was published in 1913 (five pages long), and the second group was published between 1929 and 1932. Many of these texts are marked "L. do D." by Pessoa, and several of them are also dated. Most of them are on loose sheets but a small number of fragments are handwritten in notebooks containing other writing projects.[7]

Textual and discursive divisions often coincide with the surface of inscription (for instance, most typewritten fragments fit within one page), but there also instances where paragraph spacing, horizontal rulers, and other metamarks— particularly in handwritten texts—can be used for marking semantic units and textual breaks. If we exclude the limited number of early large pieces that are several pages long, the average size of textual units marked for inclusion in the *Book of Disquiet* is only a few paragraphs long. This size suggests that Pessoa's autograph units of writing in the *Book of Disquiet* generally correspond to temporal units of writing.[8] Rather than being merely a contingent result of external circumstances, the textual fragment seems to have been the product of the temporality of the scripting act as a cognitive exploration of writing-thinking feedbacks. Each textual piece can be read as an embodied neurological unit of focused attention in the exploration of self-consciousness.

In the manuscript in Figure 4.11[9] the dynamics of filling in the page helps us to understand the material and temporal kinetics of writing as evidence of his fragmentary method. The autograph document presents material and textual

---

[7] The full list of autograph witnesses is available here: https://ldod.uc.pt/source/list.

[8] For almost three decades, Marta L. Werner's work on Emily Dickinson's manuscripts has engaged the temporality and materiality of writing acts in the minute particulars of their inscriptions as intimate recordings of writing in process. Her electronic edition of Dickinson's late fragments (Werner 1999–2010) and her analysis of the Fascicles in relation to the Master documents (2017, 2021) have contributed to my thinking about the kinetics of writing. On the problem of editing fragments, see also Dedner 2006.

[9] BNP/E3, 1-71v and 71a-v (left-hand side, bottom and top), 71 (right-hand side, bottom), 71a (right-hand side, top). Full text available at https://ldod.uc.pt/fragments/fragment/Fr064/inter/Fr064_WIT_ED_CRIT_Z_1 (Coelho 124; Sobral Cunha 371, 372; Zenith 419, 421; Pizarro 185, 186, 187).

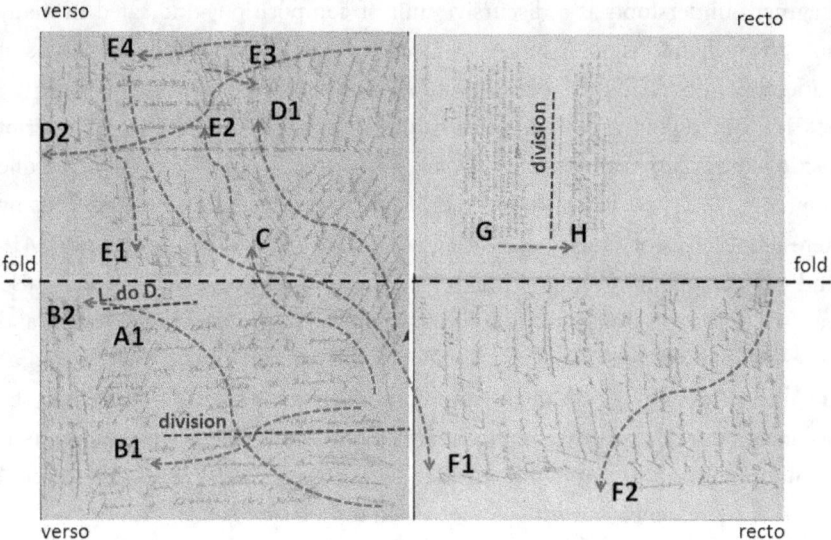

Figure 4.11 Writing in fragments: the centrifugal and contrapuntal dynamics of self-consciousness in E3, 1-71-71a. © National Library of Portugal. Reproduced with permission.

features that we find in other pieces of the *Book of Disquiet*. This folded sheet of paper contains both typescript and handwritten text, indicating at least two different moments of composition. Both the typescript and handwritten areas contain graphical marks of textual division: in the typescript area, a dashed horizontal ruler indicates that the second typed paragraph is a different semantic unit; in the manuscript area, we find the mark "L. do D." that identifies this text as a piece of writing meant for the *Book of Disquiet*, and also a handwritten horizontal ruler preceded by a title, again indicating that this part forms a particular semantic unit that can be distinguished from the paragraphs in the surrounding areas.

This example shows how a certain number of variations in textual units in each edition depend on the way editors interpret the relation between textual and material contiguity: the co-presence of textual units on the same inscription surface can be used as a criterion for transcribing those units as part of the same fragment. Material contiguity is used for constructing textual unity, as is the case in Pizarro's critical-genetic edition. Alternatively, as happens in Prado Coelho's edition, marks of textual division will justify association by semantic and thematic clustering rather than inscriptional contiguity. We may say that the fragment understood as a discursive unit of composition—indicated in many autograph manuscripts by marks of division between paragraphs or groups of paragraphs—overlaps the fragment understood as a piece of written paper.

This document contains at least four internal sections (two typescript sections and two manuscript sections), but it has been edited either as one fragment (edition by Jacinto do Prado Coelho, text no. 124), two (editions by Teresa Sobral Cunha, text nos. 371 and 372, and Richard Zenith, text nos. 419 and 421), or three (Jerónimo Pizarro, text nos. 185, 186, and 187). Editions also vary in the internal organization of paragraphs: Jacinto do Prado Coelho and Teresa Sobral Cunha place one of the typewritten paragraphs interpolated as the fifth paragraph within the handwritten text; Richard Zenith places it as the second paragraph; while Jerónimo Pizarro treats both typewritten paragraphs as an autonomous unit that follows the handwritten text. Editors organize material and textual evidence according to perceived discursive form.

The kinetics of writing on the surface of manuscript BNP/E3-1-71-v and 71a-v suggests that this sheet was rotated in clockwise and counterclockwise directions five times (Figure 4.12). The pattern of distribution on the page suggests that the temporal sequence of inscription was as indicated in A-E4 (Figure 4.13). Script areas A, C, D1, D2, E1, E2, E3, and E4 seem to belong to the same semantic unit. Areas B1 and B2 seem to form a different semantic unit. This autograph manuscript shows the process of accretion and internal differentiation of the fragment as both a kinetic register of a script act and a semantic textual unit developing towards some kind of textual whole. In the case of the *Book of Disquiet* this whole is both the self-conscious unity of the fragment, and the perceived potentiality of writing for generating stylistic and thematic coherence at larger scales. Although each piece of text desires to place itself in the larger imagined structure of the book, each piece of text is also a self-contained unit. This fragmentary logic becomes a built-in feature of Pessoa's writing process in the *Book of Disquiet*, as suggested in the previous sections.

Analysis of textual inscription on this particular page suggests the following scripting dynamics:

1. The temporal sequence of inscription on the different areas of the paper seems to be A, B, C, D, and E (this choreographic motion was also determined by the fact that this sheet was folded in half).
2. Text in area B ("A Viagem na Cabeça" ["Journey in the Mind"]) is marked by a horizontal line of division that suggests the beginning of another

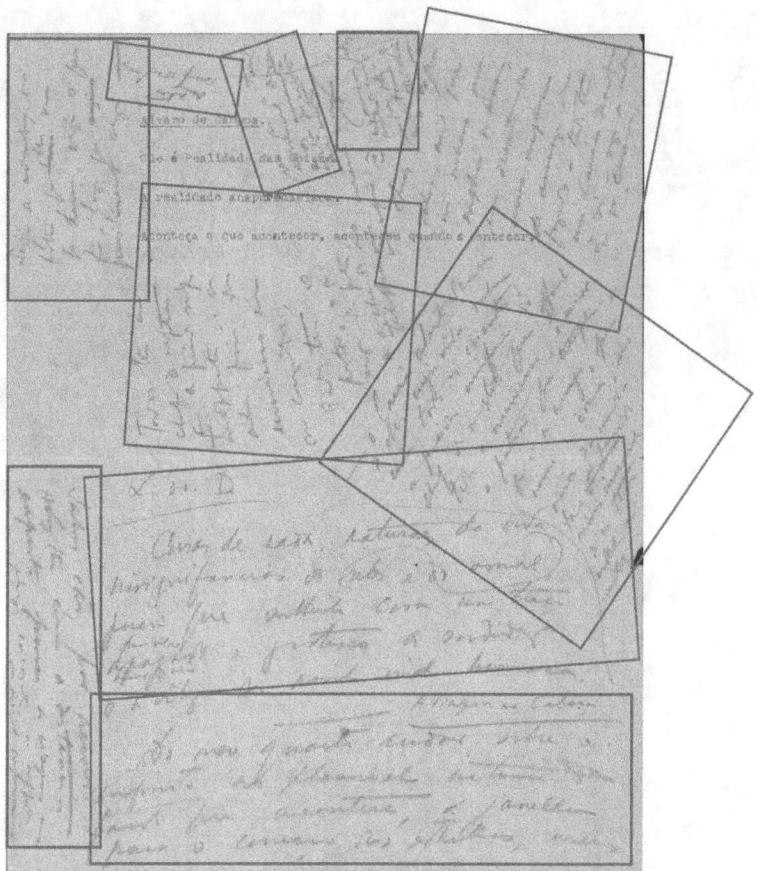

Figure 4.12 Filling in the page: the kinetics of writing for E3-1-71v. © National Library of Portugal. Reproduced with permission.

fragment. Its semantic markers are also different from those of text in area A. The title "Journey in the Mind" may belong to a later script act, since the pencil does not have the same thickness of the entries in either area A or B. Graphic markers (line of division, title) and content features (semantic unity) reinforce the process of textual differentiation.

3. After writing the text in area B, Pessoa would have reread the text in area A, which contrasts semantically with the text in area B. In this case, Bernardo Soares is presented as a dreamer in his room, in the other, Bernardo Soares is shown as a bookkeeper in the warehouse—"the sordidness and vileness of my human existence." Rereading area A may

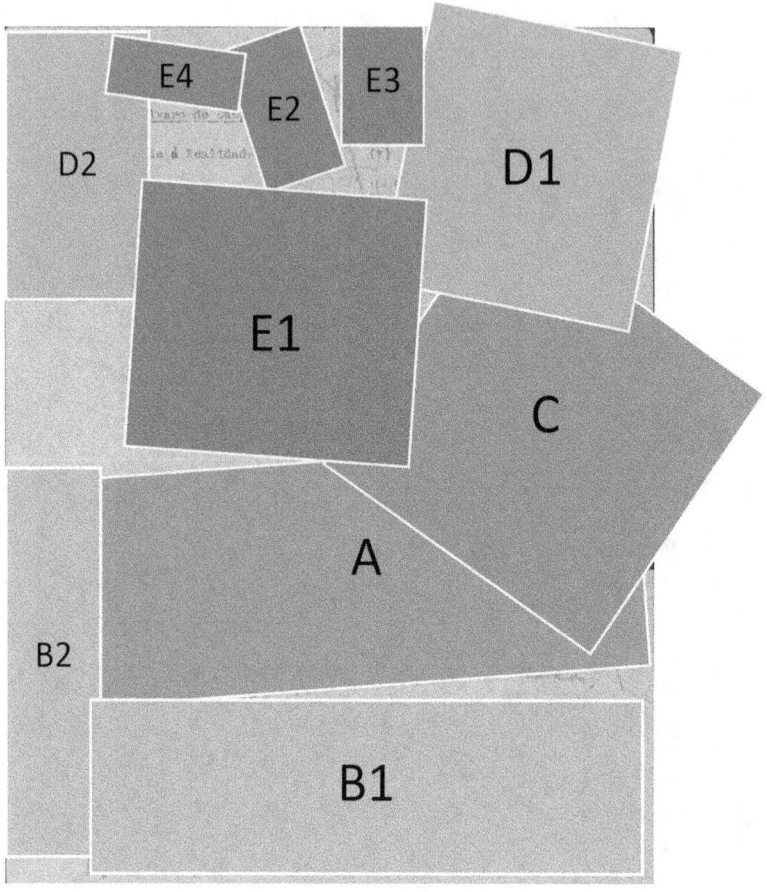

Figure 4.13 The kinetics of writing and the inner logic of fragments.

have suggested the list of topics that expand on the idea stated in the text in area A through observations about the daily business of the office.

4. Thus the temporal inscription of the page areas is A, B, C, D, and E, but semantic consistency suggests that it may be divided into two different fragments or pieces: one with the text areas A, C, D, E (+ F, on the recto face, shown above in Figure 4.11), the second text constituted only by area B (Fragment "A Journey in the Mind"). The act of assigning a title to the second fragment suggests that this paragraph could eventually be integrated or subsumed in some other text containing this topic, or that this fragment could be in itself the beginning of a possible fragment on the mental journeys of Bernardo Soares.

Through a detailed analysis of these pages it is possible to highlight several aspects of temporality and reflexivity in the act of writing:

1. Occupation of the various areas contains a chronology of inscriptions for the script acts: how each piece of text is laid out around the contours of others provides information about the relative chronology of inscription of each piece of text.
2. Writing explores the potentiality opened up by feedbacks between thought and inscription and often unfolds without a prior plan for occupying the paper: the text is not inscribed according to a linear distribution (filling in the leaf from top to bottom always in the same direction) because its development stems from the process itself. An initial area selected as a scripting field may prove insufficient, and it may trigger another circular or perpendicular movement to occupy another area of the page. The hand moves across the inscriptional surface in several directions. In this case five different paper rotations shifted the handwriting in both clockwise and counterclockwise directions. The size of the handwritten letters gets smaller as one tries to fit additional sentences into the decreasing available space.
3. The process of constructing semantic unity through the addition of sentences and paragraphs works either by contrast—a particular semantic unit can generate, by contrast, a new semantic unit (relationship between A and B)—or by similarity, i.e., by adding or subsuming topics (relationships between A, C, D, E, and F). Fragments thus take their self-conscious shape through processes of internal repetition with variation (branching, expansion, specification, etc.) and differentiation.
4. Rereading can strengthen the unity of a script act by assigning a title that gives further conceptual unity to a fragment, or by redistributing paragraphs according to later revision acts.

This analysis of the temporal and semantic dynamics of writing enables us to consider the notion of fragment at several levels:

a. The fragment as *a piece of paper*. In this case the incompleteness of the inscription is the consequence of the incompleteness of its inscriptional surface—for example, a missing or misplaced leaf, i.e., either lost or placed outside the temporal and semantic order of inscription. This type of fragmentation is contingent on partial degradation or partial loss of a document.

b. The fragment as *a piece of writing*. The incompleteness of inscription results from the incipient nature of the text—as in text B, for example—suggesting the possibility of continuation, revision, and rewriting. Loose sentences or phrases may be annotations for further expansions. This type of fragmentation is contingent on the drafting process.
c. The fragment as *a piece of writing susceptible of belonging to a larger unit*, with more or less strong semantic and narrative unity. Such fragments could then be sequenced with other fragments of the same type. In this latter instance the text may be finished as a textual unit (as is the case with many pieces of the *Book of Disquiet*, including the text published in 1913 and, more generally, with typescripts belonging to the later period of composition), but its relative position within the book as whole has not been determined. Its fragmentary condition results from this divergence between its closed internal form and its open and undetermined place within a final imagined longer textual sequence.
d. The fragment as *a genre in itself*, that is, a piece of text that asserts its fragmentariness as a stylistic and structural feature. Although these textual pieces may form a larger whole, they are self-conscious about their fragmentary unity.

Fragments of type c and d can be said to have been the unit of composition of the *Book of Disquiet* in its authorial form, while fragments of type a, b, and c are the unit of composition in the work's posthumous editorial forms. The accretion process required for the autograph production of the *Book of Disquiet* results from ordering and revising/rewriting of pieces of text that have a certain semantic unity but which are also self-consciously fragmentary in their finished forms. Dilemmas faced by the editors—reenacting dilemmas faced by the author in his notes and plans on how to organize the *Book of Disquiet*—result from this codetermination between parts and whole. The chosen fragments and the sequencing of those fragments is made with a certain conception of the whole (a certain idea about what the writing of the *Book of Disquiet* is or should be), but at the same time that perceived whole is the product of actual choices about the structure and form of its constituent parts. Its particular nature as a book project can be inferred from the style and atmosphere of certain pieces, but it is also the retrospective result of the cumulative choices from which the specific character of the work will emerge.

In the case of the *Book of Disquiet*, there are varying degrees of semantic and discursive unity, which tend to be reflected in the stages of revision that we can infer from print, typescript, and manuscript witnesses. Semantic and discursive unity is generally stronger in large printed texts ("Trechos") and typescript pieces, and weaker in short manuscript passages where there is no reiteration and expansion of a particular topic or where there are no signs of systematic revision acts. The semantic unity of textual fragments and their relative length is partly correlated with acts of revision and rewriting: it is generally stronger in typescripts than in first draft manuscripts, because these may be less self-reflexive and result from the temporality of the first act of inscription. Each sentence or phrase triggers a process of association with sets of sentences or phrases that follow at a given moment of continued and sustained writing focus. However, in the *Book of Disquiet* there are several texts where there seems to be no significant difference between manuscripts and typescripts, and several heavily corrected typescript texts may have been written directly on the typewriter without a prior handwritten draft. This kinetic temporality of handwritten or typewritten inscription produces in itself a semantic and material coherence that comes from its existence at a given moment in time.

Fragment, Book, Self

Representation of stages and layers of writing and revision has been the basis of codex critical editions that represent textual construction by marking earlier or potential forms contained in the work's archive. In the case of the *Book of Disquiet*, the work's archive is itself partially undeterminable since its textual *corpus* fluctuates according to particular editorial decisions. Editors have to select elements from the author's archive, mark them as belonging to the *Book of Disquiet* on the basis of material and stylistic evidence, place these elements in a hypothetical bibliographic sequence, and produce the result as a textual whole. Each editorial selection is different, and the relative order chosen for placing the texts and fragments selected is also unique. From these editorial interventions different *Books of Disquiet* take shape. In fact, the editorial process of selecting and ordering pieces of text to produce a book is similar to an authorial intervention on the archive of the work. Pessoa would have to edit the writings of his semi-heteronym Bernardo Soares in order for the *Book of Disquiet* to gain the psychological and stylistic unity that he imagines (cf. above, "Document, Text, Book, Work").

As we have seen, writing takes place as process that explores the potential of the fragment as a function of the writing process itself. This may be described as a major difference between the Romantic and Modernist uses of fragment: in the first instance, as quoted or constructed pieces from external sources (imaginary or not), textual and material evidence of ruins that point beyond themselves, according to an aesthetics of genre; in the second instance, as a fragmentary totality that is complete and incomplete at the same time, and whose fragmentary nature is an internal textual property. The modernist aesthetics of the fragment as genre is predicated upon types of fragment that have been described in these terms by Camelia Elias: "the fragment is essentially different from the full text as it is able to both actualize a full text's completeness and survive that actuality in becoming a totality itself" (Elias 2004: 49).

As in other modernist unfinished works—such as the *Arcades Project* (1927–40) by Walter Benjamin or *The Man Without Qualities* (1930–43) by Robert Musil—we may say that in the *Book of Disquiet* the fragment is not a contingent or circumstantial piece whose incompleteness originates in its own unfinished state, although some of its fragmentary texts would also correspond to this description (cf. instances a and b, above). It is, rather, a mode and genre of writing that produces the fragmentary as an attribute of its own internal constitution: not mere evidence of compositional hesitations and interruptions—stylistic experiments, paradoxical uses of language, repeated attempts at giving written form to thoughts, and thinking through writing—but the literary expression of the reflexive exploration of the potentiality of writing. The fragment, rather than the book or any stable and recognizable textual form or genre, emerges as the very condition of textuality. Fragmentation functions as a framework for showing writing as a process of becoming that gives form to a certain state of mind or a worldview. Pessoa is aware of these dynamics between potentiality and actuality when he describes his writing process as an accumulation of fragments: "My state of mind compels me to work hard, against my will, on the *Book of Disquiet*, but it's all fragments, fragments, fragments" (from Pessoa's letter to Armando Cortes-Rodrigues, November 19, 1914).

This experience of the fragment in writing is also an image of the discontinuous and hollow phenomenological experience of the self as constituted through language. Subjective existence cannot be captured or given form in writing except as a series of discontinuous fragments that have to be supplemented by an actual reading act, a material replication of the unity of self-consciousness as a neurological product of multiple pulses of brain activity. Pessoa's heteronyms can be described as a written dramatization of this self-differentiation process that reveals the self as a fragment to itself: "I, who dare write only passages, fragments, excerpts of the non-existent I myself—in the little that I write—am also imperfect" (Pessoa 2002: text 85).[10] Describing the *Book of Disquiet* as "Fragments of an Autobiography" (Pessoa 2002: text 251), Pessoa turns the fragmentary nature of writing into a mirror image of the fragmentary nature of the self. The potentiality of being and the potentiality of writing coalesce in the fragment.

Pessoa's textual pieces for the *Book of Disquiet* should be understood as fragments in those two distinct but related senses: expressions of the modernist genre of the fragment as both a form of writing the act of writing and a form of writing the consciousness of the self, on one hand; and also a series of written fragments of a larger text whose imagined wholeness remains in the process of being constructed. This latter tension between fragments (in various stages of completion or revision) and the projected whole (in its varied plans and versions) is essential for thinking about the dynamics of writing the self in relation to the structure and form of the book. As an artifact, the book establishes a totalizing horizon, one in which it is the very structure of the codex that is able to produce order and generate a sense of whole. And yet, Pessoa's sensationist process of writing—with its accumulation of sensations and fictional multiplication of perspectives and consciousnesses perceiving the world—generates enhanced sensations and perceptions of reality through a collection of fragments whose stylistic, narrative, and psychological coherence comes from this introspective and phenomenological experience of self-consciousness itself as a fragmentary process.

Dirk Van Hulle (2013, 2014, 2016) has argued for the value of digital collation of modern manuscripts not as a preliminary step for scholarly editing but as a tool for manuscript research. According to this perspective, digital editing can be used for studying multiple drafting as part of the cognitive process through which the act of writing and rewriting probes the workings of the extended mind through material interactions. If this cognitive approach to genetic criticism were applied to fragments of the *Book of Disquiet*, Pessoa's manuscripts and typescripts

---

[10] The fragment as a mode of understanding both world and self is a cultural trope that has gained currency since the Romantic period. Friedrich Schlegel remarks, for example, that "the fragment is the real form of universal philosophy" or that "I can give no other 'echantillon' of my entire ego than such a system of fragments because I myself am such a thing" (quoted in Elias 2004: 112). For an image of writing as a fragment of the self: "I am a fragment, and this is a fragment of me" (Ralph Waldo Emerson, quoted in Elias 2004: 112).

in their various layers of revision and emendation could also be analyzed as part of the construction of the mind of his heteronyms. The process of semantic and thematic accretion and variation found across several texts could be examined at smaller inscriptional scales of sentence, phrase, and word. Textual transcriptions mapped onto autograph markings would offer us an image of this retroactive process of invention through inscription. A layered transcription of the material writing process would provide us with another probe into Pessoa's production of the written/speaking self, offering us a view into the kinetic and cognitive procedurality of writing-in-the-making and of the book-in-the-making.

The tension between part and whole, inherent in the fragmentary kinetics of writing, implies that the form of the book works as a conceptual space of articulation that we cannot materially totalize just by selecting and ordering its writings. Contaminated by writing's and self's potentiality of becoming, it is as if the book, like the self, has turned into an open collection of fragments. Coincidence between discursive unity and material unity can only happen partially and provisionally, in a projective mode. In the *LdoD Archive*, fragmentariness—the self-contained modular textual unit and the elusive structure of an undeterminable bibliographic whole—has become the critical probe that links theoretical framework to engineering design. This notion of fragments in search for some kind of reading, editing, and writing unity through the imagination of the book is the basis for electronic textual encoding, database structure, data model, and interactive functionalities, as we have seen.

The representational layer in relation to the author-function is evident in the ability of linking topographic transcription of autograph to facsimile image of the writing autographs. This double representation of the fragmentary kinetics of scripting, in turn, is framed within the bibliographic structure of the editions: genetic transcriptions can be seen in the context of editorial transcriptions, and vice versa; fragments can be seen in the context of books, and vice versa. As shown in Figure 4.14, the right-hand side menu offers the possibility of combining vertical navigation in a particular edition (i.e., within a particular arrangement of the fragments according to a given book structure) with horizontal navigation throughout the entire archive (i.e., within the modular structure of textual pieces not yet organized according to any bibliographical principle).

This tension between writing units as self-contained autograph inscriptions and editorial units as components of a bibliographic space is reenacted for each authorial document. We can see, for instance, that authorial witness E3-1-71-71a corresponds to one fragment in Coelho, two in Sobral Cunha and Zenith,

Writing as Simulation

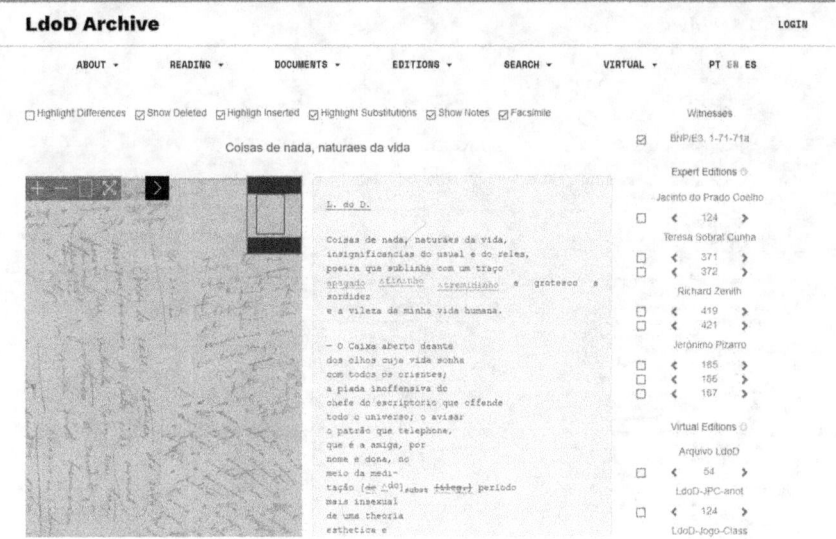

Figure 4.14 Screen capture of the *LdoD Archive*: digital facsimile vs. transcription of authorial source (E3-1-71-71a).

and three in Pizarro. We are also able to see their relative position within each of those four versions of the *Book of Disquiet*: position number 124 in Coelho; 371 and 372 in Sobral Cunha; 419 and 421 in Zenith; and 185, 186, and 187 in Pizarro. This radial structure creates the possibility of relating a genetic text view of the process of writing to a social text view of the process of editing. The back-and-forth movement between archive and edition rehearses the dynamics between written parts and projected whole.

The XML-TEI encoding of authorial and editorial variants and variations enables users of the archive to see the kinetics of the scripting acts in relation to various editorial representations of those processes. Figures 4.15 and 4.16 show one-to-one and one-to-many textual comparisons between editions represented in the *LdoD Archive*. Color highlights mark all points of variation across the various editions of this fragment, including small-scale variations—such as differences in orthography, but also authorial and editorial variants—and large-scale variations—such as differences in paragraph division and ordering. Figure 4.15 shows that Zenith and Pizarro have treated the internal textual divisions of this particular fragment differently. Figure 4.16 highlights variations at the scale of the paragraph and at the scale of words across the four critical editions. All editorial interventions—from orthographic normalization to readings

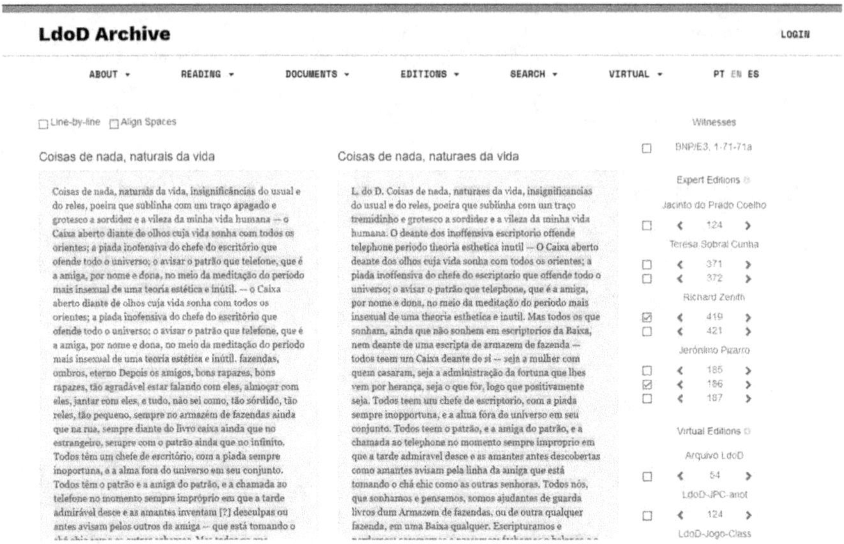

Figure 4.15 Screen capture of the *LdoD Archive*: side-by-side comparison between two transcriptions of the same fragment (E3-1-71-71a according to Zenith 2012 and Pizarro 2010).

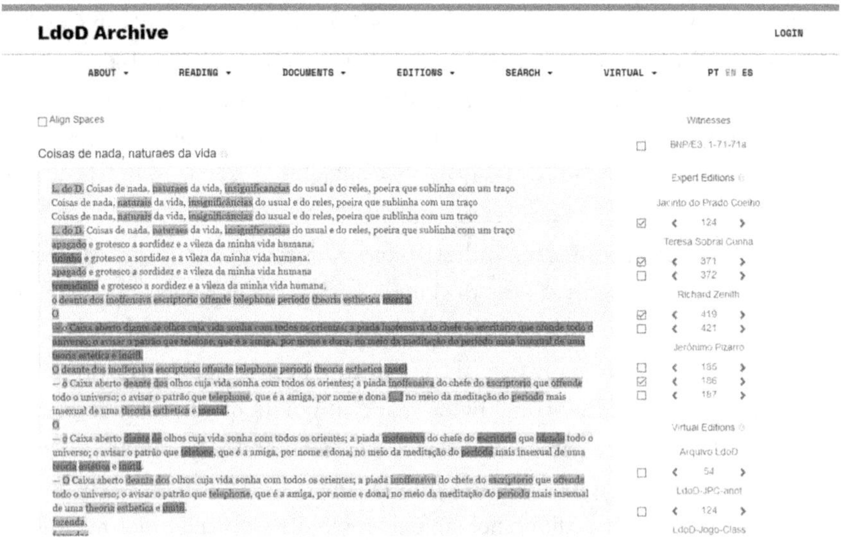

Figure 4.16 Screen capture of the *LdoD Archive*: line-by-line comparison across four editions of the same fragment (E3-1-71-71a according to Coelho 1982; Sobral Cunha 2008; Zenith 2012; and Pizarro 2010).

of particular passages to internal rearrangement of paragraphs to the general division, selection, and sequencing of texts—can be automatically visualized against each other but also against their respective authorial sources.

Every revision mark that Pessoa made on the text is a heightened moment of awareness of the writing process. How is the self made present in the fragmentary acts of writing and revising? What emerges in those layers of scripting acts? How is this writing process related to the process of creating writing selves? A systematic encoding of writing and revision acts can help us observe the textual construction of the self through this fragmentary kinetics of writing. The detailed representation of editorial interventions on the autograph materials enables us to analyze the diverse instances of mediation that lead from an open set of textual fragments to an edited book. Editorial interpretation results in the construction of a work and an image of its author. Pessoa and the *Book of Disquiet* are a collaborative construction of editors, publishers, critics, readers, and the wider academic and economic networks responsible for reproducing cultural and literary capital.

Through the encoding of authorial and editorial witnesses, users of the archive can examine not only Pessoa's writing process—by looking at revision acts represented as layers in the visualization of the transcriptions—but also the reading and interpretative processes through which the four critical editors give form and structure to Pessoa's planned book. The autograph documentary basis of the digital archive is placed in a dynamic relation with the editors' conjectural organization of textual wholes from Pessoa's archive of fragments. From this multilayered and shifting perspective—from document to text to book relations—users of the *LdoD Digital Archive* will be able to perceive the fragmentary kinetics of writing as a textual and structural feature of the *Book of Disquiet* whose variable authorial and editorial forms present us with a work in progress that remains in progress. By focusing on writing as a process of engaging with language rather than a reified output to be merely represented in its minute particulars, it is possible to extend the simulation layer to the action of writing.

From Handwriting to Language Processing

This section focuses on the author-function and explains the rationale used for virtualizing Pessoa's writing. The Web 2.0 approach adopted for this project explores annotation and writing software, but also experimental practices and electronic literature tools in order to enable user-authors to create extensions based on Pessoa's texts. These texts can be published within the virtual level of the archive. While at the editor-function level user-editors will be able to construct virtual selected editions of Pessoa's text, at the author-function level the *Book of Disquiet* becomes both a textual database and textual instrument for the networked collaborative writing of further texts. Each fragment from the *Book of Disquiet* can be appropriated for new writing acts that extend and transform the original, turning the *LdoD Archive* into literary experiment.

The process of composition of the *Book of Disquiet* results from the accretion of a few hundred script acts in both handwritten and typewritten form. With the exception of a small group of large texts, most script acts meant for the *Book of Disquiet* bear witness to these temporal units of writing, as if each one constitutes the beginning of a new text (Portela and Giménez 2016). Acts of writing are part of the writer's method for intensifying awareness of sensation and perception as "the regime of consciousness in which I began to live" (Figure 4.17). This self-conscious engagement with the action of writing provides the basis for both human and machine-assisted forms of writing at the simulatory level.

> The intensity of my sensations has always been less than the intensity of my awareness of them. I've always suffered more from my consciousness that I was suffering than from the suffering of which I was conscious.

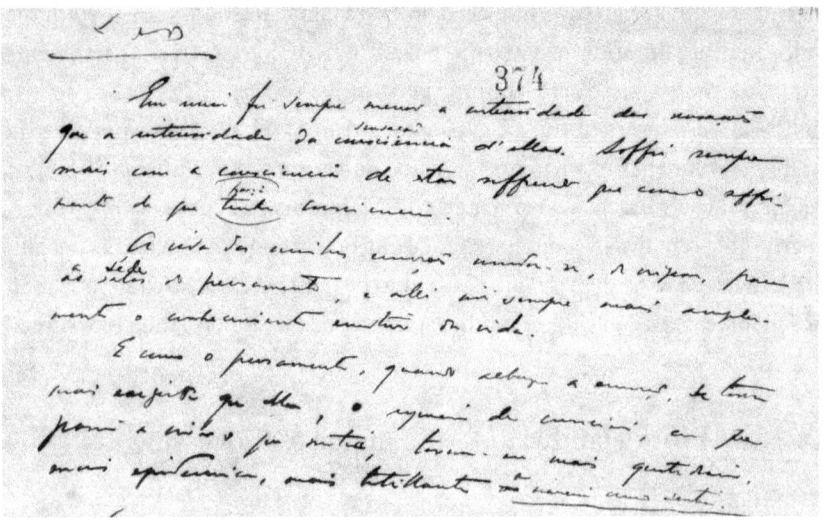

Figure 4.17 Facsimile of autograph manuscript BNP/E3, 5-19r (detail). © National Library of Portugal. Reproduced with permission.

The life of my emotions moved early on to the chambers of thought, and that's where I've most fully lived my emotional experience of life.

And since thought, when it shelters emotion, is more demanding than emotion by itself, the regime of consciousness in which I began to live what I felt made how I felt more down-to-earth, more physical, more titillating.

(Text 93[11])

Pessoa's invention of writing selves is a product of his ability to sustain self-conscious feedback loops between his thought and emotional processes on the one hand, and the material and verbal processes of writing on the other. This self-reflexive writing activity produces a sort of extended mind as if writing, functioning as an external organ of the body, participates in the neurological pulses of a conscious mind. Writing becomes a process for repeatedly invoking and constructing the self as a particular moment in the emergence of this consciousness of being conscious. The technology and practice of writing could be described as part of what Damásio refers to as sociocultural homeostasis, resulting from the interaction with the biological homeostatic impulse that favors the development of a conscious mind and the integration of neural patterns that produces a sense of self (2010: 356–63). The fact that the *Book of Disquiet* can be read, in the age of functional magnetic resonance imaging, as a book of consciousness that engages with theories of mind-brain equivalence in contemporary neuroscience, is also revealing about its continuing relevance as an inquiry into the possibilities of self-knowledge of the human mind.

Many pieces and fragments from the *Book of Disquiet* are in fact reflexive about self, consciousness, and writing. This reflexivity of the writing self is at the core of Pessoa's poetic experiments with subjectivity. His early invention of writing selves emerges from this reflexivity and constitutes the major literary effect of his understanding of language as producer of a subjectivity. Written language is not only the simulation of a series of possible subject positions, affective states, and points of view on the world, but also an introspective and metacognitive probe into the fundamental and neurological process of consciousness. The act of writing the self intensifies the neurological pathways of consciousness, i.e., the feedback circuit between thinking and writing, which results in the reiterated staging of a self being conscious of itself. The possibilities of being in the world

---

[11] Full text available at https://ldod.uc.pt/fragments/fragment/Fr309/inter/Fr309_WIT_ED_CRIT_Z (BNP/E3, 5-19r; Coelho 317; Sobral Cunha 283; Zenith 93; Pizarro 145).

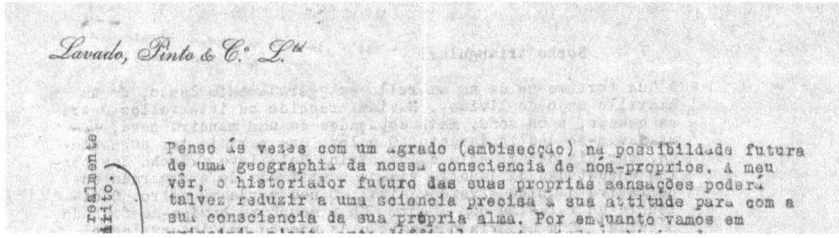

Figure 4.18 Facsimile of autograph typescript BNP/E3, 8-11v-12r (detail). © National Library of Portugal. Reproduced with permission.

are explored through the weavings of perception, memory, and imagination that make the emergence of consciousness possible. The *Book of Disquiet* teems with verbal images replete with felt, remembered, or imagined sensations, and with recursive structures that intensify these processes of consciousness, as if language and writing serve as an extended bodily and neurological organ for experiencing self-consciousness (Figure 4.18).

> I sometimes enjoy (in split fashion) thinking about the possibility of a future geography of our self-awareness. I believe that the future historian of his own sensations may be able to make a precise science out of the attitude he takes towards his self-awareness.
>
> (Text 76[12])

This understanding of the *Book of Disquiet* as an extended experiment with the self writing the self—as both record and invention of subjectivity, and as record and invention of consciousness—is one of the reasons for the *LdoD Archive*'s poetic program for opening up Pessoa's acts of writing to further reflexive processes. By taking the role of writers, readers are able to intervene in the actual textual field of the book and write their own variations based on Pessoa's pieces. Reading interventions and writing interventions are placed in a feedback circuit that simulates through material transformations the processes of self-conscious writing. Using available Web 2.0 tools, supplemented by dedicated software, the virtual dimension of the *LdoD Archive* socializes the work also at the level of writing, exploring word- and language-processing tools for rewriting the book.

---

[12] Full text available at https://ldod.uc.pt/fragments/fragment/Fr416/inter/Fr416_WIT_ED_CRIT_Z (BNP/E3, 8-11v-12r; Coelho 302; Sobral Cunha 136; Zenith 76; Pizarro 58).

Disquiet Variations

The main goal of the author-function is the extension of the *Book of Disquiet* with new texts based on original fragments. The readers of the *LdoD Archive* are able to write and publish new texts and thus perform according to the author role in the system. Central to the author-function is the functionality that provides capabilities for writing and publishing the new fragments. These capabilities range from using sentences or phrases from the *Book* as a starting point for freely written texts to the possibility of modifying sentences and phrases from the *Book*, or even to permutations and text generation based on the syntactic structures and lexicon of the work. To be considered a textual extension or variation or generation, references to the sentences and sequences of words of the original fragment (which we call *seed-fragment* in the context of the author-function) must be maintained (Figure 4.19).

Tools for textual production include text editors, textual analysis tools, and text generators of different types. Cross-references between extended fragment and seed-fragment establish an intertextual layer of inscriptions that captures users' appropriations and transformations of Pessoa's text. Similarly to the reading and editing functions, the interaction design model for the *LdoD Archive* embeds the *Book of Disquiet* into the collaborative dynamics of Web 2.0 as a writing space.

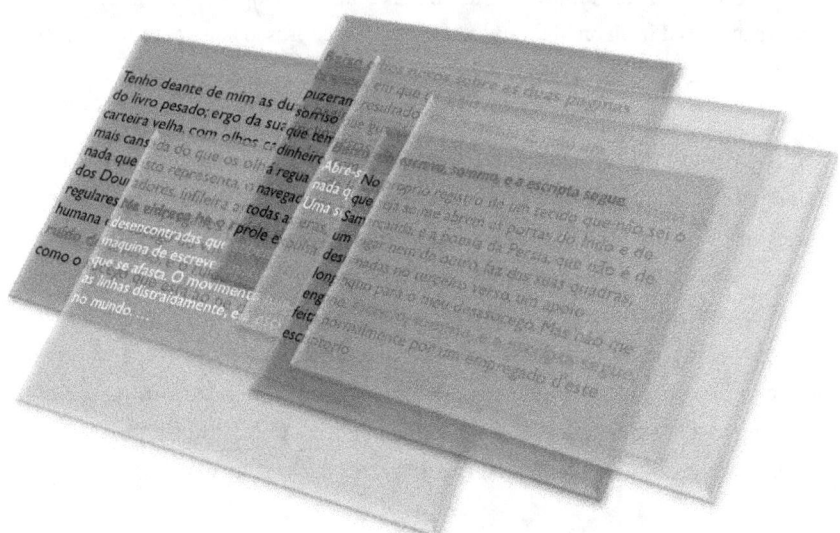

Figure 4.19 *Book of Disquiet* fragments become seed-fragments (dark gray layer) for new acts of writing that result in extended fragments (light gray layer).

References establish a network of links among Pessoa's original fragments and those produced by users of the *LdoD Archive*. As the material basis for new writing acts, seed-fragments give reader-writers an explicit awareness of the iterability of writing through the anchors and networked cross-references between sources and their extended, variational, or generated fragments. The iterative processes of rereading and rewriting become in-built elements in the participatory logic of the archive. Self-conscious writing can be experienced as an ongoing and open process of writing the self, and as a way of experimenting with the consciousness of writing acts as tools for extending the field of what can be imagined through the play of inscriptions. This ability to read and reread the self, writing itself into consciousness, is one of the sources of Pessoa's understanding of writing as self-creation:

> The entire life of the human soul is mere motions in the shadows. We live in a twilight of consciousness, never in accord with whom we are or think we are. Everyone harbours some kind of vanity, and there's an error whose degree we can't determine. We're something that goes on during the show's intermission; sometimes, through certain doors, we catch a glimpse of what may be no more than scenery. The world is one big confusion, like voices in the night.
>
> I've just reread these pages on which I write with a lucidity that endures only in them, and I ask myself: What is this, and what good is it? Who am I when I feel? What in me dies when I am?
>
> Like someone on a hill who tries to make out the people in the valley, I look down at myself from on high, and I'm a hazy and confused landscape, along with everything else.
>
> (Text 63[13])

In this passage, the process of existing in the world is deeply tainted by the ungraspable nature of self-awareness and by the impossibility of experiencing both world and self outside the fragmentary glimpses that constitute one's sense of self. As the fleeting nature of self is captured through script acts, self-awareness becomes a process of reading the writing self, as if the self were a writing-reading-writing process, conceived for exploring self-awareness through the recursive and reflexive structure of language. Pessoa is imagining the scene of writing as a landscape for observing one's process of self-production. Reading the self writing could be described as one particular instance of "lecto-escritura,"

---

[13] Full text available at https://ldod.uc.pt/fragments/fragment/Fr205/inter/Fr205_WIT_ED_CRIT_Z (BNP/E3, 3-54r-55r; Coelho 427; Sobral Cunha 501; Zenith 63; Pizarro 239).

i.e., the integrated operation of reading and writing acts (Rodríguez de la Flor and Escandell Montiel 2014: 22). In this case, however, the dynamic reciprocity of reading and writing is fed with one's own writing as the tangible presence of an evanescent and polymorphic sense of self.

Any fragment could provide a source for a new act of writing. Take, for example, the following text:

> I was already feeling uneasy. Without warning the silence had stopped breathing.
> Suddenly, the light of all hells cracked like steel. I crouched like an animal against the top of the desk, my hands lying flat like useless paws. A soulless light had swept through all nooks and souls, and the sound of a nearby mountain tumbled down from on high, rending the hard veil of the abyss with a boom. My heart stopped. My throat gulped. My consciousness saw only a blot of ink on a sheet of paper.
>
> (Text 355[14])

Fear caused by thunder and lightning is expressed through powerful images of the thunderstorm and its physiological effects on the body. The self is suddenly turned into a frightened animal hanging on to his desk, the signs of writing morphed into a "blot of ink on a sheet of paper," and consciousness is reduced to a mere visual perception of an object. Acts of writing would place specific anchors on these sentences or parts of them while exploring—through extension, variation, and generation—this visceral fear of thunder on the self and on the scene of writing.

The extension of fragments should be done in the context of a virtual edition in which Pessoa's textual witnesses are socialized at the level of writing processes by the users of the archive. After the extension, the extended fragment becomes part of a virtual writing edition and it will eventually become part of other virtual writing editions through the functionality provided by the book-function. The programming of the author-function in the virtual model assumes that writing can be experienced in its internal processes as a device for the production of consciousness and subjectivity. The technical implementation of this concept implies socializing the writing of the *Book of Disquiet*, and expanding the ludic component contained in our model for a digital virtualization according to a simulation rationale.

---

[14] Full text available at https://ldod.uc.pt/fragments/fragment/Fr211/inter/Fr211_WIT_ED_CRIT_Z (BNP/E3, 3-63r; Coelho 60; Sobral Cunha 481; Zenith 355; Pizarro 413).

The set of functionalities for extending fragments include: (1) copying a fragment for expansion and modification—by removing or replacing or adding one or more sentences and/or words; and (2) creating a new fragment and selecting a set of seed-fragments—by copying sentences and/or words from seed-fragments and by associating sentences and/or words of the extended-fragment to the seed-fragments. The two sets of functionalities described above may be used in conjunction. Note that the archive only enables the creation of extensions of fragments from the *Book of Disquiet*, and does not support extensions of already extended fragments, that is, any new fragment must reference at least one word or phrase existing in any of the fragments of the *Book*. The writing play is based on the principle that each word, phrase, sentence, or text from the *Book of Disquiet* can become the wormhole for another universe of verbal invention. Each sentence can be turned into a portal for an entirely new verbal landscape, a notational trigger for the inner workings of script acts.

References establish the link between seed-fragment and extended-fragment, and they are user-added markers of intertextual relations between fragments written by Pessoa and fragments written by readers of his fragments (Figure 4.19). The level of granularity of the cross-reference between seed-fragment and its user-created variation extends from single word to entire fragment. Although we anticipate that a group of words or a single sentence, containing powerful poetic images, will provide the most frequent chosen anchors in Pessoa's text, it is also worth considering the possibility of establishing the single word as the shortest reference element. The link to the specific quote site in the seed-fragment will always give readers access to the adjacent co-textual elements, although certain words invented by Pessoa in the *Book of Disquiet* may be said to contain their own poetic and imaginative echoes.

By default, any extended fragment must contain at least one reference to a textual passage from the *Book of Disquiet*. If the reference is to the entire fragment, then its title or its incipit will be the textual anchors. Writing operations can also be anchored on more than one seed-fragment. The search engine of the *LdoD Archive* and its tool for assisted creation of taxonomies will allow users to look for similar passages across the entire corpus of fragments, and select them for their writing experiments.

Since the author-function is highly exploratory and experimental, we are implementing different techniques for extending fragments, which means that the interface supporting this function is dependent on and will vary according to the technique in question. Generally speaking, there will be interfaces for selecting fragments intended for use in extensions, a text editor for the extension that retains and/or lets the user add references to the seed-fragment(s) and different types of text generators. The writing of the extension in the text editor is contextualized by the selected fragments, and this text editor must support ways to access those fragments and choose parts of them. The interface will also provide access to a kit of textual tools used in electronic literature, including text generation and hypertext software.

The virtual writing functions must satisfy the following conditions: (1) the possibility of selecting sources, such as selecting between transcriptions according to a particular edition contained in the archive; (2) the possibility of defining seed elements at different levels of granularity, from single word to phrase to sentence to entire fragment; (3) the possibility of defining various degrees of human-machine collaboration, from blog-like pieces of human-authored text to entirely computer-authored permutation and generation, including multimodal intermedia variations; (4) the possibility of defining anchors and links—between seed-fragment(s) and extended fragment, and also among extended fragments; (5) the possibility of defining order-specific numbering that sequences extended fragments; adopting the predefined ordering of the seed-fragments in specific editions; variable order dependent on the internal links that cross-reference extended fragments; variable order dependent on internal links that cross-reference extended and seed-fragments; and also a randomized order; (6) the possibility of defining heteronym attribution by selecting between the two original heteronyms (Vicente Guedes and Bernardo Soares) or by creating a new heteronym. Experiments include using the vocabulary and syntactic templates of other heteronyms by Pessoa, according to programmed permutations or natural language processing based on machine learning techniques.[15]

Actual writing operations in the *LdoD Archive* should be able to select from the following pool of tools according to each user's specific intentions: (1) a text editor, similar to those used in blogs; (2) a text generator, with programmed structures and behaviors that allow for user-defined parameters for combination, permutation, and generation, for instance, of algorithmic textual

---

[15] See, for example, the project "Classificador de poemas do Fernando Pessoa de acordo com os seus heterónimos" ("Classifier of poems by Fernando Pessoa according to his heteronyms") (2020) by the Turing Group (Fernando Matsumoto, Iago Nunes, Igor Câmara, Julia Pocciotti, and Lucas Sepeda), at the University of São Paulo. For this experiment, they have used texts by the following heteronyms: Bernardo Soares, Alberto Caeiro, Ricardo Reis, and Álvaro de Campos. https://github.com/GrupoTuringCodes/fernando-pessoa.

transformations, according to Oulipian[16] procedures; (3) a hypertextual tool that will facilitate the integrated development of branching structures; and (4) tools for textual analysis that enable readers to find, sort, and extract data from the *Book of Disquiet* according to specific modes of analysis, such as lexicometry, stylometry, topic modeling, textual concordances, among others. Verbal and literary knowledge produced by such textual analyses can, in turn, be used as an aid to writing with a text editor or with a text generator. A further possibility would be (5) the use of image editors (either independently or as a series of functions integrated into the text editors), for enabling users to make collages or other types of manipulations based on the authorial digital facsimiles or other images. Additional possibilities will contemplate (6) sound editors for recorded or generated voices and sounds.

The use of electronic literature tools within the writing component of the Archive will follow different strategies for textual generation. Nick Montfort's ppg256 (Perl poetry generator in 256 characters), a small text generator, applies a writing-under-constraint practice to the act of programming by setting Perl language and 256 characters of code as the constraints for the generator. Montfort specifically uses part of the code to produce graphic markers of poetic texts (such as titles and blank lines to mark stanza-breaks) in order to activate certain reading expectations about poetry, although the way the generator produces combinations of letters or combinations of words could be more or less close to dictionary words and grammatical structures (Montfort 2012). Other writers have approached text generation with other types of constraints and rules. Jean-Pierre Balpe (2013), for instance, defines knowledge representations and explicit rules of natural language grammars for the dictionarized items in ways that will guarantee grammatical and lexical cohesion.[17] The *Poemário* textual motor (Torres and Ferreira 2009–18) uses a predefined textual matrix

---

[16] Reference to writing under constraint as practiced by Oulipo (*Ouvroir de Littérature Potentielle*), a literary group founded in Paris in 1960. Historical documentation and current activities of Oulipo can be found in the official website: https://www.oulipo.net. For a glossary of Oulipian formal procedures, see https://oulipo.net/fr/contraintes. The glossary lists 146 different procedures, some of which have been appropriated from the literary tradition, and many others were invented by members of the group.

[17] Jean-Pierre Balpe calls this explicit representation a "graph of knowledge" ("*graph de connaissance*") ("Modèles en génération automatique de texts"). The output of his textual generator results from an open and recursive generation of texts, in which the programmer is able to define syntactic structures, grammar rules associated with each dictionary entry, and also graphs of knowledge that connect items according to particular semantic and lexical fields. Balpe distinguishes his open-ended textual generation from other combinatoric closed systems of permutation.

(phrase, sentence, poem), often taken from the corpus of another writer's work, and programs lexical permutations based on lists of words that result in grammatical structures. Since these lexical lists are, generally, extracted from a corpus of texts by the same author, the resulting texts can be remarkably similar to the authorial archive of existing texts, exploring the semantic productivity of certain assemblages of syntactic templates and lexicon (Portela 2012). Daniel Howe's software toolkit for generative literature offers further options for natural language experiments (Howe 2020). In particular, it provides users with the ability to work natively in the web-browser using the Processing platform (https://processing.org/).

In the case of Pessoa, textual generation could be fed, for instance, with lexical items either from the *Book of Disquiet* itself, or from the vocabularies of his major heteronyms. This would show us how heteronymic identity is a function of particular language uses and their corresponding affective states of mind, structures of feeling, and patterns of thought. Given the richness, diversity, and originality of thoughts and uses of language in the *Book of Disquiet*, there are thousands of sentences that could be harvested as seeds for new imaginings and further acts of writing of different kinds. Thus the author-function in the archive will take place in a spectrum of writing practices that includes both human-authored and machine-assisted textual production. The processes of writing represented through the genetic encoding of the Pessoa's writing acts would be cracked open for new reading-writing feedbacks.

Machines of Disquiet

The work *Machines of Disquiet*, by Luís Lucas Pereira, was designed as an ongoing electronic literature experiment based on the *Book of Disquiet* (Pereira 2017; Pereira et al. 2018).[18] Its goal is to expand the virtual writing dimension

---

[18] Earlier versions of the *Machines of Disquiet* were presented at the following exhibitions: "Textual Machines" (April 17–18, 2015, Willson Center Digital Humanities Lab, University of Georgia, Athens, USA); "Language and the Interface" (May 14–15, 2015, School of Arts and Humanities, University of Coimbra, Portugal); and "P2P: Polish-Portuguese e-lit" (August 6–8, 2015, Gallery 3.14, Bergen, Norway). A new iteration with twelve different machines was shown during the "Criatek: Criatividade Digital e Tecnologia" (Aveiro, Teatro Aveirense, May 30–June 2, 2018). An extended version (composed of twenty machines) was displayed in the ELO 2018 "Attention à la marche! / Mind the Gap!" exhibition (Gallerie du Centre de Design, Université du Québec à Montréal, August 13–17, 2018). The current version is available at http://mofd.dei.uc.pt. In the future it will be integrated within the *LdoD Archive*'s "Writing" interface.

of the *LdoD Archive* through the use of computational tools for writing in the multimedia interactive space of the web. As an expression of the simulation rationale of the Archive, *Machines of Disquiet* opens up the possibility of experiencing Fernando Pessoa's text as electronic literature. At once electronic writing and gameplay experiment, the various machines offer us textual forms and scripted interactions that are dependent on the distributed materiality of digital media. Textual applications for mobile devices (iOS and Android) and web, they can be described as literary works based on computer-assisted writing.

The series *Machines of Disquiet* is an iteration of the author-function in the *LdoD Archive*. The work uses texts from the *Book of Disquiet* as its textual database and has been designed as an exploration of electronic techniques for rewriting Pessoa's work. Permutations, combinations, substitutions, juxtapositions, and superpositions occur at different textual scales, including group of sentences, sentence, phrase, word, letter, and letter fragment. As a bilingual work, it extends the author-function to translation acts (cf. Chapter 1, above).[19] Each machine operates as a mediating tool that gives readers-players different possibilities of instantiating textual forms recreated from the *Book of Disquiet*. *Machines of Disquiet* can be seen as a catalog of specific rhetorical interaction strategies for generating symbolic effects through programmed processes. These explore relations between language and image, language and sound, language and animation, and language and gesture. Each of the twenty machines explores a distinct textual form generated through a specific electronic trope, i.e., a programmed operation that results in the coupling of instruction with textual configuration, involving particular ways of interacting with the textual machine. These JavaScript-based tropes can be described in terms of their intermedia and interactive features, i.e., according to particular combinations of textual output and interaction modalities.

---

[19] Translation is a specific form of writing. Given the translation of the *Book of Disquiet* into many languages, they could also be integrated in the *LdoD Archive* as expressions of the author-function. The representation layer would be fed with particular translations (including multiple versions in the same language), while the simulation layers would be open to the addition of new translations.

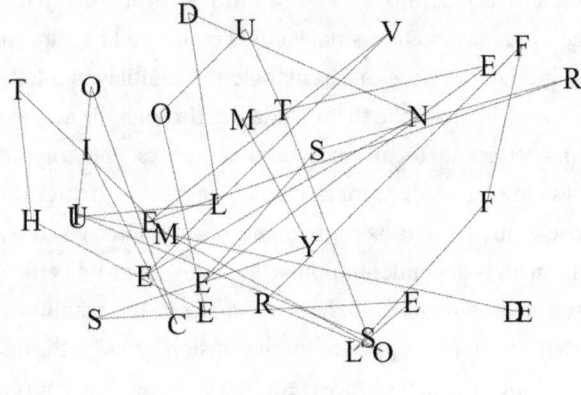

Figure 4.20 *Machines of Disquiet*, no. 1 (TP01): text as textual puzzle.

```
dragEvent = {};
   dragT1 = "";

   // drag interaction
   $(".drag").draggable({
     start: function() {
         dragEvent = {};
         dragEvent.tp = "d";
         dragEvent.index = $(this).index();
         dragEvent.x1 = $(this).position().left;
         dragEvent.y1 = $(this).position().top;
         dragEvent.t = $(this).text();
         dragT1 = Date.now()
         dragEvent.t1 = dragT1;
         //console.log("start",$(this).index(),$(this).text(),$(this).position());
},
stop: function() {
         //console.log("stop",$(this).attr("id"),$(this).text(),$(this).position());
         dragEvent.x2 = $(this).position().left;
         dragEvent.y2 = $(this).position().top;
         dragEvent.t2 = Date.now() - dragT1;
         dragEvent.i = getIntersections(points);
         pcl.addIntEvent(dragEvent);

         //console.log(getIntersections(points));
},
```

In *Machines of Disquiet*, no. 1 (TP01), short excerpts of variable lengths are turned into an entangled web of single letters connected by superimposed lines (Figure 4.20). Interactors have to disentangle the multilayered letters and place them along a line string to make them readable. Through the action of separating and connecting letters to form words and sentences, the complexities of the reading process are primed: readers cannot engage with meaning until they recognize those written letters as constituents of words in a given language. Such recognition, in turn, is dependent upon articulating letter units through spacing. Written form and linguistic form have to coalesce for reading to take place. Ordering the letters solves the puzzle, but the tension between the line connecting all the letters and the imaginary spaces required to distinguish morphological and syntactic structure remains in place. Reading requires the simultaneous cognitive parsing and matching of low-level graphic units and high-level semantic units.

As shown by the JavaScript code for this "drag interaction" function (above), the textual experience provided by this rewriting of the chosen excerpts from the *Book of Disquiet* depends on the particular figure of manipulation expressed by this script. The gestural manipulation of the letters on the screen has a specific textual form in the work's source code. Readers activate the instructions contained in the performative text of the source code: each dragging motion results in particular position of both letters and lines on the x–y coordinates of the screen. The actual configuration of each moment in the process of solving the puzzle, as well as the final constellation resulting from this gestural mode of reading, will be specific to each interaction, to each reader, and to each device and operating system.

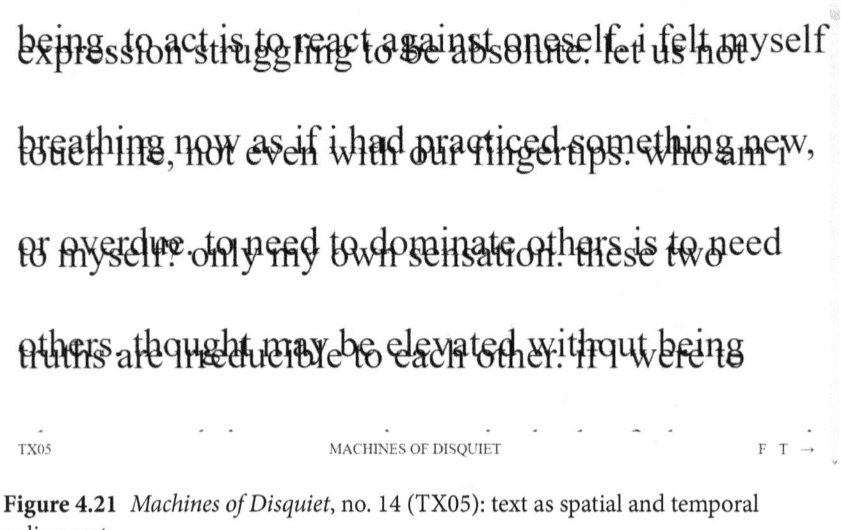

being to act is to react against oneself. i felt myself
expression struggling to be absolute. let us not
breathing now as if i had practiced something new.
touching, not even with our fingertips. who am i,
or overdue. to need to dominate others is to need
to myself? only my own sensation. these two
others. thought may be elevated without being
truths are irreducible to each other. if i were to

TX05　　　　　　　　MACHINES OF DISQUIET　　　　　　　　F T →

Figure 4.21 *Machines of Disquiet*, no. 14 (TX05): text as spatial and temporal palimpsest.

```
if (scroll < last_scroll_val) {
   //up
   dir = -vel;
} else {
   //down
   dir = vel;
}
$(".sections-class-notscroll").css("margin-top", parseFloat(margtop) + dir);
last_scroll_val = scroll;

 if (window.innerWidth < 768) {
    var adjust = 32;
 } else if (window.innerWidth ≥ 768 && window.innerWidth < 992) {
    var adjust = 25;
 } else {
    var adjust = 50;
 }
```

In *Machines of Disquiet*, no. 14 (TX05), there are two interspersed excerpts from the *Book of Disquiet*, each of which moves in opposite directions, and thus are superimposed on each other as we scroll down or up in our act of reading (Figure 4.21). Interactors have to carefully control the scroll so that they avoid superposition, while, at the same time, they have to focus on reading only alternate lines. Textual continuity depends on skipping one line in every two lines. When the lines of the two layers are entirely separate, and the reading proceeds continuously, then readers will be mixing lines from different texts and creating their reading-specific remix of both textual fragments. This particular machine seems to be based on scrambling the spatial and temporal dimensions of reading. While one needs to scroll to be able to submit the text to the linearity and temporality of reading, this sometimes results in the palimpsestic superposition of lines from two different texts, making them difficult to read. On the other hand, because successive lines come from distinct excerpts, when reading continuously readers will be mixing two lines of writing as if the palimpsest was taking place along the temporal rather than the spatial axis (in their minds instead of in front of their eyes). These two reading frustrations can only be overcome when readers are able to read alternating lines. But because the text exceeds the screen area you cannot do it without scrolling, which will then result in textual scrambling.

This machine suggests textual interference among two excerpts as both alien and constitutive of the reading process. Through the action of separating and connecting lines as components of a larger discursive unit—one that moves beyond the isolated phrase or brief sentence to the horizon of a larger descriptive or narrative or reflexive unit—this rewriting shows the intertextual presence of one text in another. As expressed by the JavaScript code for the "scroll" function (above), the textual experience depends on the particular relation between the parameters determining the orientation and velocity of scrolling for each text. Again the act of reading is forced to engage with the source code as an element that rewrites Pessoa's source text through another figure of manipulation: the simultaneous presence of two texts that become mixable through an interactive script.

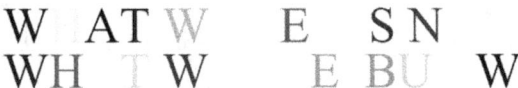

TP05   MACHINES OF DISQUIET   F T →

Figure 4.22 *Machines of Disquiet*, no. 5 (TP05): text as fade in and fade out.

```
function init() {
    $("#tx06 h1").html("");
    tr1 = random(0, text[lang].length - 1);
    tr2 = random(0, text[lang].length - 1);

    var str = text[lang][tr1].replace("[^\\p{L}\\p{N}]+", "") + " " +
    text[lang][tr2].replace("[^\\p{L}\\p{N}]+", "");
    str.replace(";", "");

    var a = str.toLowerCase().split(" ");

    for (i = 0; i < a.length; i++) {
        $("#tx06 h1").append("<span class=\"word\">" + a[i] + "</span>");
    }
```

```
$(".word").each(function(index, element) {
   o = random(1, 100) < 50 ? 0: 1;
   $(element).delay(random(1, 2000)).animate({duration: random(1, 2000),
   opacity: o});
});
         // word interaction
```

In *Machines of Disquiet*, no. 5 (TP05), letters and words from sentences from the *Book of Disquiet* appear on the screen as you touch over or mouse over them, but letters and words of the text will disappear before readers have had time to reveal the entire sentence (Figure 4.22). Interactors can only engage with scattered letters and words that belong to a longer sentence whose totality (although suggested) remains elusive. Letters are timed to fade in and fade out into the white background at varying speeds. Because this is happening in different areas of the screen at the same time, readers are forced to change their focus to slightly different areas of the screen, trying to make sense of the text before it vanishes and is replaced by the same or by another textual fragment that goes through the same procedure. In this instance, the ability to connect letters and words and form sentences is challenged by the random animation of words in and out of visibility. Once readers stop touching or mousing over the screen all letters disappear. The reading attempt can only ever be partly successful.

Textual sequence depends on connecting letters and words into larger scale units, such as sentences and groups of sentences. The process is frustrated by timing the appearance and disappearance on the screen before they coalesce into the larger unit. Excerpts from the *Book of Disquiet* are rewritten by this kinetic trope in which the temporality of the machine clashes with the temporality of reading, and in which the text cannot be seen in its entirety. The result is a fragmented experience of textual form and meaning, one that begins at the very level of perception. The readers' ability to connect letters and words into sentences and make meaning is prevented by this fragmentation through animation. Expressed in the "word interaction" source code (above) as a specific instruction for dissolving the contrast between word and background, this kinetic trope rewrites the text according to its aesthetic of frustrating perception. This partial apprehension of an elusive totality is a powerful evocation of the phenomenology of the fragmentary textual event as material fact and subjective experience.

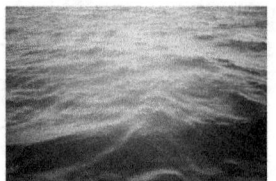

To die is to be completely other.

IM01   MACHINES OF DISQUIET   F T →

Figure 4.23 *Machines of Disquiet*, no. 20 (IM01): text as random image descriptor.

```
function init() {
    txt_num_prev = random(1, text[lang].length);
    img_num_prev = random(1, 45);

    $("img").attr("src", "../img/photos/" + img_num_prev + ".jpg");

    $("p").html(text[lang][txt_num_prev]);

    initData = {};
    initData.tid = txt_num_prev;
    initData.iid = img_num_prev;

    pcl.logData("INIT", initData);
}
init();

$("img").click(function() {
    $(".image").animate({
        opacity: 0
    }, 500, "linear");

    do {
        img_num = random(1, 45);
    } while (img_num == img_num_prev);
```

Machines of Disquiet, no. 20 (IM01) works on the basis of relations between text and image (Figure 4.23). A series of black-and-white photographs are randomly juxtaposed to a series sentences from the *Book of Disquiet*. Every time readers click on the image, a new image will be shown; every time readers click on the sentence, a new sentence will appear. Co-presence of image and text result in resignification by juxtaposition: the image can be seen through the text, and the text can be read through the image. The process through which one becomes the interpretant of the other is yet another example of machine-assisted rewriting of the work. Given the parameters for the "click function" in the source code (above), such as the database of forty-five images that can permutate randomly, exchanges between seeing and reading result in a significantly high factorial number of occurrences. Each text-image association will generate new layers of possible meanings, rewriting Pessoa's text according to principles of multimodal fragmentation and collage.

Machines of Disquiet are a series of experiments about the manipulation of media materialities and textual forms that explore the free play of signifiers. They use the *Book of Disquiet* as a modular textual database for a series of applications that engage digital modalities (text, image, sound, animation) and interactions through programmed permutations at different scales (from letter to word to sentence). When considered as a game experiment, the *Machines of Disquiet* allow us to define contexts for participation that model gameplay as a range of interactions with digital objects. When considered as a textual experiment, the *Machines of Disquiet* are about the disquiet of experience and imagination, and about the possibility of purely aesthetic enjoyment and the creation of meaning. *Machines of Disquiet* instantiate the simulation rationale of the *LdoD Archive* through programmable writing. As an instance of the author-function in the *LdoD Archive*, the *Machines of Disquiet* contribute to opening up the textual experience of the *Book of Disquiet* to acts of writing and rewriting.

5

Living on in the Web

This chapter describes the dynamics between representing and simulating the book. The notion of book-function refers to the material and conceptual unity of the book as a concrete object, and to its imaginary operation as a force field brought into being through reader-function, editor-function, and author-function. Notions of digital library, networked book, textual instability, and modular variability will be discussed, while drawing attention to the classificatory boundaries inherited from earlier media technologies in networked programmable media. Container of remediated books and an item in the digital library of the internet at the same time, the *LdoD Archive* is a microcosm of the conditionality of networked electronic documents. Subject to the socialized temporality of ongoing exchanges, its openness to interaction and socialization is an attempt to capture the flexibility of the programmable medium as an element of its poetics. Its reconfigurability through interaction explores the imagination of the book, i.e., the process through which we produce and organize a set of inscriptions towards some kind of imaginary unity.

Digital Libraries and Networked Books

The tension between their earlier media identity and their new identity as digital objects is apparent in the "Documents" interface of the *LdoD Archive* (Figure 5.1). This interface takes readers to a list of facsimile representations of the autograph documents ("Witnesses") of the *Book of Disquiet* as individual entries in the catalog of the National Library of Portugal (paper manuscripts, typescripts, and printed texts), on the one hand, and to a list of the XML files ("Encoded Fragments") as modular units in the composition of the *LdoD Archive*, on the other. In our model, the relation between potentiality and actuality—expressed in the concept of book-function—depends on opening up the textual fragmentation of witnesses to the algorithmic fragmentation of processing. The bit-mapped visual

Figure 5.1 Graphic representation of the documents interface.

emulation of the document is turned into a highly flexible machine-readable text in order to escalate the critical operations made possible by digital materiality. What happens to documents, metadata categories, and notions of library under these conditions of technical production and reproduction?

The digital library is usually imagined from the perspective of the remediation of manuscript and printed bibliographical collections and their metadata which allows for searching, location, and retrieval of digital versions of those documents. If a significant part of the structure and functions of the present and future digital library originates in the massive transcoding of written heritage and analog media into digital formats, another equally significant part—proportionally larger as the production of digital documents increases—will result from the preservation, organization, and classification of born-digital objects. These digital objects are produced according to legacy documentary units that are similar to those inherited from previous technologies, but which are, at the same time, overdetermined by the characteristic file formats and publication protocols of the internet.

Describing itself as "a non-profit library of millions of free books, movies, software, music, websites, and more" including 424 billion archived web pages, the Internet Archive proposes another concept of digital library: that of the internet itself as a kind of universal library, fueled by the desire of coincidence between all the produced information with all the collected and archived information (Figure 5.2). This desire stems from the ubiquity of recording devices for texts, sounds, and images (including moving images) and the storage capacity of digital devices, which have exponentially increased our

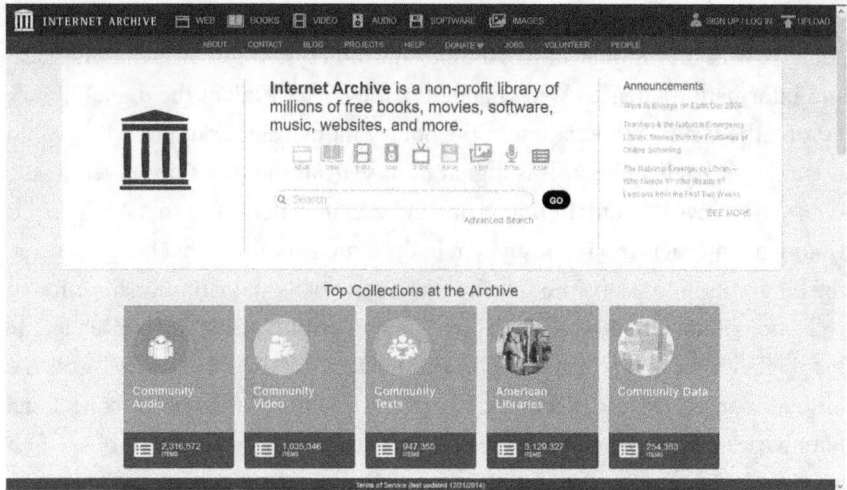

Figure 5.2 Internet Archive homepage (screenshot taken on April 23, 2020): https://archive.org/index.php.

daily practices of generating inscriptions and, therefore, documents that can be collected and classified. Given the archivability of our media-based inscriptions and the increasing ubiquity of digital devices—including their ability to turn all our actions into symbolic practices through automatic systems of numerical representation—networked cloud computing harbors the promise of a total library and a total archive, that is, an archive in which all inscription-bearing media can be collected, searched, retrieved, and reused.

In this section I briefly interrogate the notion of a digital library based on three fundamental features of digital information: the possibility of continuous reconfiguration of the data file that constitutes a digital object, with the ensuing instability at the level of both text and source code; the increased variability of document modularities and modalities since media software favors the hybridization of genres and forms by the recombination of techniques for manipulating and remixing digital objects, thus challenging the taxonomies used in metadata schemes to classify such objects; and, finally, the dynamic and collaborative nature of electronic information spaces, based on the manipulation and on the open and shared production and annotation of multiple versions of digital objects by communities of users.

Digital publishing, when conceived of as the universe of digital objects published in the electronic public space, challenges the processes of collection and classification of documents inherited from analog media, upon which the notions of library and media library were constructed. In other words: is it possible to define a digital library of digital objects whose modularities do not coincide with the modularities of the classification systems of the bibliographical and information science? What happens if we try to think of the digital library beyond the virtual remediation of the library model? For example, what would the Internet Archive be in this digital library? And the items preserved in the Internet Archive? Would the digital library be an item in the Internet Archive? Or would the Internet Archive be an item in the digital library? What happens when the library itself loses the modularity that defines it as an institutionally curated collection of documents and its content can be continuously transformed by the manipulation of different types of institutional and individual users? Is this the ultimate consequence of electronic hypertext? The dissolution of the conceptual boundaries that allow us to connect a corpus of texts and media objects to a specific classificatory practice and its authoritative institutional guardianship?

The categorial and formal hybridity of digital objects, resulting from the general process of softwarization of culture and its documentary heritage, brought about by a set of techniques shared by different computer applications, has classificatory implications regarding documentary typologies, genres, and forms (McCarty 2010; Mandell 2015). As Lev Manovich claims, a significant part of the properties of digital objects depends on the software layer that instantiates those objects:

> Strictly speaking, while it is certainly convenient to talk about properties of websites, digital images, 3D models, GIS representations, etc., it is not accurate. Different types of digital content do not have any properties by themselves. *What as users we experience as properties of media content comes from software used to create, edit, present, and access this content.*
>
> (Manovich 2013: 150; italics in the original)

This can be seen, for example, in an electronic genre such as the "weblog" (or "blog"), whose digital properties are codetermined by the features programmed in the authoring, editing, and publishing platform, many of which are common to other software applications—as happens with the text and image editing functions offered to authors or with the comment, republication, and sharing functions offered to readers. Thus, in addition to the material and stylistic properties resulting from the multimedia integration of text, image, audio, and video, the properties of the digital object "blog" depend on this layer of code that gives it the editability and manipulability specific to its form, which varies according to the technological changes of successive versions of the software.

In turn, the transfer of the notion of library to the networked electronic space implies its conceptual reconfiguration, either as a justification for recreating the structure and functions of the physical library in a given database structure, or in the sense of understanding the electronic space itself as a new type of material and technical instantiation of the library. On the other hand, the obsolescence of digital formats and protocols originates a set of epistemological dilemmas in the processes of construction of the digital library of digital objects, as for example in the case of digital literature (Namora 2013; Moulthrop and Grigar 2017) or digital files of printed books (Kirschenbaum 2020). If in the 1990s it was still possible to imagine the digital library based on the migration of the paper library into digital networks, the explosion of social media and the new affordances of Web 2.0 interaction at the beginning of the twenty-first century altered the very conceptualization of the digital library. In fact, the multiple meanings of the phrase "digital library" reflect these fast technosocial changes in the production, indexing, search, and distribution of networked information:

> The term "Digital Library" is currently used to refer to systems that are very different in scope and yield very diverse functionality. These systems range from digital object and metadata repositories, reference-linking systems, archives, and content administration systems, which have been mainly developed by industry, to complex systems that integrate advanced digital library services, which have chiefly been developed in research environments.
>
> (Candela et al. 2011: 2–3)

In this heterogeneity of systems and references one can notice the convergence of a technical redefinition and a metaphorical redefinition of the library. Thus, the reconstitution of a set of functions of document preservation and information aggregation and retrieval in the digital space may refer either to a closed network of digital objects subject to various types of institutional validation or to an open and dispersed network of digital objects, independent of institutional validation. This open network distribution of different collections of information objects potentially generates a universal repository of knowledge that does not coincide with the institutional modes of validation and cataloging, whether private or public. Thus the digital library can also be conceived as an emergent assemblage of a particular mode of technical and social intervention on this open space of publication and communication.

At the same time, the accelerated digitization of cultural heritage and cultural production leads to the reinvention of the digital library models themselves, in a strict sense, which move from a content-centric system focused on organization and structured access to data collections to a system centered on the user and on the experiences of interaction with these collections:

> Its main role has shifted from static storage and retrieval of information to facilitation of communication, collaboration and other forms of interaction among scientists, researchers or the general public on themes of relevance to the information stored in the Digital Library. Finally, it has moved from handling mostly centrally located text to combining distributed multimedia document collections, sensor data, mobile information and pervasive computing services.
> (Candela et al. 2011: 4)

The transformation of the electronic space into a space of manipulation and collaboration would therefore imply the transition from a model focused on the cataloging of content to a model centered on the flexibility of interactions, which incorporates the very dynamism of Web 2.0 in the functionalities of search, retrieval, and socialization of information. Digital searchability and relationality change the paradigm of the digital library as much as they change the paradigm of the digital museum by reconfiguring the network of possible relations among art objects and the network of possible engagements with them (Drucker 2013b). The Google Arts and Culture project has produced an equivalent ambiguity in the concept of digital museum: while it is possible to claim that the digital museum is the digitization of the collection of a given institution, the variable aggregation of many sets of digital objects from multiple institutions establishes a new conceptual and experiential museum.

One of the results of a research project on digital library models points precisely to the redefinition of the digital library as an information space inhabited by a community of users who cooperate and interact in this space.[1] The visualization of information in its context of use and the representation of the users themselves in this cooperative space materialize this model of library informed by the principles of computer-assisted cooperation. In the end, it is a matter of importing to the digital library model those interactions characteristic of the internet in its current dynamic forms. The integrated representation of the multiple perspectives inherent to this model led the cited authors to propose a general theory of digital library composed of

---

[1] Developed between 2008 and 2010 by the DL-org Consortium (National Research Council of Italy, University of Athens, and University of Glasgow) and funded by the European Union, the Digital Library Interoperability, Best Practices and Modeling Foundations project resulted in a set of documents that conceptualize this digital library model (Candela et al. 2011).

three levels—Digital Library, Digital Library System, and Digital Library Management System—defined as follows:

Digital Library (DL)
A potentially virtual organisation, which comprehensively collects, manages and preserves for the long term rich digital content, offering its targeted user communities specialised functionality on that content, of defined quality and according to comprehensive codified policies.

Digital Library System (DLS)
A deployed software system underpinned by a possibly distributed architecture providing all the facilities required by a specific Digital Library. Users interact with a Digital Library through the corresponding Digital Library System.

Digital Library Management System (DLMS)
A generic software system which provides the appropriate software infrastructure both to produce and administer a Digital Library System incorporating the suite of facilities considered fundamental for Digital Libraries and to integrate additional software offering more refined, specialised or advanced facilities.

(Candela et al. 2011: 5-6)

What is interesting in this definition, if we try to think of the relationship between a digital literary archive such as the *LdoD Archive* and the web itself as a collaborative space, is the fact that the digital library continues to be represented as an act of collection, management, and preservation of digital objects, dependent on an explicit set of quality standards and functionalities, even if the organizational entity responsible for the selection policy is potentially virtual. In addition, the tripartite model of the relationship between digital library management software systems and digital library software systems, on the one hand, and digital objects, on the other hand, establishes relationships similar to those of any other digital information system. The specificity of the digital library would not be so much in its software architecture and its information system, but in the specifications and contents of the digital objects themselves and in the functionalities defined for their user communities.

This tripartite formalization can be tested in current digital library models, which show variable configurations of collection policy and production of digital objects, interaction features with the objects of their collections, and relationship between institutional space and virtual space. The possibilities of aggregating digital objects—obtained by digitizing multiple collections from various institutions (libraries, archives, and museums)—and the integrated access to these objects through the same web interface are derived from the networked nature of digital information, development of open protocols for interoperability, and a policy of digitization and public access to archived heritage. Portals such as the National Digital Library of Portugal, Europeana, and the Digital Public Library of America, for example, represent specific implementations of these principles (Figures 5.3, 5.4, and 5.5).

Digitization and networked distribution enable the aggregation of digital versions of objects beyond the geographical and institutional boundaries of the originals, exponentiating the effects of decontextualization, recontextualization, and creative appropriation fostered by technical reproducibility. Recirculation, manipulation, and recombination of digital objects are affordances of the medium, either through functionalities offered by the platforms—such as social network sharing or making and annotating personal collections—or through import for analysis and reuse by means of specific data analytic tools or creative software applications. However, the fact that the digital library is predominantly made up of digital representations of non-digital objects, validated by the institutional systems that collected and cataloged them, means that it remains attached to the metaphor of the digital library dependent on institutional

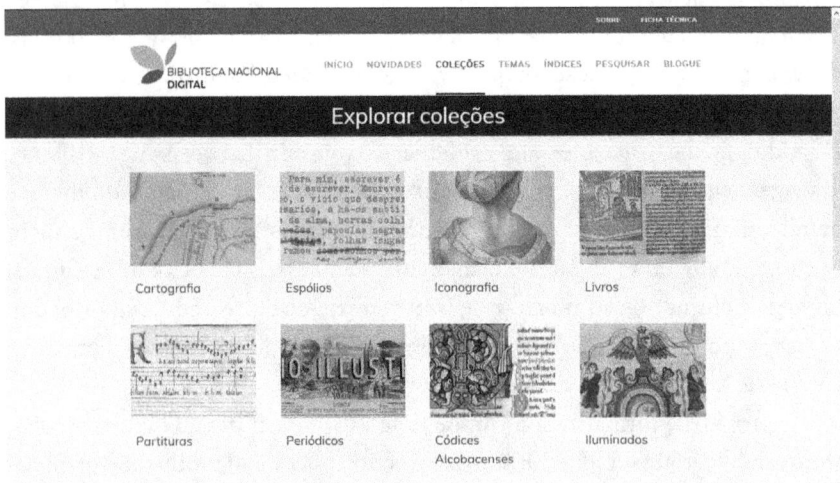

Figure 5.3 "Collections" homepage of the National Digital Library of Portugal (screen capture, April 23, 2020): https://bndigital.bnportugal.gov.pt/explorarcolecoes/.

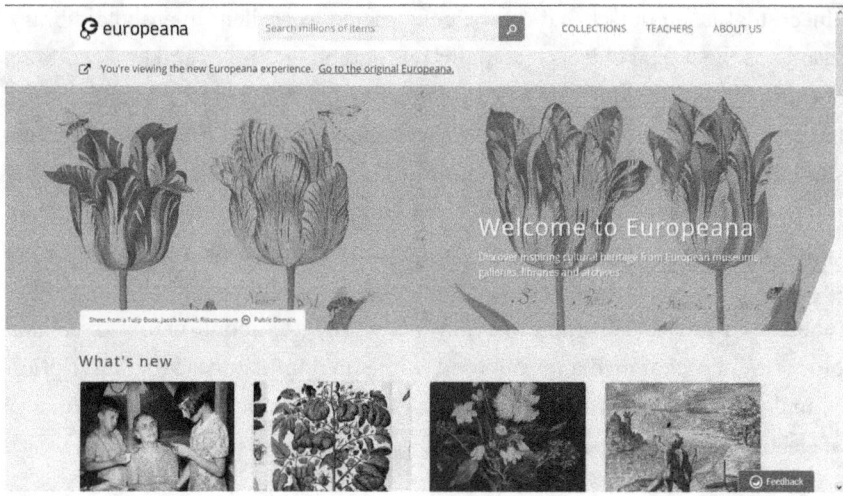

Figure 5.4 Europeana homepage (screen capture, April 23, 2020): https://www.europeana.eu/.

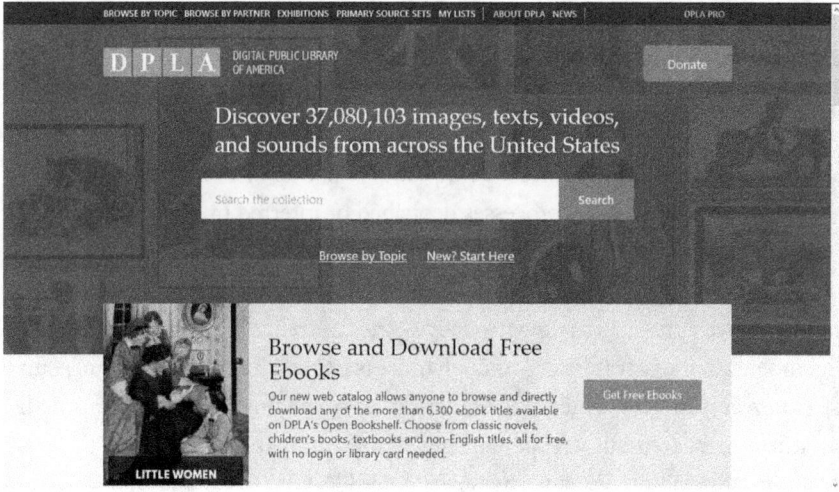

Figure 5.5 Digital Public Library of America homepage (screen capture, April 23, 2020): https://dp.la/.

boundaries, as if the identity of digital objects as library-catalogable items could only derive from this techno-institutional inscription.

It is in this interplay between electronically validated information spaces and electronic spaces as environments of open publication and collaboration that the example of the *LdoD Archive* can be illuminating in its condition of catalogable object, that is, an object that can be constructed as an item in a digital library. Insofar as the digital objects it contains (autograph facsimiles and book editions of those facsimiles) are themselves catalog objects in the library and insofar as the archive offers a set of textual collaboration and textual production features similar to those that define the communicative practices of the web, the *LdoD Archive* embodies the tension between modularity and documentary stability—which enable the stabilization of the collection, reference, and classification systems of the library—and the networked and documentary instability inherent in fast socialization and the increasingly temporal nature of textual processes in digital media (as opposed to the predominantly spatial inscription of analog media), a feature that Drucker (2014a) describes as the conditionality of electronic documents.

Textual Instability and Modular Variability

What would be the possible consequences for our knowledge of history if the contents of the books could be continuously altered? This question is interesting from the point of view of a theory of historical knowledge: in a certain sense, historical knowledge depends on the stability of documents. On the other hand, knowledge consists of the methodological production of new relations between the facts and the historical processes described or inferred from the material and documentary evidences. That is, even if the documents maintain their textual stability, the production of historical knowledge implies that we rewrite, with new tentative approaches and perspectives, the theoretical narratives in which the documents of the past appear. Although those texts remain closed in their narrative structure and in their material form, processes of reading and acts of knowledge production are constantly reopening and reconnecting them in new ways.

From this point of view, hypertext would only make the semiotic and hermeneutic process of writing and reading materially visible as a social and cognitive practice inscribed in the historical temporality that it attempts to describe. The alleged volatility of electronic documentary production would ultimately result from a conception of library and archive dependent on the reification of written inscriptions and their material surfaces outside the temporality that produced them. This archaeological fetishization of the material document would ignore the performative dimension of the symbolic acts of which the documents can only contain traces. Overabundance of inscription technologies affects the notions of archiving and collecting. By providing written discourse with certain features of spoken discourse, information technologies redefine documentability, endowing it with a kind of continuous reconfigurability, arising from the possibility of fast multiplication of versions and stages of publication. What would librarians and archivists do in this context: select and sort certain versions of these reconfigured documents? Catalog the self-documented variations in the files themselves?

How does digital mediation transform the modularity of documents, which have been institutionally stabilized as a set of textual forms that were progressively reinforced by the classificatory systems of the library and the archive? Are there genres and forms that are intrinsically digital? Or just genres and forms resulting from the adaptation and transposition of genres and forms from other media? Does remediation create new genres or is it limited to modifying previous genres? Is the website a characteristic genre of the new medium, very much like the newspaper, for example, became characteristic of the printing press? Or is it just an organizational structure that can accommodate many different genres and forms, as happens with the codex? If so, are there properties of hypertext programs and web pages that have poetic consequences? If certain properties of texts are intrinsic to genres and forms, this would mean that even when reproduced in the form of a hypertext there would be a unit of writing and reading that would define and circumscribe them according to discursive and semantic constrains. In this case, even if they could be an element of a hypertextual network and specific elements of digital transmission were added to them, they would still have the completeness, fixity, and functionality of a typographic genre.

On the one hand, hypertext and hypermedia would be more of an archive of texts and media creations that would retain their fundamental properties, though reconfigured differently from that of a library, or an anthology, or a newspaper. We may ask what do linkability and hypertextual infinity mean? Considered as a network of texts (i.e., a hypertext of hypertexts, or an archive of archives), infinity seems to characterize the online reading environment, since it is always possible to add new links that re-associate documents or add new documents. However, texts can also be published respecting the modularities characteristic of print reproduction (genre, edition, graphic design, etc.). Perhaps this is why Ted Nelson (Nelson et al. 2007) argues that the hypertext we have remains a mere imitation of paper, bound to materialize its internal and external electronic connections as metaphors of bibliographic connections.

The PDF format, for example, is generally used for the purpose of matching the unit file with a printed genre unit, such as article, chapter, or book. That is to say, it is still possible to recreate the characteristic discursive and semantic units of printed texts, since the principle-middle-end structure is also a property of genre and form and not just of material support. The continuity introduced by the insertion of the text into a network does not exclude the discontinuity of the perception of a whole, although it can no longer be perceived as the discrete material unit that would result from a printed volume. It must be seen instead as a discursive unit susceptible of remediations, rematerializations, reassociations, and remixes.

On the other hand, it is also evident that the properties of the medium are connected to the properties of genres, linking them to specific technologies. The development of the novel, for example, in its many modern subgenres, cannot be separated from the technology of the printing press. What degree of transformation of previous genres and forms is necessary for the digital medium to be more than a technology of reproduction and distribution, and to determine certain formal and discursive properties of texts? Is the use of devices such as animation, digital graphics, modes of interaction, and hyperlink sufficient to produce a digital genre? Besides, will not the digitality of current digital genres also be a function of specific computer applications? That is, are there textual properties that should be linked to specific software applications and not the general digital nature of processing and transmission? And would we have to talk about the Dreamweaver web page, the Flash poem, the StorySpace or Twine hyperfiction, the DSpace repository, the WordPress blog?

In this case, significant textual, graphic, and functional properties would depend on specific generations of applications and hardware, as happened with particular techniques of production and binding of medieval manuscripts or with the various innovations in printing techniques and formats. To the extent that such properties substantially modify the combinatorial and structural affordances of the elements that define a genre or form, computer programs and digital devices become part of the description of genres and forms.[2] Additionally,

---

[2] The CELL Project (launched in May 2015) developed a taxonomic structure for describing works of electronic literature. Its vocabulary contains four major categories: *publication types, procedural modalities, mechanisms,* and *formats* (cf. https://cellproject.net/taxonomies-definition). These vocabularies show how media-specific features operate as formal and aesthetic components of the experience of digital works. The CELL project (Consortium on Electronic Literature) "is an open access, non-commercial resource offering centralized access to literary databases, archives, and institutional programs in the literary arts and humanities scholarship." See Tabbi 2015.

let us consider the construction of hypertexts in the form of structured archives of texts linked to a work or an author. Will they not result in the creation of new genres, or meta-genres, characterized precisely by a certain way of connecting files and producing a new discursive web? In this case, the electronic edition in the form of a digital archive, when designing a particular meta-documentary cyberspace with an author's documentary corpus, would also be defining a specific genre or digital form.

The Dynamic Digital Archive and the Library

The editing of works for the digital medium in the form of archives in progress (some of which remain in progress for decades) is a case in which we can simultaneously observe the instability that results from the continuous reconfiguration of the data files, and the production of modularities that seem to challenge the metadata schemes inherited from bibliographic culture. In the *LdoD Archive* we recognize the presence of earlier documentary and genre modularities, that is, the facsimiles of the autograph documents (in manuscript, typescript, and print form) that are part of the collection kept in the National Library of Portugal and the printed books produced by the four major editors of the work (Coelho, Sobral Cunha, Zenith, and Pizarro). We can also see the reconfiguration of those legacy units by the modularities of the digital files that encode them as processable units in a structured database. They become a network of files that can be modified and incremented through the manipulation and intervention of interactors, who, over time, change the form and contents of digital objects contained in the dynamic layer of the archive through their annotations, re-editings, and rewritings. If, like much Web 2.0 content, the *LdoD Archive* is designed to be continually reconfigured by the collective action of its users, how can we represent its documentary identity as a digital genre?

Figure 5.6 presents the various layers and functionalities provided by the *LdoD Archive* as poetic instantiations of the ecology of the web. The static layer of the archive contains facsimiles of the autograph documents, topographic transcriptions, and also textual transcriptions corresponding to the four main editions. Transcriptions can be automatically compared to each other, searched, arranged, and manipulated according to multiple criteria. Named as "expert editions" in the context of the archive, those transcriptions are also the material

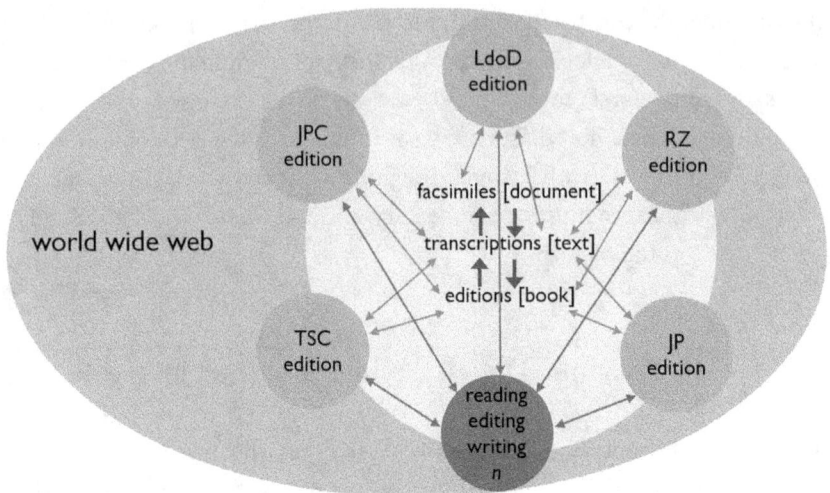

Figure 5.6 Diagram depicting the dynamic nature of the *LdoD Archive* within the ecosystem of the World Wide Web. © Manuel Portela, 2020.

basis for the dynamic layer, which encourages interactors to reread, re-edit, and rewrite—individually or collectively—the fragments contained in the database.

In turn, all of these interventions can be published and become permanent elements at the virtual level of the *LdoD Archive*, creating a collaborative and open feedback loop between the interactions and the dynamic contents of the archive. Through the subject-oriented actions of reading, editing, and writing, the book is simulated as an imaginary operator in literary performativity within the network. Reading traversals, editing selections (including annotation and classification), and writing interventions are scripted back into the dynamic content layer, becoming available for the recursive processes of creative production and analysis. The book is simulated as an emergent reading-editing-writing process involving the temporized and situated presence of the subject. The *LdoD Archive* loses its self-contained authoritative unity: its borders become porous to the hypertext and social rationale of the World Wide Web as a literary space.

One question triggered by the presence of the ecology of web within the structure and functionalities of the *LdoD Archive* is the following: what would be a digital library of digital archives like this? Would the digital library work as an instrument for the production of order in the chaotic branching out of hypertext, capable of conforming to the Dublin Core fields even those objects that fell outside the bibliographic taxonomy? Another way of asking the same question: will the library concept survive in an entirely digital information universe? What happens if, instead of thinking of the digital library as a remediation of paper and media libraries or as collections of institutionally classified and validated digital objects, we think of the digital library as the mere combination of the functions of search, location, and presentation of the information and the meta-information contained in the files themselves? That is, as a form of structured search in the documentary universe of the internet itself? Can the digital library be conceived of as the conjunction of a metadata system with a set of algorithms, supported by the electronic infrastructure that allows for data transfers? Is the library an emergent function of the relation among structured and annotated data, connectivity, findability, and usability?

The *LdoD Archive*, like similar digital archive projects of literary works, shows the reconfiguration of the documentary modularities that underlie the concepts of editing, archive, and library, as well as the relations between content and container. The flexibility of digital numerical representation allows documents to be modularized according to the specific materiality of the digital medium regardless of the modularity of the original objects. Thus, while it contains a set of editions that would correspond to printed books or to single autograph documents, the *LdoD Archive* is susceptible of constituting itself as a webliographic or bibliographic item in a digital library. As a digital representation, part of its function is to preserve and make accessible a specific authorial archive as well as the editorial configurations of a particular work over time. The archive itself, as conceptual creation and experimental technique, is subordinate to the protocols for the preservation and classification of digital information. However, by establishing itself as an open archive, capable of being transformed by their users, the *LdoD Archive* assimilates the logic of the internet in its poetic form, thus exceeding the fields of the catalog that attempts to describe it.

A result of the change in the physical scale of information objects is that they can now be represented photo-electronically on the screens and in the circuits of our digital devices and distributed through a network. One of the effects of digitization, i.e., the transformation of media objects into numerical representations, lies in the variability of their aggregations, that is, how we can define search units and manipulate the corresponding objects. The file format as a specific computational encoding has become another documentary unit for the purpose of classification, search, and preservation. A digital literary archive is, from this perspective, a documentary ecosystem where it is possible to observe the reconfiguration of the relations between analog documentary units and digital documentary units, due to the interferences between bibliographic classification categories and computational classification categories (Portela 2014). The unity between material form and discursive form that identifies a genre can now be digitally represented through different file formats, giving rise to new modularities available for crossings, mixes, and aggregations. The search algorithms characteristic of the bibliographic catalog can be extended and combined with associative and reticular possibilities of the semantic web.

It is certainly true that the collaborative digital literary archive is catalogable in the sense that its unity as an archive can be referenced as a unit, that is, through a unique identifier, on which the remaining elements depend hierarchically or associatively. However, its dynamic nature implies a changing content over time through a partial reconfiguration of the data files and the metadata that constitute it and describe it as a digital object, making it exceed the library frame according to the proliferative and socialized logic of networked programmable media. This is perhaps the point at which the digital library metaphor ceases to be operational as a cataloged meta-representation of a collection of objects in order to be redefined on the basis of the abstract specificity of the digital medium as a certain type of relationship between data structures and algorithms.

The Monograph, the Work, and the Archive

Given the situatedness of this monograph in a postdigital and cross-media ecology, what is its relation to the literary work and to the literary archive? How does it participate in the production of the *Book of Disquiet* as a readable, editable, and writable work, and in the production of the *LdoD Archive* itself as a space for simulating those comings into being of the work? What kind of interpellation is it making to its readers? In other words, how can we understand this monograph performatively, i.e., as a theoretical framework for imagining and designing the literary in the digital medium, and as a scholarly argument in book form?

One possible answer would be to say that this monograph is part of a transmedia network that includes both the dynamic remediation of the multiple versions of the *Book of Disquiet* as they evolve within this unfinished literary machine, and the *LdoD Archive* itself as a heterogenous evolving unit in the World Wide Web. As a print-based artifact, the monograph is a supplement to the web application, and their relation bears witness to our postdigital situation.

From this perspective, *Literary Simulation and the Digital Humanities*, the digital rereadings, re-editings, and rewritings of the *Book of Disquiet*, and the *LdoD Archive* constitute a transmedia network in which scholarly argument, literary practice, and interface design intersect without coinciding. Media divergence is an expression of their postdigital condition.

Another possible answer would be to say that this monograph is a self-contained textual and material instantiation of the idea and form of the book. To use the terms of its own theory, it is an expression of the constellation of reading, editing, and writing acts within the force field of the book as physical and metaphysical operator. The monograph is evidence of a particular literary practice embedded in the international scholarly system of knowledge validation. It points towards a media ecology in which books are self-sustained units of discourse in discrete material formats attributable to individual authors, and produced according to the quality control and market principles of the publishing industry.

As a postdigital book about a dynamic digital archive about a predigital book in progress, *Literary Simulation and the Digital Humanities* demonstrates the heightened critical awareness created by the metamedia features of the computer as a simulation machine. It provides an interpretative framework for establishing relations between a cluster of concepts and the metaphorical and technical translation of those concepts into an evolving computational simulation of the acts of reading, editing, and writing. Its strong relation with a computational environment further suggests that this monograph could also be seen as an output of that digital artifact. Not in the strict sense of being the inevitable result of its permutational parameters, but in the broad sense of being retroactively informed by the workings of code and the computational modeling of interpretations and interactions.

The scholarly argument for exploring digital mediation as a second-degree time-based model of the performativity of textual production is theoretically expressed in the monograph, and artifactually embodied in the *LdoD Archive*'s database, algorithms, and interfaces. By constantly gesturing towards the digital literary machine, the monograph tries to make the *LdoD Archive* intelligible as a new kind of DH experiment. Reciprocally, several theoretical arguments in *Literary Simulation and the Digital Humanities* have to be understood through the actual workings of the *LdoD Archive*. Uncoincidences between machine workings and theoretical descriptions, as well as mismatches between those two dimensions and their appropriations by subjects in diverse contexts, open up self-descriptions and textual computability to further revisions and modifications,

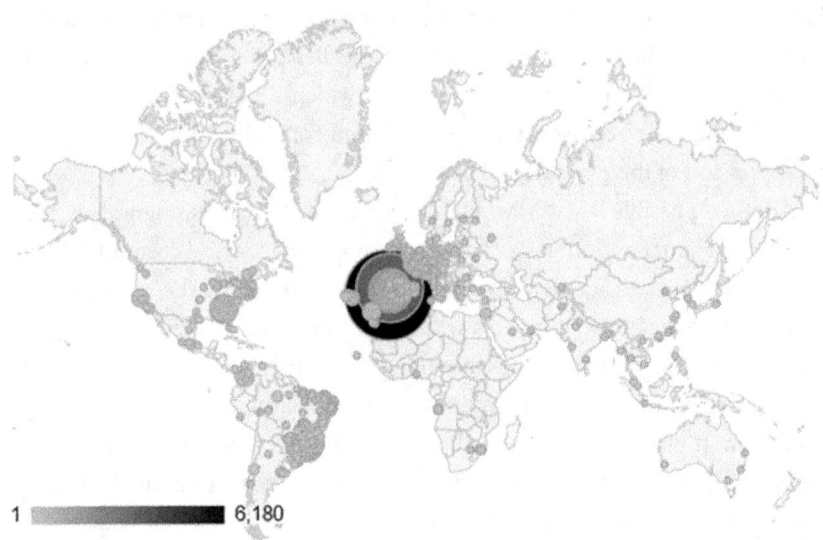

Figure 5.7 Google Analytics map representing the geographical distribution of the 35,000 users of the *LdoD Archive* (December 2017–June 2021).

and to the actuality of situated practices with their insights and creativity, but also to misunderstandings and communication failures (Figure 5.7).

Every technical implementation of each concept will bring its own ensemble of programming tools and techniques to the model. The theoretical framework has to be mediated through specific affordances enabled by working code. But the challenges of developing a computational simulation of the processuality of reading, editing, and writing are not limited to the constraints of computational modeling of a given theory of literary performativity. Given the *LdoD Archive*'s rhetorical appeal to the collaborative socialization of textual production, transmission, and reception, the actual outcome will depend on the situated uses and appropriation of its affordances and ideas by its intended communities of interactors (lay persons, students, experts).

The ongoing reception of the *LdoD Archive* shows precisely this double tension: between theory and computation, on the one hand, and between production and reception, on the other. Critical essays and reviews of the platform have recognized its rigorous critical apparatus, the productivity of its meta-editorial approach, and the novelty of its deep interactivity (Barbosa and Pittella 2017; Aldabalde and Pittella 2018; Boto 2020). At the same time, they have also stressed the limitations imposed to its dynamic and community-based orientation for being subordinated to the editorial interventions of a predefined set of canonical editions (Dionísio 2021). To what extent do the interaction design and collaborative affordances match our theoretical descriptions? How does the monograph converse with the Archive, and vice versa?

A clear example of compromise between theoretical emphasis on variability and the need to offer a tractable computational representation of variability was that it was necessary to limit the fluctuation that occurs in each expert's edition over time. A specific version of the book had to be selected to stand in for all the versions of that particular expert. However, the logic underlying the *LdoD Archive* would require that all variations be marked up not only across the four editions of the selected experts, but also within the corpus of each of them before and after the launch of the Archive. The exhaustive encoding of all variation points would make the task endless. It was necessary to reduce the variability to make it computationally representable. Theoretical description and computational implementation do not entirely match.

Additionally, ethnographic descriptions of the situated practices of appropriation have shown the challenges of navigating the platform and the institutional constraints on performing literary roles in an open, non-scripted performance (Magalhães 2022).[3] One of the communication problems created by the *LdoD Archive*'s interaction model comes from its intentional and programmatic confusion between the role of common reader and the role of expert. While the first group is invited to reorganize, annotate, and comment on the text even without knowing the entire work, the second group is encouraged to see what can be done with a text when we multiply its fragmentation and stop worrying about historical or philological principles. The *LdoD Archive* seems to say to both groups that any text, even if it was written by Fernando Pessoa, can become a space for rereading, re-editing, and rewriting.

Articulation between the theoretical claims of the monograph and the interaction injunctions of the *Archive* can be tested through the remix of those actions. Although the "Reading" interface tries to respect the role of the "reader who only reads," it is already contaminated by the multiplication of reading paths by juxtaposing the four editions and the reading recommendation, that is, it turns the reading order into an interpretative problem. Additionally, the

---

[3] Cecília Magalhães (2022) has produced an ethnographic analysis of the uses of the *LdoD Archive* by multiple groups of users: university students and lecturers, secondary school students and teachers, performative arts practitioners, experts on Pessoa's works, and general readers. Based on workshops, video interviews, and observations in various informal and formal contexts, these analyses highlight how the situated expectations of users inflect their understanding and their engagement with the platform. The playful element has been appropriated with varying degrees of success.

"Virtual" interface invites readers to transition to the role of editors and move around selecting and organizing text, thus contaminating "reading" with "editing." Even the "Editions" and "Documents" interfaces (those that conform to the circumspect expectations of the digital critical edition) are not sufficiently separated from the other interfaces, since their texts can easily transition to the "Reading" interface or to the "Virtual" editing interface.

Readers' cognitive disorientation (the fact that they are thrown into the middle of the Archive right at the front page without the possibility of a panoramic view) is reinforced, to a certain extent, by the performative disorientation, that is, the mixture of roles they are invited to play and which, in turn, collide with the type of subject they bring to the platform: that of the reader who sees the text as an object independent of his/herself and his/her action. This could be, perhaps, a criterion to assess the success or failure of the enunciative proposal of the *LdoD Archive* as an embodiment of this monograph's notion of literary simulation. To what extent does the experience of exploration and use manage to transform readers' awareness about their role and about the text? How far can they understand the interpretative and simulatory nature of the platform as a semiotic space where their actions are inscribed?

Experimentation with the material and conceptual potentiality of the book opens up the literary imagination beyond the bibliographic horizon. Starting from the philological and historical question "what is the *Book of Disquiet*?" we moved from a performative representation of this book as unfinished authorial project and conjectural editorial construct to a performative simulation of how a book comes into being. Instead of merely fetishizing particular acts of reading, editing, and writing as recorded marks to be remediated, we reconceptualized them as iterative actions that are dynamically open to the social processuality of meaning production. This opening up of the processuality of the work is experimented with through the performativity of a collaborative space. The textual practices of the web redefined the textual condition of the *LdoD Archive*. In this way, the presentation of the processes of production of the *Book of Disquiet* is reconfigured and diffracted by the possibility of changing its content, structure, and form in tentative acts of reading, editing, and writing. Networks of inscriptions and interpretations come into the world: reading becoming reading, editing becoming editing, writing becoming writing.

Explicit: No Problem Has a Solution

Foresight

After six years of software development and textual encoding, the *LdoD Archive: Collaborative Digital Archive of the Book of Disquiet* was finally published, in December 2017, as a free online resource (Figure 6.1) (https://ldod.uc.pt/). At once textual archive and textual machine, the multifunctional and multilayered digital artifact that we published on the web had evolved into something quite different from what I had been able to conceive when the first ideas were set to paper. In April 2009, I wrote down for the first time the title for what would turn out to be a decade-long research project: "No Problem Has a Solution: A Digital Archive of the *Book of Disquiet*."

The phrase "No Problem Has a Solution" is the English translation of the incipit from one of the fragments belonging to Fernando Pessoa's *Book of Disquiet*. I came to the project title entirely by chance: a series of autograph notebooks by

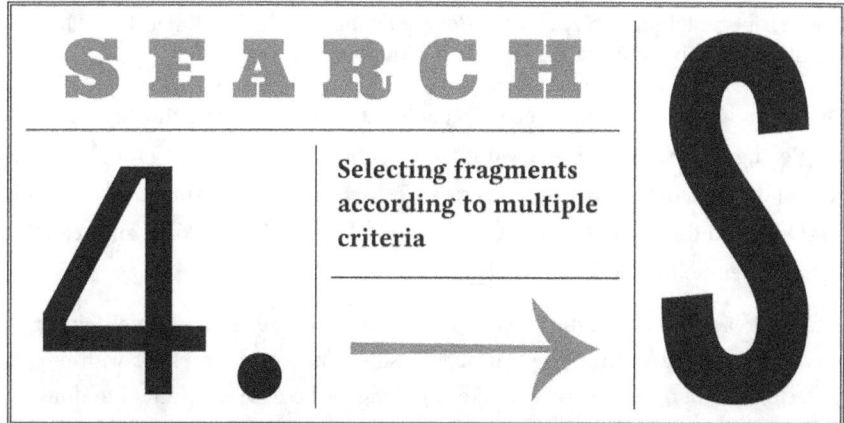

Figure 6.1 Graphic representation of the search interface.

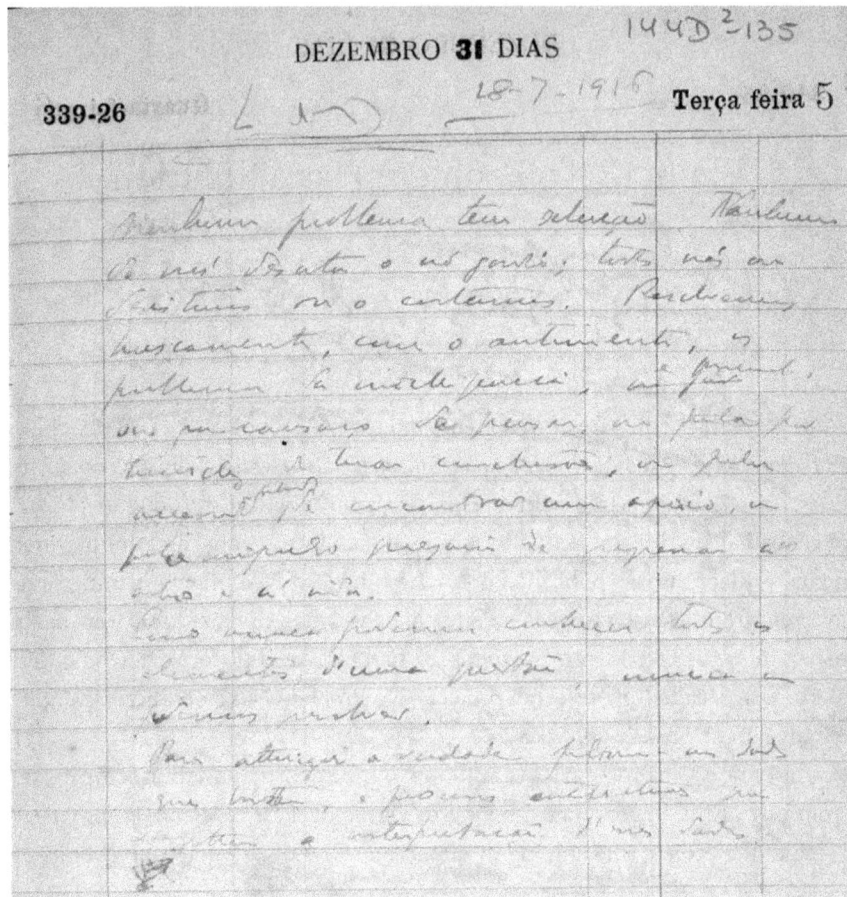

Figure 6.2 "L. do D. 18-7-1916 Nenhum problema tem solução." Autograph manuscript containing a piece for the *Book of Disquiet* (BNP/E3, 144D(2)-135r). © National Library of Portugal. Reprinted with permission.

Pessoa had just been made freely available, as digital facsimile images, through the Portuguese National Library digital collection. After searching for "L. do D." within the metadata for those notebooks, I discovered the facsimile of notebook 144D(2), and then browsed it until I came to folio 135r (Figure 6.2), and read the handwritten text dated July 18, 1916:

> No problem has a solution. None of us can untie the Gordian knot; either we give up or we cut it. We brusquely resolve intellectual problems with our feelings, either because we're tired of thinking, or because we're afraid to draw conclusions, or because of an inexplicable need to latch on to something, or because of a gregarious impulse to return to other people and to life.

> Since we can never know all the factors that a problem entails, we can never solve it.
>
> To arrive at the truth we would need more data, along with the intellectual resources for exhaustively interpreting the data.
>
> (Text 333[1])

Pessoa's reflection (or rather, the reflection of the first heteronym he created for this particular work) about the impossibility of pursuing a course of inquiry to its ultimate consequences, and the somewhat uncanny notion of *data interpretation*, resonated with my own sense that digital mediation of textual processes offered unchartered possibilities asking for further conceptual and technical exploration. So this textual fragment was unconsciously invested with an allegorical and speculative significance for the entire enterprise: it was both a material instance of textual processes in the *Book of Disquiet* whose digital remediation posed challenging intellectual problems, and a philosophical comment on the impossibility of thinking problems through towards some satisfactory solution.

Somehow, the phrase "no problem has a solution" implied the need for an entirely open-ended artifactual and theoretical inquiry into the nature of reading, editing, writing, and digital materiality which could use the textual space of this particular work to produce a more general model of literary action. Or, in another equally appropriate implication, "no problem has a solution" also suggested the inevitability of failure. Given the technical and conceptual difficulties I anticipated and the uncertain outcome of our efforts, the building of this artifact could turn out to be a generator of unsolvable problems. Somehow the unsolvability of the *Book of Disquiet* puzzle would be replicated in the puzzle of its digital incarnation.

Besides, the co-occurrence of the tokens "problem," "solution," and "data" provided yet another layer of meaning, in which this piece of text could be read in parodic relation to the typical vocabulary and discourse fields of software engineering. This parodic echo also reverberated through the growing dislocation of discourses and practices of Digital Humanities towards empirical validation and data solutionism. Its overinterpreted resonance in my mind thus extended from the material level of autograph inscription to the philosophical and literary level of meaning production, and to the methodological level of computational

---

[1] Full text available at https://ldod.uc.pt/fragments/fragment/Fr553/inter/Fr553_WIT_ED_CRIT_Z (BNP/E3, 144D(2)-135r; Coelho 157; Sobral Cunha 173; Zenith 333; Pizarro 133).

parsing and processing. Which were the problems that could only *not be solved?* That had to *not be solved?*

My interest in digital editing had started in the early 2000s when I began looking at and working with various digital literary archives that had been under development since the mid-1990s. Those early projects were addressing the problem of re-editing literary works by adapting established principles of critical and documentary editing in print media to the hypertext and hypermedia capabilities of the networked computer. Computational advances were changing the technologies and practices of textual production and reproduction. Digital editors used those changes not only for migrating the archive of literary production to the new medium, but also for testing forms of textual encoding made according to specific editorial theories, such as genetic criticism or social editing. Although their initial focus was on making accessible and linkable many different types of source materials in verbal and visual media, research gradually shifted to explore other possibilities created by the machine readability of digitized texts and, later, by the collaborative and socialized processes of the evolving ecology of the web.

It was within this technical and intellectual context that I began to look for a work that would sustain a set of relevant literary interrogations related to material and social processes of textual mediation. As an unfinished modular work composed of an open set of a few hundred witnesses in various stages of completion, the *Book of Disquiet* seemed the most likely candidate for making a new experiment in digital critical editing. Its modular and fragmentary structure matched the modular nature of digital objects. Furthermore, the *Book of Disquiet* is a major literary achievement of modernist awareness of the performative nature of the self, representative of Pessoa's writing practice and of European modernism, and it continues to interest all kinds of contemporary readers. It is the most often quoted text by Pessoa on the internet, as well as his most translated work worldwide. Material form and literary significance thus came together in justifying this choice.

When I started working on the project, it was mostly as a meta-editorial representation of four versions of the *Book of Disquiet*, which would allow interactors to automatically compare them against the autograph sources and against each other at the micro-scale of textual transcription and at the macro-scale of bibliographic structure. The focus would be placed on representing the processuality of editing rather than making a claim for an improved, definitive, or final edition of the work. The archive would be data modeled in ways that would give us a sense of the authorial and social processes of textual production that resulted in several versions of the work. This was the version of the project that was written into the original February 2011 application for funding.

Once we started working, in March 2012, the concept of the archive gradually morphed into the concept of the dynamic archive and, soon after that, of the literary simulator. By early 2013 all of the dynamic functionalities had subsumed the initial archival meta-editorial logic, which by then had been reconceived as one set of functions among several other functionalities to be programmed into the ongoing literary machine. For five years we continued to develop both the critical editing and meta-editing component, on the one hand, and the interactive simulation component, on the other. Each of those components was refined and integrated into a common textual space which was intended to model literary performativity beyond the bibliographic horizon. The *Book of Disquiet* thus became a digital literary space for probing into textual processuality in general. It was as if the data processing of this particular work had opened up the entire field of literary performance.

The notions of literary simulation and evolutionary textual environment were unintended creative outcomes of this project, two artifactual embodiments of the intersection between scholarly practice and literary imagination (Portela 2021). Conceived as a meta-editorial archive containing several editorial versions of Fernando Pessoa's unfinished work *Book of Disquiet*, the project evolved into a new kind of conceptual and technical artifact, which I now see, in retrospect, as both a scientific and literary invention. Many threads of ideas have fed into this invention, among which I highlight the following: the hypertext rationale for electronic editing as theorized and put into practice by Jerome McGann and other digital critical editors in the 1990s and 2000s; the notion of speculative computing, performative materiality, and humanistic display as expressed in Johanna Drucker's analyses of codependence between material form and interpretative action; John Cayley's creative and critical explorations of programmability and reading, synthesized in the concept of grammalepsy (Cayley 2018).

The ideas contained in this book resulted from the process of designing a computational architecture and modeling textual relations and subject-text interactions as a highly variable interpretative space. Retroaction between computational performativity and literary performativity can be seen in the programming of functions and roles as simulations. The generative feedback of the computational tooling and retooling is expressed in a theory of literary performance that uses the digital medium to try and apprehend the network sustained by the actions of reading, editing, and writing through the material and imaginary operations of the book. An extended experiment in reimagining the computational for reimagining the literary, this book and its companion archive must confront their own historicity as intellectual and artifactual constructions for our transmedia present.

Hindsight

And you may find yourself in a beautiful house, with a beautiful archive
And you may ask yourself
Well ... How did I get here?

Letting the days go by
Let the code hold me down
Letting the days go by
XML flowing underground
Into the blue again
After the money's gone
Once in a lifetime
XML flowing underground[2]

A – So now you finally see it ...
B – Now I see *what*?
A – You see just how ominous it was for your archive that you have chosen such a title.
B – What do you mean?
A – The question is not *what do I mean*, but rather: *what did you expect*?
B – I am not following you.
A – Why did you pick that title?
B – I don't know. I guess it was just an intuition.
A – Intuitions have consequences, you know. I ask you again: *what were you expecting*?
B – I really don't know. I think that we only have knowledge in hindsight. We always have to start in the dark, with only a vague sense of direction, with only the blind anticipation of desire.

---

[2] Parody of "Once in a Lifetime" (1980) by David Byrne.

A – But why did you have to call it *"no problem has a solution"*? Don't you think it sounds somewhat *desperate*?

B – When I started, my feeling was that I didn't even know what the problem was. I was looking for the problem, and that sentence just popped in front of my eyes.

A – Well, sentences don't just pop up in front of people, you have to pick them.

B – OK, I admit: I picked the sentence without realizing that I would not be able to control what it would come to mean as the project advanced.

A – Now, you have lost me. Please explain.

B – You see, my first thought was: I don't know what the problem is so I don't know what the solution might be for a problem that I don't know what it is.

A – And so you thought that would be the best thing that you could write in your grant application?

B – I don't need your sarcasm. Let me explain further: I also thought what I wanted to do was perhaps too difficult, and that it might not even be possible to achieve. So that even when I would come to the point where I would have a problem I still would not know if I could find a solution.

A – So first *you had no problem and no solution*. Then *you would have a problem and no expectation of finding a solution*. I still don't see how you could sell that to the research council.

B – I didn't say that I had a problem with no solution. I found a sentence in the book that said that "no problem has a solution." I thought of it as a strategic title, a way of hinting at the intractable nature of what I was attempting, and also, at the same time, as *a way of saying that it was impossible to fail*.

A – I am sure the evaluation panel wasn't versed in subtle paradox.

B – Well, you see: I thought the sentence could mean that *even if we failed we would have succeeded*. It was a self-ironic title. If no problem has a solution we could always claim that our problem also had no solution.

A – "No problems" and "no solutions." Is this the kind of state-of-the art research that they are funding these days?

B – Well, regardless of the title, I think the research was sound enough, but I soon realized that I could not control what the title would come mean.

A – How so?

B – The world is a messy place, you know. Texts are messy too. We have ideas and plans, and we test them, but materials and texts always resist to those plans and ideas, and we doubt what we are doing, and then *we get to totally different points from what we had first imagined.*

A – And how do you see that in your title?

B – I saw that I could not control what I wanted it to mean. We think *we have found problems and we think we have found solutions*, but we also have problems without solutions, and we continue looking for problems that we don't really know what they are.

A – So *your title doesn't mean anything, really*. Is that what you are saying?

B – I don't know. I was implying that we would succeed even if we failed, but maybe we just failed.

A – So now you see why I said that you had chosen an ominous title. You finally *see it.*

B – I don't think it's in the title. It's just that we have to fail. Trying and failing. In research as in life. We have to try. We only have knowledge in hindsight. We love in the dark. We code in the dark.

Acknowledgments

The software architecture, data model, and code for the *LdoD Archive* infrastructure were developed by António Rito Silva. Close collaboration with him was essential for giving technical expression to the conceptual development of the model as our research advanced. Without his enthusiasm for the *Book of Disquiet* and his ability to translate all the concepts into working code in a software system, the *LdoD Archive* and its generative ideas would not exist as an actual computational artifact and textual environment. Our continuing conversations—reflected in several coauthored papers—have created the intellectual space for many new ideas to emerge. This book is deeply indebted to him as coauthor of the *LdoD Archive* and software researcher whose questioning helped us turn a speculative thought experiment into a functional literary invention. Without those many iterations of our conversations neither the *LdoD Archive* nor this book would exist. This book is dedicated to him, long-time friend and light-hearted engineer.

I would also like to acknowledge several other people who, over the last ten years (2012–21), have contributed directly to the *LdoD Archive*: Ana Marques, André Santos, Cecília Magalhães, Daniela Côrtes Maduro, Diego Giménez, Duarte Oliveira, Gonçalo Montalvão Marques, José Maria Cunha, José Raposo, Luís Lucas Pereira, Miguel Cruz, Nuno Gonçalves, Rita Catania Marrone, and Tiago Santos. Without their dedication to the tasks of transcription, encoding, revision, programming, designing, and testing, there would be no literary machine. In some cases, our collaborative work was carried out in the context of postgraduate research supervision (MA theses in Information Systems and Computing Engineering, at the University of Lisbon, and PhD dissertations in Materialities of Literature, at the University of Coimbra). I am also grateful to all other members of the research team of the "No Problem Has a Solution" project (2012–15): Abel Barros Baptista, António Sousa Ribeiro, John David Mock, Osvaldo Manuel Silvestre, Paulo Silva Pereira, Pedro Serra, Ricardo Namora, and Samuel Teixeira.

During its development, the *LdoD Archive* benefited from the external collaboration of several individuals and institutions. My gratitude is due, first and foremost, to the editors Jerónimo Pizarro, Richard Zenith, and Teresa Sobral Cunha, for sharing their knowledge of the editorial problems of the *Book of Disquiet*. Our team of project consultants also included three leading digital humanities scholars whose critical insights contributed to the advancement of our ideas: Johanna Drucker, Matthew G. Kirschenbaum, and Susan Schreibman have generously shared their expertise and have been a continuing source of support and inspiration.

I am grateful to all beta-users who, in September 2014 and May 2017, participated in usability tests of the functionalities and web design of the *LdoD Archive*, and to all the participants in our ongoing series of workshops on the *LdoD Archive*. These workshops help us understand how interactors appropriate the functionalities of the platform in situated contexts (such as in secondary schools and universities, as well as several informal online groups), and also how we can improve our interface design and our communication strategies. Given the collaborative and playful nature of the platform as an open-ended interactive space, their creative contributions are an integral component of the *LdoD Archive* as both literary experience and literary experiment.

These acknowledgments are extended to the organizers and participants of national and international seminars and conferences, in which several conceptual and technical components of the *LdoD Archive* were first presented, namely in universities and research centers in Portugal, Australia, Brazil, Canada, Colombia, Cyprus, France, Germany, Greece, Indonesia, Ireland, Italy, Japan, Spain, Sweden, the United Kingdom, and the United States of America. Peer review and interaction with diverse communities of researchers (digital humanities, computer science, information science, textual encoding, textual criticism, Pessoa studies, electronic literature, cultural and social studies) are reflected in many papers and articles, several of which have been rewritten, adapted, and remixed for this book. Articles partially reused have appeared in the following journals: *Digital Scholarship in the Humanities*, *Digital Humanities Quarterly*, *Journal of the Text Encoding Initiative*, *Textual Cultures*, *Variants*, *Gramma*, *Colóquio Letras*, and *Materialities of Literature*. I would also like to acknowledge the anonymous reviewers of this book, whose perceptive reading has helped me clarify important points. The expertise of the Bloomsbury editors and designers was instrumental in giving a final bibliographic form to the imagined book. I would like to mention, in particular, Haaris Naqvi, editorial director, and the members of the editorial and production team: Rachel Moore, Megan Jones, and Linda Fisher.

Finally, I express my gratitude to the following institutions: Foundation for Science and Technology (FCT), Center for Portuguese Literature at the University of Coimbra (CLP), Instituto de Engenharia de Sistemas e Computadores, Investigação e Desenvolvimento em Lisboa (INESC-ID), National Library of Portugal (BNP), Department of English at the University of Maryland (UMD), and School of Arts and Humanities (FLUC) at the University of Coimbra. Their support was crucial in the development of the *LdoD Archive* and, generally, in advancing the research now presented in this book.[1]

---

[1] The *LdoD Archive* was developed under the research project "No Problem Has a Solution: A Digital Archive of the *Book of Disquiet*," coordinated by Manuel Portela (PTDC/CLE-LLI/118713/2010). Project funded by the Foundation for Science and Technology (FCT), and co-funded by the European Regional Development Fund (FEDER), through Axis I of the Competitiveness Factors Operational Program (POFC) of the National Strategic Framework (QREN)—European Union (COMPETE: FCOMP-01-0124- FEDER-019715). Additional national funds by the Foundation for Science and Technology (FCT), under the "Plurianual Funding—Unit 759" projects: "PEst-OE/ELT/UI0759/2013" and "PEst- OE/ELT/UI0759/2014."

References

Aldabalde, Taiguara Villela, and Carlos Pittella. 2018. "A trajetividade do Pessoa digital: contributos para uma história do espólio pessoano." *Património Cultural e Transformação Digital.* Eds. Fernando Ilharco, Peter Hanenberg, and Marília dos Santos Lopes. Lisboa: Universidade Católica Editora. 102–30.

Allen, Graham. 2006. *Intertextuality.* New York: Routledge.

André, Julie, and Elena Pierazzo. 2013. "Le codage en TEI des brouillons de Proust: vers l'édition numérique." *Genesis* 36: 155–61. https://doi.org/10.4000/genesis.1159

Apollon, Daniel, Claire Bélisle, and Philippe Régnier, eds. 2014. *Digital Critical Editions: Exploring the Interweaving of Traditional and Digital Textual Scholarship.* Chicago, IL: University of Illinois Press.

Balpe, Jean-Pierre. 2013. "Modèles en génération automatique de textes." *Timsal n Tamazight* 5.1: 117–21. https://www.asjp.cerist.dz/en/downArticle/244/5/1/7813

Balpe, Jean-Pierre. 2015–21. *Jean-Pierre Balpe—Un Univers de Génération Automatique Littéraire.* http://www.balpe.name/ (Accessed 21 September 2021).

Barad, Karen. 2003. "Posthumanist Performativity: Toward an Understanding of How Matter Comes to Matter." *Signs* 28.3: 801–31. https://doi.org/10.1086/345321

Barad, Karen. 2007. *Meeting the Universe Halfway: Quantum Physics and the Entanglement of Matter and Meaning.* Durham, NC: Duke University Press.

Barbosa, Nicolás, and Carlos Pittella. 2017. "The Website of Disquiet: The First Online Critical Edition of Fernando Pessoa." *Pessoa Plural: A Journal of Fernando Pessoa Studies* 12: 725–32. https://doi.org/10.7301/Z07S7KZD

Barney, Brett. 2012. "Digital Editing with the TEI Yesterday, Today, and Tomorrow." *Textual Cultures* 7.1: 29–41. https://doi.org/10.2979/textcult.7.1.29

Bartalesi, Valentina, Carlo Meghini, Daniele Metilli, Mirko Tavoni, and Paola Andriani. 2018. "A Web Application for Exploring Primary Sources: The DanteSources Case Study." *Digital Scholarship in the Humanities* 33.4: 705–23. https://doi.org/10.1093/llc/fqy002

Barthes, Roland. 1977. *Image, Music, Text.* Ed. and trans. Stephen Heath. London: Fontana Press.

Barthes, Roland. 2002. *S/Z.* Trans. Richard Miller. Oxford: Blackwell [First French edition, 1970].

Bénel, Aurélien, and Christophe Lejeune. 2009. "Humanities 2.0: Documents, Interpretation and Intersubjectivity in the Digital Age." *International Journal on Web Based Communities* 5.4: 562–76. https://doi.org/10.1504/ijwbc.2009.028090

Biblioteca Nacional Digital. Lisboa: Biblioteca Nacional de Portugal, 2002–21. https://bndigital.bnportugal.gov.pt/

Bloome, David, and Huili Hong. 2012. "Reading and Intertextuality." *The Encyclopedia of Applied Linguistics*. Oxford: Wiley-Blackwell. 4872–9. https://doi.org/10.1002/9781405198431.wbeal0996

Bolter, Jay David. 2001. *Writing Space: Computers, Hypertext, and the Remediation of Print*. New York: Routledge. 2nd ed.

Boto, Sandra. 2020. "Reseña—Archivo LdoD: Archivo digital colaborativo del Libro del desasosiego." *RHD: Revista de Humanidades Digitales* 5: 189–96. http://revistas.uned.es/index.php/RHD/article/view/24237/22269

Brown, Nathan C., and Caitlin T. Mueller. 2019. "Design Variable Analysis and Generation for Performance-Based Parametric Modeling in Architecture." *International Journal of Architectural Computing*, 17.1: 36–52. https://doi.org/10.1177/1478077118799491

Brüning, Gerrit, Katrin Henzel, and Dietmar Pravida. 2013. "Multiple Encoding in Genetic Editions: The Case of 'Faust'." *Journal of the Text Encoding Intiative* 4 (March): §1–37. https://doi.org/10.4000/jtei.697

Bryant, John. 2002. *The Fluid Text: A Theory of Revision and Editing for Book and Screen*. Ann Arbor: University of Michigan Press.

Burnard, Lou, Katherine O'Brien O'Keeffe, and John Unsworth, eds. 2006. *Electronic Textual Editing*. New York: Modern Language Association of America.

Burnard, Lou, Fotis Jannidis, Elena Pierazzo, and Malte Rehbein. 2011. "An Encoding Model for Genetic Editions." Revised draft. https://tei-c.org/Vault/TC/tcw19.html

Bush, Vannevar. 1945. "As We May Think." *The Atlantic Monthly* 176 (July 1945): 101–108. https://www.theatlantic.com/magazine/archive/1945/07/as-we-may-think/303881/

Butler, Judith. 1988. "Performative Acts and Gender Constitution: An Essay in Phenomenology and Feminist Theory." *Theatre Journal* 40.4: 519–31. https://doi.org/10.2307/3207893

Candela, L., G. Athanasopoulos, D. Castelli, K. El Raheb, P. Innocenti, Y. Ioannidis, A. Katifori, A. Nika, G. Vullo, and S. Ross. 2011. "A Digital Library Manifesto." DL.org Consortium, 2011. http://www.dlorg.eu/uploads/Booklets/booklet21x21_manifesto_web.pdf (Accessed 21 September 2021).

Castro, Ivo. 1993. "Intenções finais e mais intenções." *Defesa da Edição Crítica de Fernando Pessoa*. Cleonice Berardinelli and Ivo Castro. Lisboa: published by the authors. 35–99.

Caughie, Pamela L., Nick Hayward, Mark Hussey, Peter Shillingsburg, and George K. Thiruvathukal, eds. 2013. *Woolf Online*. Center for Textual Studies and Digital Humanities, Loyola University Chicago. Web. http://www.woolfonline.com/

Cayley, John. 2018. *Grammalepsy: Essays on Digital Language Art*. London: Bloomsbury. https://doi.org/10.5040/9781501335792

Cheema, Muhammad Faisal, Stefan Jänicke, and Gerik Scheuermann. 2016. "AnnotateVis: Combining Traditional Close Reading with Visual Text Analysis." Workshop on Visualization for the Digital Humanities, IEEE VIS 2016,

Baltimore, Maryland, USA, October 24, 2016. http://www.informatik.uni-leipzig. de/~stjaenicke/annotatevis.pdf (Accessed 21 September 2021).

Ciula, Arianna, Øyvind Eide, Cristina Marras, and Patrick Sahle. 2018. "Modelling: Thinking in Practice. An Introduction." *Historical Social Research* Supplement 31: 7–29. https://doi.org/10.12759/hsr.suppl.31.2018.7-29

Coelho, Jacinto do Prado, ed. 1982. Fernando Pessoa, *Livro do Desassossego por Bernardo Soares*. Collection and transcription by Maria Aliete Galhoz and Teresa Sobral Cunha. Lisboa: Ática, 1982. 2 vols.

Cohen, Matt, Ed Folsom, and Kenneth M. Price, eds. 1995–2021. *The Walt Whitman Archive*. Institute for Advanced Technology in the Humanities (1995–2007) / Center for Digital Research in the Humanities at the University of Nebraska–Lincoln (2007–21). https://www.whitmanarchive.org/

Colclough, Stephen. 2007. *Consuming Texts: Readers and Reading Communities, 1695–1870*. New York: Palgrave Macmillan.

Cordell, Ryan, and David Smyth. 2017. *The Viral Texts Project: Mapping Networks of Reprinting in 19th-Century Newspapers and Magazines*. Northeastern University. https://viraltexts.org/

Cruz, Miguel. 2018. *Reusable Framework for Digital Humanities: A Case Study with the LdoD Archive*. Lisboa: Instituto Superior Técnico da Universidade de Lisboa. MA thesis in Information Systems and Computer Engineering. https://fenix.tecnico. ulisboa.pt/cursos/meic-a/dissertacao/283828618790314

Damásio, António. 2010. *Self Comes to Mind: Constructing the Conscious Brain*. New York: Pantheon Books.

Darnton, Robert. 2009. *The Case for Books: Past, Present, and Future*. New York: PublicAffairs.

Darnton, Robert. 2015. "Digitize, Democratize: Libraries and the Future of Books." *A Biblioteca da Universidade: Permanência e Metamorfoses*. Eds. José Augusto Bernardes, Ana Maria Miguéis, and Carla Alexandra Ferreira. Coimbra: Imprensa da Universidade de Coimbra. 123–32.

Dedner, Burghard. 2006. "Editing Fragments as Fragments." *Text* 16: 97–111. https:// www.jstor.org/stable/30227961

Deegan, Marylin, and Katherine Sutherland, eds. 2009a. *Text Editing, Print and the Digital World*. London: Ashgate.

Deegan, Marylin, and Katherine Sutherland. 2009b. *Transferred Illusions: Digital Technology and the Forms of Print*. London: Ashgate.

Del Turco, Roberto Rosselli. 2019. "Designing an Advanced Software Tool for Digital Scholarly Editions: The Inception and Development of EVT (Edition Visualization Technology)." *Textual Cultures* 12.2: 91–111. https://doi.org/10.14434/textual.v12i2.27690

Derrida, Jacques. 1988. "Signature Event Context." *Limited Inc*. Trans. Samuel Weber and Jeffrey Mehlman. Evanston, IL: Northwestern University Press. [First French edition, 1972]. 1–23.

Digital Public Library of America. 2013–21. Boston: Boston Public Library. https://dp.la/

Dionísio, João. 2021. "Fazer Edições com Edições: Peritos e Comunidades." *Todas as Letras: Revista de Língua e Literatura* 23.1: 1–17. https://doi.org/10.5935/1980-6914/eLETDO2114243

Dobson, James E. 2019. *Critical Digital Humanities: The Search for a Methodology*. Chicago, IL: University of Illinois Press.

Driscoll, Matthew James, and Elena Pierazzo, eds. 2016. *Digital Scholarly Editing: Theories and Practices*. Cambridge: Open Book Publishers.

Drucker, Johanna. 2009. *SpecLab: Digital Aesthetics and Projects in Speculative Computing*. Chicago, IL: University of Chicago Press.

Drucker, Johanna. 2013a. "Performative Materiality and Theoretical Approaches to Interface." *Digital Humanities Quarterly* 7.1: §1–43. http://digitalhumanities.org:8081/dhq/vol/7/1/000143/000143.html

Drucker, Johanna. 2013b. "Is There a 'Digital' Art History?" *Visual Resources* 29.1–2: 5–13. https://doi.org/10.1080/01973762.2013.761106

Drucker, Johanna. 2014a. "Distributed and Conditional Documents: Conceptualizing Bibliographical Alterities." *MATLIT: Materialidades da Literatura* 2.1: 11–29. https://doi.org/10.14195/2182-8830_2-1_1

Drucker, Johanna. 2014b. *Graphesis: Visual Forms of Knowledge Production*. Cambridge, MA: Harvard University Press.

Drucker, Johanna. 2020. *Visualization and Interpretation: Humanistic Approaches to Display*. Cambridge, MA: MIT Press.

Earhart, Amy E. 2012. "The Digital Edition and the Digital Humanities." *Textual Cultures* 7.1: 18–28. https://doi.org/10.2979/textcult.7.1.18

Eaves, Morris, Robert Essick, and Joseph Viscomi, eds. 1995–2021. *The William Blake Archive*. Institute for Advanced Technology in the Humanities, University of Virginia (1996–2006) / University of North Carolina at Chapel Hill and University of Rochester (2007–present). http://www.blakearchive.org/

Elias, Camelia. 2004. *The Fragment: Towards a History and Poetics of a Performative Genre*. London: Peter Lang.

Engelbart, Douglas. 1962. *Augmenting Human Intellect: A Conceptual Framework*. Menlo Park, CA: Stanford Research Institute. http://cognitivemedium.com/tat/assets/Engelbart1962.pdf

Ericsson, K. Anders, and Herbert A. Simon. 1993. *Protocol Analysis: Verbal Reports as Data*. Cambridge, MA: MIT Press. 2nd rev. ed.

Estibeira, Maria do Céu. 2008. *A Marginalia de Fernando Pessoa*. Lisboa: Faculdade de Letras da Universidade de Lisboa. PhD Dissertation. https://repositorio.ul.pt/handle/10451/534

Estibeira, Maria do Céu. 2013. "Porquê Editar a Marginalia Pessoana?" *MATLIT: Materialidades da Literatura* 1.1: 75–87. https://doi.org/10.14195/2182-8830_1-1_4

Europeana. 2008–21. Europeana Foundation. The Hague: National Library of the Netherlands. www.europeana.eu/

Eve, Martin Paul. 2019. *Close Reading with Computers: Textual Scholarship, Computational Formalism, and David Mitchell's* Cloud Atlas. Stanford, CA: Stanford University Press.

Ferrari, Patricio, 2012. *Meter and Rhythm in the Poetry of Fernando Pessoa*. Lisboa: Faculdade de Letras da Universidade de Lisboa. PhD Dissertation. https://repositorio.ul.pt/handle/10451/7424

Ferrari, Patricio, ed. 2018. *Inside the Mask: The English Poetry of Fernando Pessoa*. Providence, RI: Gávea-Brown, 2018.

Ferrer, Daniel. 1998. "The Open Space of the Draft Page: James Joyce and Modern Manuscripts." *The Iconic Page in Manuscripts, Print, and Digital Culture*. Eds. George Bornstein and Theresa Tinkle. Ann Arbor: University of Michigan Press. 249–67.

Ferrer, Daniel. 2001. "Un imperceptible trait de gomme de tragacanthe …" *Bibliothèques d'écrivains*. Eds. Paolo D'Iorio and Daniel Ferrer. Paris: CNRS éditions. 7–27.

Filipe, Teresa. 2018. "Pessoa, tradutor sucessivo de Shakespeare." *Pessoa Plural: A Journal of Fernando Pessoa Studies* 14: 120–283. https://doi.org/10.26300/xvx9-pt32

Fiormonte, Domenico. 2018. *Per una critica del testo digitale: Letteratura, filologia e rete*. Roma: Bulzoni.

Fish, Stanley E. 1976. "Interpreting the Variorum." *Critical Inquiry* 2.3: 465–85. https://www.jstor.org/stable/1342862

Fish, Stanley E. 2000. *Is There a Text in This Class? The Authority of Interpretive Communities*. Cambridge, MA: Harvard University Press. [1st ed. 1980].

Flanders, Julia, and Fotis Jannidis, eds. 2019. *The Shape of Data in Digital Humanities: Modeling Texts and Text-Based Materials*. London: Routledge.

Forstall, Christopher W., and Walter J. Scheirer, eds. 2019. *Quantitative Intertextuality: Analyzing the Markers of Information Reuse*. Cham: Springer.

Foucault, Michel. 1977. "What is an Author?" Trans. Donald F. Bouchard and Sherry Simon. *Language, Counter-Memory, Practice: Selected Essays and Interviews*. Ed. Donald F. Bouchard. Ithaca, New York: Cornell University Press. 113–38.

Fraistat, Neil, and Steven Jones. 2009. "Editing Environments: The Architecture of Electronic Texts." *Literary and Linguistic Computing* 24.1: 9–18. https://doi.org/10.1093/llc/fqn032

Fraistat, Neil, Elizabeth Denlinge, and Raffaele Viglianti, eds. 2013–21. The Shelley-Godwin Archive. College Park, MD: Maryland Institute for Technology in the Humanities. http://shelleygodwinarchive.org/

Frischer, Bernard. 2011. "Art and Science in the Age of Digital Reproduction: From Mimetic Representation to Interactive Virtual Reality." *Virtual Archaeology Review* 2.4: 19–32. https://doi.org/10.4995/var.2011.4544

Gabler, Hans Walter. 2010. "Theorizing the Digital Scholarly Edition." *Literature Compass* 7: 43–56. https://doi.org/10.1111/j.1741-4113.2009.00675.x

Ganascia, Jean-Gabriel, Peirre Glaudes, and Andrea Del Lungo. 2014. "Automatic Detection of Reuses and Citations in Literary Texts." *Literary and Linguistic Computing* 29.3: 412–21. https://doi.org/10.1093/llc/fqu020

Genette, Gérard. 1997. *Paratexts*. Cambridge: Cambridge University Press. [First French edition, 1987].

Giménez, Diego. 2020. "Problemas de Intertextualidade Filosófica no Livro do Desassossego." *Novos Estudos Pessoanos 2020: Ponto da Situação*. Lisboa: Casa Fernando Pessoa. 21–30.

Google Books. 2005–21. https://www.google.com/googlebooks/about/history.html

Gonçalves, Nuno. 2019. *A Product Family for Digital Humanities Repositories*. Lisboa: Instituto Superior Técnico da Universidade de Lisboa. MA thesis in Information Systems and Computer Engineering. https://fenix.tecnico.ulisboa.pt/cursos/meic-a/dissertacao/1691203502343425

Grésillon, Almuth. 1994. *Éléments de critique génétique: Lire les manuscrits modernes*. Paris: Presses universitaires de France.

Grüne-Yanoff, Till, Stéphanie Ruphy, John Simpson, and Paul Weirich. 2011. "Philosophical and Epistemological Issues in Simulation and Gaming." *Simulation & Gaming* 42.2: 151–4. https://doi.org/10.1177/1046878110394034

Haberer, Adolphe. 2007. "Intertextuality in Theory and Practice." *Literatūra* 49.5: 54–67.

Hayles, N. Katherine. 2017. *Unthought: The Power of the Cognitive Nonconscious*. Chicago, IL: University of Chicago Press.

Hoffman, Gretchen L. 2019. *Organizing Library Collections: Theory and Practice*. Lanham: Rowman & Littlefield Publishers.

Howe, Daniel C. 2020. *RiTa: Tools for Natural Language and Generative Writing*. Version 2.4. https://rednoise.org/rita/

Internet Archive. San Francisco: Internet Archive, 1996–2021. https://archive.org/index.php

Israel, Susan E., ed. 2015. *Verbal Protocols in Literacy Research: Nature of Global Reading Development*. New York: Routledge.

Jänicke, Stefan, Greta Franzini, Muhammad Faisal Cheema, and Gerik Scheuermann. 2017. "Visual Text Analysis in Digital Humanities." *Computer Graphics Forum* 36.6: 226–50. https://doi.org/10.1111/cgf.12873

Kay, Alan. 2002. "User Interface: A Personal View." *Multimedia: From Wagner to Virtual Reality*. Eds. Randall Packer and Ken Jordan. New York: Norton. 121–31.

Kay, Alan, and Adele Goldberg. 1977. "Personal Dynamic Media." *Computer* 10.3: 31–41. Republished in *The New Media Reader*. Eds. Noah Wardrip-Fruin and Nick Montfort. Cambridge, MA: MIT Press, 2003. 391–404.

Kirschenbaum, Matthew G. 2008. *Mechanisms: New Media and the Forensic Imagination*. Cambridge, MA: MIT Press.

Kirschenbaum, Matthew G. 2013. "The .txtual Condition: Digital Humanities, Born-Digital Archives, and the Future Literary." *Digital Humanities Quarterly* 7.1: §1–42. http://www.digitalhumanities.org/dhq/vol/7/1/000151/000151.html

Kirschenbaum, Matthew G. 2016. *Track Changes: A Literary History of Word Processing*. Cambridge, MA: The Belknap Press of Harvard University Press.

Kirschenbaum, Matthew G. 2020. *Books.Files: Preservation of Digital Assets in the Contemporary Publishing Industry: A Report*. April 2020. https://hcommons.org/deposits/objects/hc:29224/datastreams/CONTENT/content

Kirschenbaum, Matthew G., and Sarah Werner. 2014. "Digital Scholarship and Digital Studies: The State of the Discipline." *Book History* 17: 406–58. https://www.jstor.org/stable/43956362

Kristeva, Julia. 1986. "Word, Dialogue and Novel." *The Kristeva Reader*. Ed. Toril Moi, trans. Alice Jardine. New York: Columbia University Press. [First French edition, 1969]. 35–61.

Landow, George P. 2006. *Hypertext 3.0: Critical Theory and New Media in an Era of Globalization*. Baltimore, MD: The Johns Hopkins University Press.

Latour, Bruno. 1996. "On Actor-Network Theory: A Few Clarifications." *Soziale Welt* 47.4: 369–81. https://www.jstor.org/stable/40878163

Lavocat, Françoise. 2014. "Facts, Fiction, Cognition." *Neohelicon* 41.2: 359–70. https://doi.org/10.1007/s11059-014-0244-y

Liao, T. Warren, and Guoqiang Li. 2020. "Metaheuristic-Based Inverse Design of Materials—A Survey." *Journal of Materiomics* 6.2: 414–30. https://doi.org/10.1016/j.jmat.2020.02.011

Lopes, Teresa Rita. 2016. "Livros do Desassossego – No Plural." *Abriu* 5: 79-93. https://doi.org/10.1344/abriu2016.5.6

Magalhães, Cecília. 2022. *Fragmentos em Prática: Interação, Colaboração e Criatividade no Arquivo LdoD*. Coimbra: University of Coimbra. PhD thesis in Materialities of Literature. [forthcoming]

Mandell, Laura. 2015. *Breaking the Book: Print Humanities in the Digital Age*. Oxford: Wiley-Blackwell.

Mangen, Anne, and Adriaan van der Weel. 2016. "The Evolution of Reading in the Age of Digitisation: An Integrative Framework for Reading Research." *Literacy* 50.3 (September): 116–24. https://doi.org/10.1111/lit.12086

Mangen, Anne, Gérard Olivier, and Jean-Luc Velay. 2019. "Comparing Comprehension of a Long Text Read in Print Book and on Kindle: Where in the Text and When in the Story?" *Frontiers in Psychology: Cognitive Science*. Volume 10. Article 38. 15 February 2019. https://doi.org/10.3389/fpsyg.2019.00038

Manovich, Lev. 2011. "What is Visualisation?" *Visual Studies* 26.1: 36–49. https://doi.org/10.1080/1472586X.2011.548488

Manovich, Lev. 2013. *Software Takes Command: Extending the Language of New Media*. London: Bloomsbury.

Marques, Ana, and Manuel Portela. 2020. "Representação e Análise da Receção Crítica do *Livro do Desassossego* no *Arquivo LdoD*." *Novos Estudos Pessoanos—Ponto de Situação*. Lisboa: Casa Fernando Pessoa. 5–11.

Marques, Gonçalo Montalvão. 2018. *Virtual Editions in the LdoD Archive using Crowdsourcing and Gamification*. Lisboa: Instituto Superior Técnico da Universidade de Lisboa. MA thesis in Information Systems and Computer Engineering. https://fenix.tecnico.ulisboa.pt/cursos/meic-a/dissertacao/1972678479054238

Marrone, Rita Catania. 2016. "Fernando Pessoa e a alquimia como ciência do espírito." *Colóquio/Letras* 192 (May): 112–23.

Marrone, Rita Catania. 2017. "Os «Livros Ocultos» da Biblioteca Particular de Fernando Pessoa." *Congresso Internacional Fernando Pessoa 2017*. Lisboa: Casa Fernando Pessoa. 352–71.

Martinho, Fernando J.B. 2014. "Autoconsciência literária em Bernardo Soares, com uma coda sobre o Livro como um livro de sabedoria." *Central de Poesia II, O Livro do Desassossego*. Eds. Patrícia Soares Martins, Golgona Anghel, and Fernando Guerreiro. Lisboa: Lemon Spring/Esfera do Caos Editores. 33–42.

Martins, Fernando Cabral. 2014. "O Livro do Desassossego e a escrita heteronímica." *Central de Poesia II, O Livro do Desassossego*. Eds. Patrícia Soares Martins, Golgona Anghel, and Fernando Guerreiro. Lisboa: Lemon Spring/Esfera do Caos Editores. 43–8.

McCarty, Willard, ed. 2010. *Text and Genre in Reconstruction: Effects of Digitalization on Ideas, Behaviours, Products and Institutions*. Cambridge: Open Book Publishers. https://books.openedition.org/obp/630

McGann, Jerome, ed. 1993–2008. *Rossetti Archive*. Charlottesville, VA: Institute for Advanced Technology in the Humanities, University of Virginia. http://www.rossettiarchive.org/

McGann, Jerome J. 2001. *Radiant Textuality: Literature after the World Wide Web*. New York: Palgrave.

McGann, Jerome. 2006. "From Text to Work: Digital Tools and the Emergence of the Social Text." *Text* 16: 49–62. https://www.jstor.org/stable/30227956

Millis, Keith, Joseph Magliano, and Stacey Todaro. 2006. "Measuring Discourse-Level Processes with Verbal Protocols and Latent Semantic Analysis." *Scientific Studies of Reading* 10.3: 225–40. https://doi.org/10.1207/s1532799xssr1003_2

Montfort, Nick. 2012. "XS, S, M, L: Creative Text Generators of Different Scales." *Trope* 12.2: 1–18. Web. https://dspace.mit.edu/bitstream/handle/1721.1/78887/TROPE-12-02.pdf

Moulthrop, Stuart, and Dene Grigar. 2017. *Traversals: The Use of Preservation for Early Electronic Writing*. Cambridge, MA: MIT Press.

Muñoz, Trevor, Raffaele Viglianti, and Neil Fraistat. 2013. "Texts and Documents: New Challenges for TEI Interchange and the Possibilities for Participatory Archives." *The Linked TEI: Text Encoding in the Web. Book of Abstracts. Abstracts of the TEI Conference and Members Meeting 2013*. Eds. Fabio Ciotti and Arianna Ciula. Roma: DIGILAB, Università La Sapienza and Text Encoding Initiative Consortium. 91–6. http://digilab2.let.uniroma1.it/teiconf2013/wp-content/uploads/2013/09/book-abstracts.pdf (Accessed 21 September 2021).

Murray, Janet H. 2012. *Inventing the Medium: Principles of Interaction Design as Cultural Practice*. Cambridge, MA: MIT Press.

Musil, Robert. 2009. *Kommentierte Edition Samtlicher Werke, Briefe und Nachgelassener Schriften. Mit Transkriptionen und Faksimiles Aller Handschriften*. Eds. Walter Fanta, Klaus Amann, and Karl Corino. Robert Musil-Institut der Alpen-Adria Universitat Klagenfurt.

Namora, Ricardo. 2013. "El concepto de biblioteca digital como cuestión epistemológica." *La Biblioteca de Occidente en Contexto Hispánico*. Ed. Miguel Ángel Garrido Gallardo. Logroño: Universidad Internacional de La Rioja. 73–84.

Nell Smith, Martha, Marta Werner, Julie Enszer, Jessica Beard, and Ellen Louise Hart, eds. 2012–21. *DEA2—Dickinson Electronic Archives*. College Park, MD: Maryland Institute of Technology in the Humanities [First version, *DEA1*, 1994–2012]. https://www.emilydickinson.org/

Nelson, Theodor H. 1965. "A File Structure for the Complex, the Changing, and the Indeterminate." *Association for Computing Machinery: Proceedings of the 20th National Conference*, 84–100.

Nelson, Theodor H. 1987. *Literary Machines*. Swarthmore, PA: published by the author. 2nd ed.

Nelson, Theodor H. 1995. "The Heart of Connection: Hypermedia Unified by Transclusion." *Comunications of the ACM* 38.8: 31–3. https://doi.org/10.1145/208344.208353

Nelson, Theodor H., Robert Adamson Smith, and Marlene Mallicoat. 2007. "Back to the Future: Hypertext the Way It Used to Be." *HT 2007: Proceedings of the Eighteenth Conference on Hypertext and Hypermedia*. September. 227–8. https://doi.org/10.1145/1286240.1286303

Nielsen, Michael. 2016a. "Thought as a Technology." http://cognitivemedium.com/tat/index.html (Accessed 21 September 2021).

Nielsen, Michael. 2016b. "Toward an Exploratory Medium for Mathematics." http://cognitivemedium.com/emm/emm.html (Accessed 21 September 2021).

Nunberg, Geoffrey, ed. 1996. *The Future of the Book*. Berkeley, CA: University of California Press.

Oatley, Keith. 2016. "Fiction: Simulation of Social Worlds." *Trends in Cognitive Sciences* 20.8: 618–28. https://doi.org/10.1016/j.tics.2016.06.002

Oliveira, Duarte, António Rito Silva, and Manuel Portela. 2019. "Social Media Aware Virtual Editions for the Book of Disquiet." *Digital Libraries at the Crossroads of Digital Information for the Future. ICADL 2019. Lecture Notes in Computer Science*, vol. 11853. Eds. Adam Jatowt, Akira Maeda, and Sue Yeon Syn. Cham: Springer. 271–82. https://doi.org/10.1007/978-3-030-34058-2_25

Oliveira, Duarte. 2018. *Automatic Collection of Citations in the LdoD Archive*. Lisboa: Instituto Superior Técnico da Universidade de Lisboa. MA thesis in Information Systems and Computer Engineering. https://fenix.tecnico.ulisboa.pt/cursos/meic-a/dissertacao/1972678479054227

Opitz, Sven. 2017. "Simulating the World: The Digital Enactment of Pandemics as a Mode of Global Self-Observation." *European Journal of Social Theory* 20.3: 392–416. https://doi.org/10.1177/1368431016671141

Ott, Brian, and Cameron Walter. 2000. "Intertextuality: Interpretive Practice and Textual Strategy." *Critical Studies in Media Communication* 17.4: 429–46. https://doi.org/10.1080/15295030009388412

Pereira, Luís Lucas. 2017. *Machines of Disquiet*. Coimbra: Department of Informatics Engineering. http://mofd.dei.uc.pt (Accessed 21 September 2021).

Pereira, Luís Lucas, Manuel Portela, and Licínio Roque. 2018. "Machines of Disquiet: Textual Experience in the *LdoD Archive*." *MATLIT: Materialities of Literature* 6.3: 59–71. https://doi.org/10.14195/2182-8830_6-3_5.

Pessoa, Fernando. 1982. *Livro do Desassossego por Bernardo Soares*. Collection and transcription by Maria Aliete Galhoz and Teresa Sobral Cunha. Ed. Jacinto do Prado Coelho. Lisboa: Ática, 1982. 2 vols.

Pessoa, Fernando. 1990. *Livro do Desassossego por Vicente Guedes, Bernardo Soares*. Ed. Teresa Sobral Cunha. Lisboa: Presença. Vol. 1.

Pessoa, Fernando. 1991. *Livro do Desassossego por Vicente Guedes, Bernardo Soares*. Ed. Teresa Sobral Cunha. Lisboa: Presença. Vol. 2.

Pessoa, Fernando. 1998. *Livro do Desassossego, composto por Bernardo Soares, ajudante de guarda-livros na cidade de Lisboa*. Ed. Richard Zenith. Lisboa: Assírio & Alvim.

Pessoa, Fernando. 2002. *The Book of Disquiet by Bernardo Soares, Assistant Bookkeeper in the City of Lisbon*. Ed. and trans. Richard Zenith. London: Penguin Books.

Pessoa, Fernando. 2008. *Livro do Desassossego por Vicente Guedes, Bernardo Soares*. Ed. Teresa Sobral Cunha. Lisboa: Relógio d'Água.

Pessoa, Fernando. 2010. *Livro do Desasocego. Edição Crítica das Obras de Fernando Pessoa, Vol.* XII (Tomos I e II). Ed. Jerónimo Pizarro. Lisboa: Imprensa Nacional-Casa da Moeda.

Pessoa, Fernando. 2012. *Livro do Desassossego, composto por Bernardo Soares, ajudante de guarda-livros na cidade de Lisboa*. Ed. Richard Zenith. Lisboa: Assírio & Alvim.

Pessoa, Fernando. 2013a. *Livro do Desassossego*. Ed. Teresa Sobral Cunha. Lisboa: Relógio d'Água.

Pessoa, Fernando. 2013b. *Livro do Desassossego*. Ed. Jerónimo Pizarro. Lisboa: Tinta-da-china.

Pessoa, Fernando. 2015. *Livro(s) do Desassossego*. Ed. Teresa Rita Lopes. São Paulo: Global Editora.

Phillips, Gary A. 2016. "Poststructural Intertextuality." *Exploring Intertextuality: Diverse Strategies for New Testament Interpretation of Texts*. Eds. B.J. Oropeza and Steve Moyise. Eugene, OR: Cascade Books. 106–27.

Pierazzo, Elena. 2011. "A Rationale of Digital Documentary Editions." *Literary and Linguistic Computing* 26.4: 463–77. https://doi.org/10.1093/llc/fqr033

Pierazzo, Elena. 2015. *Digital Scholarly Editing: Theories, Models and Methods*. Farnham: Ashgate.
Pierazzo, Elena, Julie André, and Raffaele Viglianti. 2012. "Around a Sequence and Some Notes of Notebook 46: Encoding Issues about Proust's Drafts." http://peterstokes.org/elena/proust_prototype/ (Accessed 21 September 2021).
Pisarski, Mariusz. 2011. "Hypertext and Intertextuality: Affinities and Divergences." *Porównania* 8: 183–94.
Pizarro, Jerónimo, ed. 2009. *Fernando Pessoa: O Guardador de Papéis*. Lisboa: Texto Editores.
Pizarro, Jerónimo, ed. 2010. Fernando Pessoa, *Livro do Desasocego. Edição Crítica das Obras de Fernando Pessoa*, Vol. XII (Tomos I e II). Lisboa: Imprensa Nacional-Casa da Moeda.
Pizarro, Jerónimo. 2012. *La Mediación Editorial: Sobre la Vida Póstuma de lo Escrito*. Madrid: Iberoamericana / Vervuert.
Pizarro, Jerónimo. 2016a. "Os Muitos Desassossegos." *Revista do Centro de Estudos Portugueses* 36.55: 11–27. http://dx.doi.org/10.17851/2359-0076.36.55.11-27
Pizarro, Jerónimo. 2016b. "A Ansiedade da Unidade: Uma Teoria da Edição." *LEA—Lingue e letterature d'Oriente e d'Occidente* 5: 284–311. https://doi.org/10.13128/LEA-1824-484x-20038
Pizarro, Jerónimo. 2018. "*Livro do Desassossego*." Ler Pessoa. Lisboa: Tinta-da-china. 141–56.
Pizarro, Jerónimo, Antonio Cardiello, and Patricio Ferrari, eds. 2010. *A Biblioteca Particular de Fernando Pessoa*. Lisboa: D. Quixote.
Portela, Manuel. 2012. "Autoauthor, Autotext, Autoreader: The Poem as Self-Assembled Database." *Writing Technologies* 4: 43–74. https://www.ntu.ac.uk/__data/assets/pdf_file/0030/827085/Manuel-Portela-Autoauthor,-Autotext,-Autoreader-The-Poem-as-Self-assembled-Databas.pdf
Portela, Manuel. 2013a. *Scripting Reading Motions: The Codex and the Computer as Self-Reflexive Machines*. Cambridge, MA: MIT Press.
Portela, Manuel. 2013b. "Nenhum Problema Tem Solução: Um Arquivo Digital do *Livro do Desassossego*." *MATLIT: Materialidades da Literatura* 1.1: 9–33. https://doi.org/10.14195/2182-8830_1-1_1
Portela, Manuel. 2014. "Multimodal Editing and Archival Performance: A Diagrammatic Essay on Transcoding Experimental Literature." *Digital Humanities Quarterly* 8.1: §1–44. http://www.digitalhumanities.org/dhq/vol/8/1/000175/000175.html
Portela, Manuel. 2016a. "Writing the Archive: An Experiment in Literary Self-Consciousness." *Gramma: Journal of Theory and Criticism* 23: 15–32. http://ejournals.lib.auth.gr/gramma/article/download/5401/5295
Portela, Manuel. 2016b. "A Simulação da Performatividade Literária no *Arquivo LdoD*." *Cultura e Digital em Portugal*. Eds. José Luís Garcia, João Teixeira Lopes, and Teresa Duarte Martinho. Porto: Afrontamento. 89–101.
Portela, Manuel. 2017. "Atos de Escrita no *Livro do Desassossego*." *Congresso Internacional Fernando Pessoa 2017*. Lisboa: Casa Fernando Pessoa. 224–39.

Portela, Manuel. 2018. "Re-Produzir Pessoa, isto é, P1 + P2 = Autor / Re-Producing Pessoa, i.e. P1 + P2 = Author." *Pessoa Plural: A Journal of Fernando Pessoa Studies* 12: 402–15. https://doi.org/10.26300/a107-eb54

Portela, Manuel. 2021. "An Evolutionary Textual Environment: The Unfinished Machine." *Textual Cultures* 14.2 [forthcoming].

Portela, Manuel. 2022. "From Meta-Editing to Virtual Editing: The *LdoD Archive* as a Computer-Assisted Editorial Space." *Approaches to Teaching Pessoa's The Book of Disquiet*. Eds. Paulo de Medeiros and Jerónimo Pizarro. New York: Modern Language Association [forthcoming].

Portela, Manuel, and Diego Giménez. 2015. "The Fragmentary Kinetics of Writing in the *Book of Disquiet*." *Textual Cultures* 9.2: 52–78. https://www.jstor.org/stable/26500730

Portela, Manuel, and Cecília Magalhães. 2020. "The *Book of Disquiet Digital Archive* as a Role-playing Experiment." *Mind The Gap! Thinking Electronic Literature in a Digital Culture / Attention à la marche! Penser la littérature électronique en culture numérique*. Eds. Bertrand Gervais and Sophie Marcotte. Montréal: Les presses de l'écureuil—ALN/NT2. 307–25. http://nt2.uqam.ca/en/elo-2018

Portela, Manuel, and António Rito Silva. 2015a. "A Model for a Virtual *LdoD*." *Digital Scholarship in the Humanities* 30.3: 354–70. https://doi.org/10.1093/llc/fqu004

Portela, Manuel, and António Rito Silva. 2015b. "A Dinâmica entre Arquivo e Edição no *Arquivo LdoD*." *Colóquio Letras* 188: 33–47.

Portela, Manuel, and António Rito Silva. 2016a. "Fernando Pessoa's *Book of Disquiet* as a Dynamic Digital Archive. " *Edizioni Critiche Digitali: Edizioni a confronto / Digital Critical Editions: Comparing Editions*. Eds. Paola Italia and Claudia Bonsi. Roma: Sapienza Università Editrice. 37–50.

Portela, Manuel, and António Rito Silva. 2016b. "Encoding, Visualizing, and Generating Variation in Fernando Pessoa's *Livro do Desassossego*." *Variants* 12–13: 189–210. https://doi.org/10.4000/variants.356

Portela, Manuel, and António Rito Silva, eds. 2017–21. *Arquivo LdoD: Arquivo Digital Colaborativo do Livro do Desassossego [LdoD Archive: Collaborative Digital Archive of the Book of Disquiet]*. Coimbra: Centre for Portuguese Literature at the University of Coimbra. https://ldod.uc.pt/

Pressley, Michael, and Peter Afflerbach. 1995. *Verbal Protocols of Reading: The Nature of Constructively Responsive Reading*. Mahwah, NJ: Lawrence Erlbaum Associates.

Price, Leah. 2004. "Reading: The State of the Discipline." *Book History* 7: 303–20. https://www.jstor.org/stable/30227365

Price, Leah. 2019. *What We Talk About When We Talk About Books*. New York: Basic Books.

Purcell, Aaron D. 2016. *Digital Library Programs for Libraries and Archives: Developing, Managing, and Sustaining Unique Digital Collections*. Chicago, IL: ALA Neal-Schuman, American Library Association.

Ramsay, Stephen. 2011. *Reading Machines: Toward an Algorithmic Criticism*. Chicago, IL: University of Illinois Press.

Raposo, José, António Rito Silva, and Manuel Portela. 2021. "LdoD Visual—A Visual Reader for Fernando Pessoa's *Book of Disquiet*: An In-Out-In Metaphor." *Digital Humanities Quarterly* 15.3 [forthcoming].

Raposo, José. 2019. *LdoD Visualization: Reading the Book of Disquiet with Information Visualization Techniques*. Lisboa: Instituto Superior Técnico da Universidade de Lisboa. MA thesis in Information Systems and Computer Engineering. https://fenix.tecnico.ulisboa.pt/cursos/meic-a/dissertacao/283828618790395

Reisenzein, Rainer. 2009. "On Literary Works as Simulations that Run on Minds." *Emotion Review* 1.1: 35–6. https://doi.org/10.1177/1754073908097183

Riffaterre, Michael. 1994. "Intertextuality vs. Hypertextuality." *New Literary History* 25.4: 779–88. https://www.jstor.org/stable/469373

Rito Silva, António, and Manuel Portela. 2013. "Social Edition 4 *The Book of Disquiet*: The Disquiet of Experts with Common Users." In *ECSCW 2013 Adjunct Proceedings: The 13th European Conference on Computer-Supported Cooperative Work*. Eds. Matthias Korn, Tommaso Colombino, and Myriam Lewkowicz. Aarhus, Denmark: Department of Computer Science, Aarhus University. 45–50. https://doi.org/10.7146/dpb.v40i596.13587

Rito Silva, António, and Manuel Portela. 2015. "TEI4LdoD: Textual Encoding and Social Editing in Web 2.0 Environments." *Journal of the Text Encoding Initiative* 8: §1–46. https://doi.org/10.4000/jtei.1171

Rito Silva, António *et al.* 2013–21. *Social Edition – LdoD*. https://github.com/socialsoftware/edition

Robinson, Peter. 2013. "Towards a Theory of Digital Editions." *Variants* 10: 105–31.

Robinson, Peter. 2016a. "Social Editions, Social Editing, Social Texts." *Digital Studies/Le champ numérique* 6.6: Chapter 7. http://doi.org/10.16995/dscn.6

Robinson, Peter 2016b. "The Digital Revolution in Scholarly Editing." *Ars Edendi Lecture Series*, vol. IV. Eds. Barbara Crostini, Gunilla Iversen, and Brian M. Jensen. Stockholm: Stockholm University Press. 181–207. http://dx.doi.org/10.16993/baj.h

Rodríguez de la Flor, Fernando, and Daniel Escandell Montiel. 2014. *El Gabinete de Fausto: "Teatros" de la Escrituray la Lectura a un Lado y Otro de la Frontera Digital*. Madrid: Consejo Superior de Investigaciones Científicas.

Roland, Meg. 2011. "Facsimile Editions: Gesture and Projection." *Textual Cultures* 6.2: 48–59. https://doi.org/10.2979/textcult.6.2.48

Romanello, Matteo. 2016. "Exploring Citation Networks to Study Intertextuality in Classics." *Digital Humanities Quarterly* 10.2: §1–46. http://www.digitalhumanities.org/dhq/vol/10/2/000255/000255.html

Sahle, Patrick. 2016. "What is a Scholarly Digital Edition?" *Digital Scholarly Editing: Theories and Practices*. Eds. Matthew J. Driscoll and Elena Pierazzo. Cambridge: Open Book Publishers. 19–39. https://books.openedition.org/obp/3397

Santos, Irene Ramalho. 2003. *Atlantic Poets: Fernando Pessoa's Turn in Anglo-American Modernism*. Lebanon, NH: University Press of New England.

Santos, André. 2015. *Arquivo Digital do Livro do Desassossego: Pesquisa e Recomendações*. Lisboa: Instituto Superior Técnico da Universidade de Lisboa. MA thesis in Information Systems and Computer Engineering. https://fenix.tecnico.ulisboa.pt/cursos/meic-a/dissertacao/846778572211152

Scheirer, Walter, Christopher Forstall, and Neil Coffee. 2014. "The Sense of a Connection: Automatic Tracing of Intertextuality by Meaning." *Digital Scholarship in the Humanities* 31.1: 204–17. https://doi.org/10.1093/llc/fqu058

Schreibman, Susan. 2016–21. *Letters 1916–1923*. Maynooth University. http://letters1916.maynoothuniversity.ie/

Schreibman, Susan, Vinayak Das Gupta, and Neale Rooney. 2017. "Notes from the Transcription Desk: Visualising Public Engagement." *English Studies* 98.5: 506–25. https://doi.org/10.1080/0013838X.2017.1333754

Sena, Jorge de. 1984. "Introdução ao Livro do Desassossego." *Fernando Pessoa & Ca. Heterónima: Estudos Coligidos, 1940–1978*. Lisboa: Edições 70. 177–242.

Sepúlveda, Pedro. 2013. "Listas do Desassossego." *MATLIT: Materialidades da Literatura* 1.1: 35–55. https://doi.org/10.14195/2182-8830_1-1_2

Sepúlveda, Pedro. 2014. "Pessoas-livros: Arquivo Bibliográfico de Fernando Pessoa." *MATLIT: Materialidades da Literatura* 2.1: 55–77. https://doi.org/10.14195/2182-8830_2-1_3

Sepúlveda, Pedro, and Ulrike Henny-Krahmer, eds. 2017. *Edição Digital de Fernando Pessoa: Projetos e Publicações*. Editorial coordination by Pedro Sepúlveda, technical coordination by Ulrike Henny-Krahmer. Lisbon and Cologne: IELT, New University of Lisbon and CCeH, University of Cologne. http://www.pessoadigital.pt/en/index.html

Shillingsburg, Peter L. 2006. *From Gutenberg to Google: Electronic Representations of Literary Texts*. Cambridge: Cambridge University Press.

Shillingsburg, Peter L. 2009. "How Literary Works Exist: Convenient Scholarly Editions." *Digital Humanities Quarterly* 3.3. :§1–43. http://digitalhumanities.org/dhq/vol/3/3/000054/000054.html

Shillingsburg, Peter L. 2017. *Textuality and Knowledge: Essays*. University Park, PA: The Pennsylvania State University Press.

Siemens, Ray, Mike Elkink, Alastair McColl, Karin Armstrong, James Dixon, Angelsea Saby, Brett D. Hirsch, and Cara Leitch. 2010. "Underpinnings of the *Social* Edition? A Narrative, 2004–9, for the Renaissance English Knowledge Base (REKn) and Professional Reading Environment (PReE) Projects." *Online Humanities*

Scholarship: The Shape of Things to Come. Eds. Jerome McGann, Andrew M. Stauffer, Dana Wheeles, and Michael Pickard. Houston, TX: Rice University Press. 401–60. http://cnx.org/content/col11199/1.1/ (Accessed 21 September 2021).

Siemens, Ray, Meagan Timney, Cara Leitch, Corina Koolen, and Alex Garnett, with the ETCL, INKE, and PKP Research Group. 2012. "Toward Modeling the Social Edition: An Approach to Understanding the Electronic Scholarly Edition in the Context of New and Emerging Social Media." *Literary and Linguistic Computing* 27.4: 445–61. https://doi.org/10.1093/llc/fqs013

Silva, Patrícia. 2016. "Pessoa's *The Mad Fiddler*: Sensationism in English." *Pessoa Plural: A Journal of Fernando Pessoa Studies* 10: 89–105. https://doi.org/10.7301/Z0Z899MQ

Silva, Patrícia. 2018. "The Poetic Drama of Fernando Pessoa and W.B. Yeats and the Symbolist Theatre Tradition." *Pessoa Plural: A Journal of Fernando Pessoa Studies* 14: 5–28. https://doi.org/10.26300/9cpf-wd41

Silvestre, Osvaldo Manuel. 2014. "O Que Nos Ensinam os Novos Meios sobre o Livro no *Livro do Desassossego*." *MATLIT: Materialidades da Literatura* 2.1: 79-98. https://doi.org/10.14195/2182-8830_2-1_4

Sinclair, Stéfan, and Geoffrey Rockwell. 2016. "Text Analysis and Visualization: Making Meaning Count." *A New Companion to Digital Humanities*. Eds. Susan Schreibman, Ray Siemens, and John Unsworth. Oxford: Wiley-Blackwell. 274–90.

Sobral Cunha, Teresa, ed. 2008. Fernando Pessoa, *Livro do Desassossego por Vicente Guedes, Bernardo Soares*. Lisboa: Relógio d'Água

Sula, Chris Alen, and Matthew Miller. 2014. "Citations, Contexts, and Humanistic Discourse: Toward Automatic Extraction and Classification." *Literary and Linguistic Computing* 29.3: 452–64. https://doi.org/10.1093/llc/fqu019

Tabbi, Joseph. 2010. "Electronic Literature as World Literature; or, The Universality of Writing under Constraint." *Poetics Today* 31.1: 17–50. https://doi.org/10.1215/03335372-2009-013

Tabbi, Joseph. 2015. "Manifesto." *CELL Project: Consortium on Electronic Literature*. NT2 Laboratory at Université du Québec à Montréal (UQAM). https://cellproject.net/manifesto

Tamir, Diana I., Andrew B. Bricker, David Dodell-Feder, and Jason P. Mitchell. 2016. "Reading Fiction and Reading Minds: The Role of Simulation in the Default Network." *Social Cognitive and Affective Neuroscience* 11.2: 215–24. https://doi.org/10.1093/scan/nsv114

Tatar, Kıvanç, and Philippe Pasquier. 2019. "Musical Agents: A Typology and State of the Art Towards Musical Metacreation." *Journal of New Music Research* 48.1: 56–105. https://doi.org/10.1080/09298215.2018.1511736

Terras, Melissa. 2016. "Crowdsourcing in the Digital Humanities." *A New Companion to Digital Humanities*. Eds. Susan Schreibman, Ray Siemens, and John Unsworth. Oxford: Wiley-Blackwell. 420–38.

The TEI Consortium. 2021. *TEI P5: Guidelines for Electronic Text Encoding and Interchange*. Version 4.2.2. Last updated April 9, 2021. Text Encoding Initiative Consortium. https://tei-c.org/release/doc/tei-p5-doc/en/Guidelines.pdf

Torres, Rui, and Nuno F. Ferreira. 2009–18. *Poemário*. https://telepoesis.net/curso-breve/tutorial.html

Trillini, Regula Hohl, and Sixta Quassdorf. 2010. "A 'Key to All Quotations'? A Corpus-Based Parameter Model of Intertextuality." *Literary and Linguistic Computing* 25.3: 269–86. https://doi.org/10.1093/llc/fqq003

Turing Group. 2020. "Classificador de poemas do Fernando Pessoa de acordo com os seus heterônimos." Fernando Matsumoto, Iago Nunes, Igor Câmara, Julia Pocciotti, and Lucas Sepeda, University of São Paulo. https://github.com/turing-usp/fernandopessoa

UK RED. 2011. *The Reading Experience Database (RED), 1450–1945*. Milton Keynes: Open University. http://www.open.ac.uk/Arts/reading/ (Accessed 21 September 2021).

Van Hulle, Dirk. 2013. "The Stuff of Fiction: Digital Editing, Multiple Drafts and the Extended Mind." *Textual Cultures* 8.1: 23–37. https://doi.org/10.14434/TCv8i1.5048

Van Hulle, Dirk. 2014. *Modern Manuscripts: The Extended Mind and Creative Undoing from Darwin to Beckett and Beyond*. London: Bloomsbury Academic, 2014.

Van Hulle, Dirk. 2016. "Exogenetic Digital Editing and Enactive Cognition." *Digital Scholarly Editing: Theories and Practices*. Eds. Matthew James Driscoll and Elena Pierazzo. Cambridge: Open Book Publishers. 107–18. https://books.openedition.org/obp/3404

Van Hulle, Dirk, and Mark Nixon, eds. 2011–21. *Samuel Beckett Digital Manuscript Project*. Centre for Manuscript Genetics (University of Antwerp), The Beckett International Foundation (University of Reading), Harry Ransom Humanities Research Center (Austin, Texas) and the Estate of Samuel Beckett. https://www.beckettarchive.org/

Vanhoutte, Edward. 2006. "Prose Fiction and Modern Manuscripts: Limitations and Possibilities of Text-Encoding for Electronic Editions." *Electronic Textual Editing*. Eds. Lou Burnard, Katherine O'Brien O'Keeffe, and John Unsworth. New York: Modern Language Association of America. 161–80.

Victor, Bret. 2013. "Media for Thinking the Unthinkable." (April 4, 2013; video talk). https://vimeo.com/67076984

Wallen, James Ramsey. 2013. "'Let us italicize': Blurring Form and Content in Derrida." *European Journal of English Studies* 17.1: 41–53. https://doi.org/10.1080/13825577.2012.755001

Werner, Marta L. 1999–2010. *Radical Scatters: Emily Dickinson's Late Fragments and Related Texts, 1870–1886*. University of Michigan, 1999–2007 / University of Nebraska–Lincoln, 2007–10. http://radicalscatters.unl.edu/

Werner, Marta L. 2011. "'Reportless Places': Facing the Modern Manuscript." *Textual Cultures* 6.2: 60–83. https://doi.org/10.2979/textcult.6.2.60

Werner, Marta L. 2017. "Emily Dickinson: Manuscripts, Maps, and a Poetics of Cartography." Michael Kelly, Marta L. Werner, Carolyn Vega, Susan Howe, Richard Wilbur, *Emily Dickinson: The Networked Recluse*. Amherst, MA: Amherst College Press. 89–112.

Werner, Marta L. 2021. *Writing in Time: Emily Dickinson's Master Hours*. Amherst, MA: Amherst College Press.

Wilson, Eric. 2012. "Criminogenic Cyber-Capitalism: Paul Virilio, Simulation, and the Global Financial Crisis." *Critical Criminology* 20: 249–74. https://doi.org/10.1007/s10612-011-9139-7

Wise, M. Norton. 2017. "On the Narrative Form of Simulations." *Studies in History and Philosophy of Science* Part A 62: 74–85. https://doi.org/10.1016/j.shpsa.2017.03.010

Wittern, Christian. 2013. "Beyond TEI: Returning the Text to the Reader." *Journal of the Text Encoding Intiative* 4 (March): §1–42. https://doi.org/10.4000/jtei.691

Wright-Maley, Cory. 2015. "Beyond the 'Babel Problem': Defining Simulations for the Social Studies." *The Journal of Social Studies Research* 39.2: 63–77. https://doi.org/10.1016/j.jssr.2014.10.001.

Zenith, Richard, ed. 2012. Fernando Pessoa, *Livro do Desassossego*. Lisboa: Assírio & Alvim.

Zenith, Richard, 2013. "*Livro do Desassossego*: o romance possível (*var.*: impossível)." *Comunicações do III Congresso Internacional Fernando Pessoa*. Lisboa: Casa Fernando Pessoa. 1–12. https://www.blogletras.com/2013/12/livro-do-desassossego-o-romance.html

Zenith, Richard. 2016. "*Livro do Desassossego*: Translating, Reading, and Deciphering the Text." *Abriu* 5: 65–77. https://doi.org/10.1344/abriu2016.5.5

Zenith, Richard. 2021. *Pessoa: A Biography*. New York: W.W. Norton & Co.

Zundert, Joris J. van, and Tara L. Andrews. 2017. "Qu'est-ce qu'un texte numérique?—A New Rationale for the Digital Representation of Text." *Digital Scholarship in the Humanities* 32, Supplement 2: ii78–ii88. https://doi.org/10.1093/llc/fqx039

Index

Afflerbach, Peter 74
affordance(s)
    collaborative 15, 50, 197
    computational 30
    of the digital medium 25, 26, 38, 186
    encyclopedic 38
    of machine-readable text 18
    participatory 16, 36, 41, 129
    of the platform 94
    procedural 38
    programmed 11
    social media 89
    spatial 38
    of Web 2.0 interaction 183
    of the working code 196
    writing 50
Aldabalde, Taiguara Villela 196
algorithm(s) 194, 195
    for collection of citations 89
    intertextual 85, 87
    search 194
    set of 193
    text similarity 95
algorithmic
    analysis 102
    critical reading 68
    modeling 21
    procedures 1
    processes/ing 5, 20, 71, 107, 121
    readings, editings, and writings 47
    sequences 16, 61, 95
    textual transformations 167–8
Allen, Graham 68, 71
André, Julie 33
Andrews, Tara L. 30
Apollon, Daniel 30
author-function 13–14, 40–5, 50–1, 179,
    see also virtual writing

Balpe, Jean-Pierre 168
Barad, Karen 42, 46–7

Barbosa, Nicolás 60 n.1, 196
Barthes, Roland 68, 69
Beckett, Samuel 31–3
Bénel, Aurélien 41
Benjamin, Walter 154
bibliographic
    codes 40
    structure(s) 22, 41, 48, 61, 104, 106,
        121, 129, 156, 202
Blake, William 62–3
Bloome, David 68, 88
Bolter, Jay David 70
book, *see also* codex
    digital 24–5, 29
    networked 179
    in progress 1, 14, 37, 54, 111–15, 131,
        159, 195
    under construction 3, 38, 41, 49, 52–4
book-function 14, 40–5, 51–2, 165, 179,
    see also book
Book of Disquiet—editions
    by Jacinto do Prado Coelho 37, 83,
        103–5, 113
    by Jerónimo Pizarro 37, 103–5, 113–14
    by Richard Zenith 37, 103–5, 113
    by Teresa Sobral Cunha 37, 103–5,
        113–14
Book of Disquiet—editors
    Coelho, Jacinto do Prado 37, 83
    Lopes, Teresa Rita 104 n.3
    Pizarro, Jerónimo 37
    Sobral Cunha, Teresa 37
    Zenith, Richard 37
Book of Disquiet—in the *LdoD Archive*
    modeling the 38–41
    simulating the 52–6
    virtualization of/virtualizing the 41–5
Book of Disquiet—quoted texts by title or
    incipit
    "After I've slept many dreams" (1930)
        126

"Aspects" (c. 1918) 37
"B. of D. (Note)" (c. 1931) 112–13
"During the first days of Autumn" (c. 1929) 63, 138–9
"Even writing has lost its appeal" (c. 1917) 139–40
"Fragments of an Autobiography" (undated) 155
"I have the most conflicting opinions" (c. 1931) 64
"I know no pleasure like that of books" (c. 1930) 12, 64
"I sometimes enjoy (in split fashion)" (c. 1914) 162
"I was already feeling uneasy" (c. 1932) 165
"I write with a strange sorrow" (1930) 140–1, 144
"I'm astounded whenever I finish something" (c. 1930) 50
"In one of those spells of sleepless somnolence" (c. 1930) 13, 51
"In the faint shadows cast by the last light" (1931) 11, 13
"It sometimes occurs to me, with sad delight" (c. 1919) 142–3
"Journey in the Mind" (c. 1929) 147–50, 157–8
Letter to Mário de Sá-Carneiro (1916) 132–3
"Millimeters" (c. 1914) 126
"My soul is a secret orchestra" (c. 1914) 109
"No problem has a solution" (1916) 200
"Note concerning the actual editions" (c. 1929) 49
"Nothing is more oppressive than the affection of others" (1932) 65
"Page by page I slowly and lucidly reread" (c. 1931) 64
"Perystile" (c. 1913) 5–6
"… that episode of the imagination" (c. 1931) 126
"The Art of Effective Dreaming for Metaphysical Minds" (c. 1914) 13
"The entire life of the human soul is mere motions" (1930) 48, 164
"The higher a man rises" (1931) 63
"The idea of travelling seduces me" (c. 1929) 64
"The intensity of my sensations has always been less" (c. 1917) 160–1
"The trivial things that make up life" (c. 1929) 147–50, 157–8
"What's primordial in me" (c. 1914) 126
"When I consider all the people I know" (c. 1930) 155
"With a Shrug" (c. 1930) 135–6
Book of Disquiet—reception
 expert critical reception 15, 48, 66–73, 73–9
 modeling of 73–9
 social media reception 15, 48, 66–73, 88–94
Boto, Sandra 196
Bryant, John 30
Butler, Judith 1, 46

Candela, Leonardo 183–5
Castro, Ivo 105
Cayley, John 203
citability 68, 70, 72, 76, 85
Ciula, Arianna 30
codex 24–6, 115, 189, *see also* book
 as a communication artifact 24
 conventions 71
 critical editions 153
 as a dynamic literary object 16
 editing and the 15
 printed 1, 24, 25
 structure(s) of the 29, 155
 totalization 114
Colclough, Stephen 58
Consortium on Electronic Literature (CELL) 190 n.2
Cortes-Rodrigues, Armando 154
crowdsourcing 67, 71, 72, 127
Cruz, Miguel 42 n.14

Damásio, António 134, 161
Deegan, Marylin 25
Derrida, Jacques 68, 70
Dickinson Electronic Archives, 35
digital humanities 2, 5, 9, 18, 72, 75, 201
digital library 18, 179–94
 classification systems 180–94

digital literary archives 31–5
Digital Public Library of America (DPLA) 186–7
Dionísio, João 197
discourse/discursive fields 44, 53, 61, 77, 201
Driscoll, Matthew 30
Drucker, Johanna 22–3, 30, 47, 68, 184, 188, 203
Dynabook 20

editing
  meta-editing 15, 115, 203
  process(es) 24, 53, 107, 117, 129, 144, 153
  process of 109, 157
editor-function 12, 40–5, 49–50, 179,
    see also virtual editing
Ericsson, K. Anders 74
Escandell Montiel, Daniel 165
Europeana 186–7
evolutionary textual environment 1–7, 18, 203

Ferreira, Nuno F. 168
Ferrer, Daniel 62
Fish, Stanley 68, 75–6
Flanders, Julia 30
Foucault, Michel 40
fragment
  definitions 37, 151–3
  extended fragment 51, 163–7
  in relation to author-function 51
  in relation to book-function 52
  in relation to editor-function 49
  in relation to reader-function 48–9
  seed-fragment 163–7
  as unit of the *Book of Disquiet* 7–9, 17, 23, 37–9
  as unit of the *LdoD Archive* 7–9, 17, 23, 37–9, 116–17
fragmentation
  algorithmic 179
  textual 179
Fraistat, Neil 41
Frischer, Bernard 20

Gabler, Hans Walter 107
genetic edition 26, 31, 34, 120

Genette, Gérard 68
Giménez, Diego 62 n.3, 160
Gonçalves, Nuno 42 n.14
Google Books 28
Google Arts and Culture 184
graphical user interface 20–2, 119
Grigar, Dene 183
Grüne-Yanoff, Till 19
Guedes, Vicente (Pessoa's heteronym)
  as heteronym 7, 37
  as narrator 131
  psychology and style 112–13

Haberer, Adolphe 68
Hayles, N. Katherine 47
Henny-Krahmer, Ulrike 37 n.13, 105 n.5
heteronym(s) 7, 13, 14, 37, 80–3, 90, 104–6, 113–15
  semi-heteronym 7, 37, 90, 104, 106, 115, 145, 153
Hong, Huili 68, 88
Howe, Daniel C. 169
hypertext 21–22
  and intertext 57, 71
hypermedia 21, 35, 189

interaction design 29, 39, 163, 197
interactive
  environment 41, 129
  feature(s) 38, 122, 170
  functionalities 156
  interfaces 95
  literature 21, 22
  script 174
  simulation 203
  space 21, 170, 208
Internet Archive 180–2
intertextuality 68–72, 73, 76
  computational model of 77–87
Israel, Susan E. 74
iterability 40, 53, 164

Jannidis, Fotis 30
Jones, Steven 41

Kay, Alan 20–1
Kirschenbaum, Matthew G. 20, 30, 183
Kristeva, Julia 68

Landow, George P. 70, 71 n.12
Latent Semantic Analysis (LSA) 83
Latour, Bruno 47–8
Lavocat, Françoise 19
LdoD Archive: Collaborative Digital Archive of the Book of Disquiet 2, 8, 199
LdoD Archive—computational aspects
  data model 3, 23, 34, 36, 101–2, 110, 116, 156, 202
  interaction design 4, 29, 39, 163, 197
  JavaScript 170–6
  as a literary machine 8, 11, 42, 53, 54, 125, 131, 169–70, 194, 195, 199, 203
  source code 3, 42 n.14, 172, 174–5, 177, 181
  textual encoding 33, 30, 36, 38, 54, 95, 156, 199, 202
  textual encoding template 117–19
  visualization, *see* visualization
  web applications 42 n.14
  XML-TEI 66, 85, 102, 117–19, 122, 157
LdoD Archive—interfaces
  documents interface 179
  editions interface 102
  reading interface 58
  search interface 199
  virtual interface 122
  writing interface 132
LdoD Archive—virtual editions
  "Twitter Citations" 94, 125
  "Daydreaming Machine" 126
  "Jacinto do Prado Coelho—Annotated Edition" 125–6
  "Mallet" 124–5
LdoD Archive—web applications
  "Citations on Twitter" 42 n.14, 67, 89–94
  "Classification Game" 42 n.14, 127–9
  "Visual Book" 42 n.14, 95–100
lecto-escritura 164
Lejeune, Christophe 41
literary performativity 1–5, 11–16, 43–8, 192, 196, 203–4
literary simulation 1, 8, 16, 23, 198, 203
literary simulator 10, 16, 23, 203

machine learning 124, 167
macro-variations 17, 110, 117, 120–21

Magalhães, Cecília 197
Mallet (MAchine Learning for LanguagE Toolkit) 124
Mandell, Laura 25, 182
Manovich, Lev 21, 182
Marques, Ana 67
Marques, Gonçalo Montalvão 127
Martinho, Fernando J. B. 80, 81–2
Martins, Fernando Cabral 80, 82–3
McCarty, Willard 182
McGann, Jerome 22, 43, 203
meta-edition 101, 102, 121
metamedia 16, 18, 21, 52, 195
micro-variations 17, 110, 117, 120–21
Millis, Keith 83–4
modeling/model of
  electronic reading, editing, and writing space 37–40
  intertextuality 76, 88
  library 184, 185
  literary action 201
  literary performance 8
  literary performativity 2, 3, 16, 18
  processuality 10, 11, 43, 53–4
  performative materiality 47
  performativity of textual production 195
  procedural nature of textuality 43
  reading 71
  reception analysis 69
  recursive processes of consciousness 142
  remediation 42
modularity
  of the *Book of Disquiet* 7, 10, 23
  of digital materiality, 18, 115
  as editing unit, 124
  of forms, genres, and documents 182, 188–9, 193
  of the *LdoD Archive* 7, 10
  as writing unit, 145
Montfort, Nick 168
Moulthrop, Stuart 183
Muñoz, Trevor 41
Murray, Janet H. 38
Musil, Robert 154

Namora, Ricardo 183
National Digital Library of Portugal 186

Index

National Library of Portugal (BNP) 6, 179, 191
Nelson, Theodor Holm 21-2, 69-70, 189
network of quotations 66, 71, 95
networked
  book 179
  cloud computing 181
  collaborative writing 22, 160
  computational media 41, 129
  computer 202
  electronic documents 179, 188
  electronic space 183
  information 183, 186
  LdoD Archive 125
  programmable media 5, 179, 194
  reading, editing, and writing spaces 15
  systems for electronic books 58
Nixon, Mark 30-1
Nunberg, Geoffrey 28

Oatley, Keith 19
Oliveira, Duarte 89, 125
Opitz, Sven 19
Ott, Brian 68
Oulipo (Ouvroir de Littérature Potentielle) 168

Pereira, Luís Lucas 169
  Machines of Disquiet 169-77
performativity, *see* literary performativity
Pessoa, Fernando (1888-1935)
  Book of Disquiet (1913-1934) 1-16, 18-24, 37-8
  as editor
    "B. of D. (Note)" (c. 1931) 112-13
    "Bibliographic Table" (1928) 82-3
  heteronyms
    Caeiro, Alberto 37, 90, 167 n.15
    Campos, Álvaro de 37, 167 n.15
    Guedes, Vicente, *see* Guedes, Vicente
    Reis, Ricardo 37, 167 n.15
    Soares, Bernardo, *see* Soares, Bernardo
    Teive, Barão de 104 n.3
  as reader
    marginalia 62 n.2, 63 n.4, 120
    private library 62 n.2, 63 n.4, 120
  as writer
    handwriting (witnesses) 139, 141, 142, 147, 149, 160, 200
    typewriting (witnesses) 133, 135, 138, 162
Perl (programming language) 168
potentiality
  and actuality 5, 154, 179
  of becoming 156
  of being 155
  of the book 43, 198
  of the digital medium 15, 42
  literary 15, 16
  of self-production 54
  of the typewriter 139
  of writing, reading, and editing 23, 53, 148, 151, 154
processuality 1-16
  of the book 3-5, 14, 43
  of editing 2-5, 14, 101, 116, 117, 196, 202
  of reading 2-5, 14, 196
  reflexive 53
  textual 14, 203
  of writing 2-5, 14, 131, 132, 145, 196
Phillips, Gary A. 68
Pierazzo, Elena 30, 31, 33, 34, 107
Pittella, Carlos 60 n.1, 196
Pizarro, Jerónimo 62 n.2, 79-81, 105, 106, 124, *see also* Book of Disquiet— editors
Pisarski, Mariusz 71
Portela, Manuel 23, 40, 43, 53, 67, 71, 122, 160, 169, 194
Pressley, Michael 74
Price, Leah 57-8
Proust, Marcel 31, 33-4

Radical Scatters 35
Ramsay, Stephen 68
Raposo, José 95 n.30
reader-function 12-13, 40-5, 48-9, 179, *see also* reading
reading
  emersive 57, 66, 97-100
  immersive 57, 66, 95-6, 100
  mark(s) 57-59, 62
  meta-reading 15

paths 1, 3, 10, 15, 16, 48, 53, 60, 94, 100, 197
process(es) 49, 57, 61, 66, 68, 69, 78, 85, 95–100, 164, 172, 173
reading-writing 11, 53, 64, 70, 78, 90, 164
recommendation 60, 94, 197
sequence(s) 16, 49, 57–61, 95–100
trails 4, 15, 52, 60, 70
traversals 8, 17, 49, 53, 192
reading protocols 56, 63, 66–8, 71, 73–9, 84–7
Reisenzein, Rainer 19
representation 1–16, *see also* simulation
    meta-editorial 202
    and simulation 20–22, 101
representation layer 3, 55–6, 170 n.19
Riffaterre, Michael 68
Rito Silva, António 23, 40, 42 n.14, 43, 95, 119 n.12, 125
Robinson, Peter 30, 107–8
Rodríguez de la Flor, Fernando 165
Roland, Meg 30
role playing 1–16, 45, 54
    literary roles 40–6, 197–8
Rossetti Archive 35

Sá-Carneiro, Mário de 131
Sahle, Patrick 30
Samuel Beckett Digital Manuscript Project 31–3, 35
Schreibman, Susan 72
script acts 17, 32–3, 50, 112, 143–66
self, *see also* writing
    enunciating self 132, 145
    enunciated self 132, 145
    self-conscious 66, 90, 148, 152, 160, 162, 164
    self-consciousness 114, 131, 146–7, 154–5, 162
    writing self 11, 50, 135, 139, 144, 161, 164
    written self 15, 139
Sepúlveda, Pedro 37, 105 n.5
Shelley-Godwin Archive, 35
Shillingsburg, Peter L. 30, 112, 143
Siemens, Ray 41
Simon, Herbert A. 74
simulation layer 3, 52, 55–6, 57, 159, 170 n.19

simulation(s) 1–16, *see also* representation
    of the acts of editing 10, 117, 195–6, 198
    of the acts of reading 10, 17, 95, 195–6, 198
    of the acts of writing 10, 131, 195–6, 198
    of cognitive processes 21–2
    of literary performativity 56
    of literary processes 40
    of subject-positions 161
Soares, Bernardo (Pessoa's heteronym)
    as character 67, 82–3, 106
    as heteronym 7, 37, 65–6, 79–83, 145, 153
    Lisbon 63, 73, 79–81, 145
    as narrator 131
    psychology and style 112–13
    as reader 90
social media 15, 17, 48, 57, 61, 66, 183, *see also* Twitter
    reception 88–94
    "Twitter Citations" virtual edition 125
social text edition 120, 157
speech act(s) 44, 54, 56, 112
Sutherland, Katherine 25

Tabbi, Joseph 190 n.2
Tamir, Diana I. 19
Terras, Melissa 72
Text Encoding Initiative (TEI) 27, 30
textual marks 31, 34, 36, 43, 131
Torres, Rui 168
transliterature 70
Twitter 42 n.14, 67, 89–94, 125, *see also* social media

UK RED (Reading Experience Database) 58

variability
    editorial 49, 197
    modular 179, 181, 188, 193
    reading 57, 61
    textual 43, 104
virtual editing 8, 10, 17, 94, 108, 121–9, *see also* editing
    annotations 15, 17, 49, 50, 120, 121–9, 191, 192

classifications 4, 42 n.14, 84, 97, 127–9, 180–94
selections 15, 41, 50, 121–9, 192
taxonomies 4, 9, 15, 95, 97, 121–9, 166, 181
virtual reading, *see also* reading
  multiple reading paths 1, 10, 16
  spacetime of reading 66, 94, 100
  visualizing reading 56
virtual writing 8, 10, 51, 132, 159–77, *see also* writing
  Disquiet variations 163–9
  Machines of Disquiet 169–77
  writing variations 9, 17, 56
Van Dam, Andries 70, 71 n.12
Van Hulle, Dirk 30–1, 155
Vanhoutte, Edward 112
visualization
  comparative 17, 109
  of intertextual networks 67, 95
  macro-visualization 4, 49, 57
  manipulation and abstraction 21
  of reading trails 15, 94, 97
  of taxonomies 125
  temporized 33, 34

tools 61, 94–7, 102
of transcription 34, 48–9, 119–20, 159

Walt Whitman Archive 35
Walter, Cameron 68
Werner, Marta L. 112, 146 n.8
William Blake Archive 35
Wilson, Eric 19
Wise, M. Norton 19
Woolf Online 31–5
Woolf, Virginia 34–5
Wright-Maley, Cory 19
writing, *see also* self; virtual writing
  act of 135–45, 151, 155, 161, 165
  mark(s) 31, 50, 63
  meta-writing 15
  process(es) 15, 41, 43, 134, 140, 143–53, 157, 164, 188
  writing-reading 68, 70, 77, 78, 164
  writing the self 155, 161–4

Zenith, Richard 67, 81 n.22, 82 n.23, 106, *see also Book of Disquiet*—editors
Zundert, Joris J. van 30

www.ingramcontent.com/pod-product-compliance
Lightning Source LLC
Chambersburg PA
CBHW051809230426
43672CB00012B/2671